Computer Graphics User's Guide

Andrew S. Glassner has been creating pictures with computers for over six years. His graphics experience includes programming at Rutgers University and real-time three-dimensional modeling and programming at Case Western Reserve University, where he developed a system for visualizing the probability shells for electrons in the hydrogen atom. He has spent a year modeling and programming at the New York Institute of Technology (NYIT) Computer Graphics Laboratory, and a year at NYIT's Digital Sound Lab, where he synthesized digital music and designed a digital sound editor. Mr. Glassner has also worked in computer graphics at the IBM T.J. Watson Research Laboratory.

Mr. Glassner has written several three-dimensional modeling and rendering systems, one of which was used to generate most of the illustrations in this book. He currently lives in Cleveland, Ohio, where he attends Case Western Reserve University and consults in computer graphics.

Andrew's current computer graphics research interests include techniques for high-speed ray tracing, computer-generated holography, three-dimensional interactive games, computer-assisted polyhedron design, and a host of crackpot schemes. Andrew reports that he is 23, a "Torus," and that this is his first book.

Computer Graphics User's Guide

by
Andrew S. Glassner

Howard W. Sams & Co., Inc.
4300 WEST 62ND ST. INDIANAPOLIS, INDIANA 46268 USA

FIRST EDITION
FIRST PRINTING—1984

International Standard Book Number: 0-672-22064-4
Library of Congress Catalog Card Number: 83-50378

Edited by: *Pryor Associates*
Illustrated by: *T.R. Emrick*

Printed in the United States of America.

Preface

For several years now I've been convinced that as soon as computer graphics got out of the research labs and large animation studios, a lot of artists would be attracted to the field. But, there hasn't existed any kind of reference material to teach non programmers and nonmathematicians what computer graphics is all about.

I initially thought of a series of short films that described the ideas behind computer graphics. That project was later whittled down to a series of filmstrips. But after a while, it became clear that the best way to present this material was in a book, where difficult ideas could be reviewed, and each reader can go at his or her own pace.

I am indebted to Bill Mahar for his encouragement and support when this text was first being planned. Without his enthusiasm, it is possible that this book would never have been written.

I would also like to thank the various people who were kind enough to review the manuscript at various stages of development and offer suggestions for improvement. Roberta Glassner reviewed some early drafts, made substantial suggestions about the overall tone, and helped me plan the book with a consistent style. She also suggested the format for the summary sections at the end of the more difficult chapters.

Several people read a complete but rough draft of the manuscript without illustrations, but managed to make very helpful suggestions nonetheless. These imaginative reviewers were Eric Braun, Bruce Glassner, Chris Jones, David Labuda, and Barak Pearlmutter. When an initial set of illustrations had been made, the combination of rough draft and illustrations was considered by artists Anne Beekman and Mark Howard.

The text for the entire book was created with the text editor "vi" running under the UNIX™* Operating System on the VAX 11/780 computer operated by the Computer Engineering Department at Case Western Reserve University. I am indebted to Department Chair Chuck Rose for his kind permission to use this facility to write the text, and Professor K. Gopinath for his assistance in getting me set up on the computer. Without the support and help of Professor Frederic Way, III, I would probably never have had the time nor freedom to write this book. If this book has a guardian angel, it is he.

*UNIX is a trademark of Bell Laboratories.

The fractal line drawings in Chapter 7 were created using CWRU's plotter with a general fractal-generating system I wrote.

Most of the shaded graphics in the book were generated during the summer when I was working at the IBM T.J. Watson Research Laboratory. Here I wrote a new version of a three-dimensional polygon modeling system I originally wrote at CWRU. The code was written in APL and run under the VM operating system. Most of these pictures were taken at a screen resolution of 640 by 512 or 320 by 256.

I would never have had the time or opportunity to make these pictures without the support and encouragement of Dave Bantz, whose trust and help I am most grateful for. I can certainly say that without his help there would be virtually no shaded pictures in this book.

Another vital helper and friend was Paul Sholtz. Once I had generated a picture on the machine, I needed some way to get it out of the computer's memory, onto a frame buffer screen, and then to a camera. It turns out that this was a very formidable task, and I could easily have spent my entire summer just figuring out how to accomplish it. Paul, however, generously offered the use of his existing software, which performed flawlessly when used as advertised.

Paul also contributed to this book with several of the illustrations in Chapter 11. Having tried my hand at making slides, I can truly appreciate the work involved in creating such fine-looking images.

When I was having trouble with the illustrations for Chapter 12, Claire Albahae offered her help and artistic ability at refining my rough sketches. Her work helps illuminate some ideas that would otherwise remain obscure.

A valuable contribution came from Benoit Mandelbrot, who graciously read the manuscript for Chapter 7 and offered constructive suggestions for its improvement. He also offered me several of the more stunning pictures in this book, which in turn came from his book.

The illustrations of mountains, islands, and planets were made by Richard Voss using fractal geometry. Certainly among the most realistic pictures ever created by computer, I am proud to present them in my book.

The more abstract fractal shapes in Chapter 7 were created by Alan Norton. Alan has developed a very robust set of techniques for generating these mathematical objects, and I watched one day as he followed a particular mathematical expression from a blackboard equation to a stunning picture.

All the people mentioned above work at the Watson lab, where I was made to feel comfortable and at home. Everyone mentioned was willing to spend time with me to discuss this project and related ideas, and for all their help and generosity, I offer my thanks.

Thanks are also due to Paula Sweeney. During the final phases of production of this manuscript, life got very hectic and complications abounded. Without Paula's help and support I would probably never have been able to complete this book. Paula's contribution can be seen in every computer-generated photograph produced at three in the morning, and there are plenty!

Writing a book while attending college full time is a very difficult enterprise. I'd like to thank my friends who (among other favors) took notes for me in classes I cut while writing the text!

I've had to walk a fine line in this book between enough description of technical processes to give their flavor and methods, and too much detail that would swamp and lose the reader. I think that I found reasonable compromise in the more difficult chapters and patterned the rest of the book around them.

The text is broken up into three general sections. First, the introductory material regarding geometry and computers that we need to know for the technical descriptions to come is presented. Then the techniques and processes of computer graphics are given. This discussion is really an explanation of what goes on inside the computer. Another way of looking at it is to say that the inventors of computer graphics basically have ideas, and then write computer programs that implement these ideas. We also discuss these ideas and how they are used. Finally, the different production techniques, or ways of getting your computer images onto film or videotape, and producing professional-looking animation are covered.

This book is written primarily for artists and hobbyists. The artist doesn't care about how the computer implements the various techniques in actual computer programs but has to know the mechanics of those programs to understand why they make the pictures they do.

The hobbyist may someday write his or her own computer graphics programs, or may use someone else's programs on the machine he or she owns. Either way, it's important for the hobbyist to understand the principles behind computer graphics before plunging into the technical details of good computer programming of these principles. This book does not cover the mathematics necessary to write the computer programs, but provides a solid explanation of everything that those mathematics do. The clever hobbyist who has had some calculus background may be able to reinvent some of the mathematics needed strictly from the descriptions in this text. To help those hobbyists who are not in the position to reinvent the entire field virtually from scratch, I suggest reading this book carefully to understand the principles behind computer graphics.

To all those who are interested in the field of computer graphics, I offer my encouragement to not be bound by the ideas and techniques in this book. The field is still brand new, and new ideas and methods are invented all the time. Once you have mastered where computer graphics is today, you will be able to create pictures of a professional caliber, and you may have ideas that will prove so popular, they will have to be included in future books like this. Enjoy!

ANDREW S. GLASSNER

To Bertram and Roberta Glassner

Contents

CHAPTER 5

CHAPTER 6

CHAPTER 7

CHAPTER 8

CHAPTER 9

CHAPTER 10

CHAPTER 11

CHAPTER 12

CHAPTER 13

Introduction

When I was writing this book, I spoke with several artists about computer graphics and asked them what they would want out of a book that described the field to them. Usually, I was asked a number of questions, and by the time I was through answering them, I felt like I had described a pretty good introduction to the book.

So in that spirit, here is a bunch of questions and the answers to them that describe what this book is all about and who it's for.

What Is Computer Graphics All About?

Computer graphics is the name given to all the computer hardware and all the programs that people have written that are directed to one common goal: getting computers to draw pictures.

It became clear several years ago that with special hardware and clever programming, you could get a computer to draw pictures that would look good. In fact, some people said that pictures drawn by computer could be made so good that they would almost look like photographs of real objects!

Well, that has been the general thrust of shaded computer graphics over the last few years: making pictures that look almost real. A lot of people have also been working on ways to make stylized pictures as well with the idea that the computer can help us make images that we otherwise couldn't have made so that instead of being a camera, the computer was actually a new artistic device.

Most of the computer graphics you've probably seen have either been in some recent science-fiction movies or on television. Many commercials and station identifications are now done with computer graphics, but a lot of the graphics are so well done that unless they have been deliberately stylized to look "computerish," you would probably not have guessed they weren't animated by hand.

Whos's Been Doing All This Animation With Computers?

Well, generally it's been a blend of research scientists with an artistic flair and commercial animation houses. Computer graphics is just now beginning to take off and get outside the few research labs where it was invented and the few big professional animation studios that could afford it.

Several small companies are now coming out with computer graphics equipment for television stations to run themselves, for corporate art departments, for newspapers, and for fine art.

Okay, So the Computer Can Draw Pictures. How Do I Do It?

As far as I know, there aren't any places an artist can go to learn state-of-the-art, three-dimensional computer graphics besides a research lab or production house that is doing it. In other words, to learn computer graphics you have to find someone who knows and is willing to teach you.

That's why this book was written. This is a book for artists who want to learn computer graphics.

But I Don't Know Anything About Computers! And I Really Hate Math . . .

That's fine. There's no reason an artist has to be a computer programmer or a mathematician to work in computer graphics. This book contains no computer programs and except for a couple of simple equations in one paragraph (which is optional!) no mathematical equations. This is a book for artists, not mathematicians or programmers.

But we're not going to gloss over the whole field. Think about how well you would be able to paint with oils if you never worked with them before? You know something about how they thin with turpentine, and how they change with temperature. So you really do know some technical details about your materials. And photographers understand a great deal about the technical mechanics and optics that make their cameras work. They probably don't know the equations for designing lenses, but they know explicitly and completely just what those lenses do.

In the same spirit this book will go into the details of computer graphics. We won't talk about computer programming at all, but we will talk about the ideas that people are thinking about when they write computer graphics programs. This discussion will give you an understanding of how those programs work. And when you understand how those programs work and why they work, you're free.

When you understand the programs that are computer graphics, you're free to do the unexpected. You're free to use those programs in ways that the programmer never thought of. You're free to design objects for the computer to draw that no one else ever considered. But to be able to do these things, you have to really know what these programs do. You need to know why they work in order to know why they don't work when you get unexpected results. You need to understand the reasons behind the information you type into the computer to be really creative with that information.

This book is designed to tell you everything you need to know about how computer graphics programs work, so you'll be free to use those programs creatively with confidence and competence.

I've Always Thought Computers Were Pretty Complicated

They are, but remember: we're not going to study computers in this book. We're going to study the ideas behind the programs. Reading this book will be an exercise in imagination and visualization. When you understand the reasons why the programs work they way they do, you'll understand how to control those programs to do what you want them to do. You may even think of new ways, better or different ways, to do the same things. If you find a programmer and share your ideas, you may find yourself the inventor of a whole new technique in the field!

Computer graphics is less than 20 years old. There's a lot of growth ahead, and artists who understand the methods that are used today will be the creators who invent the methods of tomorrow.

Chapter ONE

Approaches to Modeling

This chapter is an introduction to the ideas of computer graphics and an introduction to the hardware of computer graphics machines. It turns out that this hardware greatly influences how a user gets along with the computer graphics equipment, so we'll examine it in some detail.

In this chapter we're going to look at some of the basic concepts central to creating and manipulating shapes with a computer. We'll talk about the different ways of defining a complicated shape (anything from an egg to a spaceship). This way we'll have some idea right from the start of how we create objects with the computer, and we'll also briefly look at the different appearances of the final computer-generated picture, using different techniques for drawing the picture.

We'll then look at the various pieces of hardware, or equipment, that is likely to be found associated with computer graphics. The different pieces of equipment available to the user greatly influence the style of interaction and communication between the artist and computer. And since the computer should be just another tool, it's important to understand the mechanisms that control that tool.

WHAT IS A COMPUTER MODEL?

One of the most essential concepts in computer graphics is the idea of "models." In this book we will consider the word *model* to have one of two meanings:

A *scale model*—a scaled up (or down) copy of some other object, usually built up with many smaller pieces, or a *mathematical model*—a description of physical laws, useful for representing an object's motion, the brightness of a light source, and other applications.

Anyone who has ever built a plane or car from a plastic hobby kit is familiar with the idea of a scale model. A scale model is a copy of some object, recreated either larger or smaller than the original. A mathematical model, though widely used in scientific areas, is less familiar. Economists predict trends through the use of a mathematical model. Another kind of mathematical model is used by engineers planning the flight path for the space shuttle. They supply the model with various data called *input*, such as the earth's size, its motion around the sun, its gravity, etc. The model then supplies them with *output,* or new information derived from the given information; in this case, specifics on the flight path of the shuttle. The model itself is usually considered a set of mathematical equations that are linked intricately in some way.

In this book we will look at computer modeling from the point of view of someone who wants to represent a real object (like a person or a spaceship) on a computer screen, with the freedom to manipulate that object as if it were real. The spaceship we will consider a scale model, the description of its planned flight a mathematical model.

To make a scale model, you assemble it out of smaller pieces, or surfaces. We will examine the various popular kinds of surfaces used today in computer modeling, and how they are used to build realistic-looking models.

INTERACTIVE VERSUS PREPARED MODELING

Once you have an object in mind, there are two routes you may take in getting your vision into the computer.

One method is to make accurate engineering drawings of the model, and measure the drawings themselves for the sizes of the different shapes that make up the model. This information is then typed into the computer in terms of three-dimensional points, lines, spheres, and other shapes and surfaces. The computer takes this information and builds a complete description in its memory.

The other technique is to model interactively, sitting in front of a video screen, manipulating various switches, knobs, and joysticks, juggling shapes around on the screen, creating new shapes and deleting old ones, putting shapes together and taking them apart until you have a satisfactory model. Although this technique requires less preparation than prepared modeling, it is today a very difficult and awkward process and, except for straightforward mechanical assemblies, it is rarely used.

ADDITIVE VERSUS SUBTRACTIVE MODELING

There's an old joke about a hobby kit that claims to be a complete kit for a scale model of an elephant. Inside the box is a block of wood and a knife, and the instructions, "To make an elephant, just carve away everything that doesn't look like an elephant!" That kind of technique is called *subtractive modeling,* and in general it means you start off with too much material and gradually take away pieces until the shape you desire emerges. For example, carving marble is accomplished by cutting away chunks of marble to create a sculpture, so we can call marble carving a subtractive process.

A more popular modeling technique is called *additive modeling,* and it means building up a model by assembling many simple pieces. This method, used in more traditional plastic models, is the technique we will consider exclusively in this book. Sculpting with clay is primarily an additive process since you add clay to a basic form to build up the final sculpture. Sometimes the words *solid modeling* are used to mean the same thing as additive modeling.

LINE DRAWINGS AND SHADED DRAWINGS

The two main types of drawings provided by computer graphics are *line drawings* and *shaded drawings.* Line drawings are similar to arcade-style asteroid games, which we couldn't call very realistic. Usually drawings produced with lines are only meant to indicate the structure of an object, not to fool you into thinking you're looking at the object itself. Shaded drawings, on the other hand, can look very much like photographs of real objects. Most shaded graphics today wouldn't fool you into thinking you're looking at real objects; they're usually too metallic, or crisp-edged, or otherwise unreal. This look isn't always a drawback, because it gives computer-generated images a very special kind of look. Nevertheless, many people are working on improving the realism that shaded graphics can produce. In this book we'll concentrate on methods that produce realistic pictures, and mention special effects that can also be done to make "impossible" and stylized pictures.

Line drawings are often faster and cheaper to generate than shaded drawings and sometimes can be all you need. They serve admirably for charts and graphs, engineering drawings, and other precise line-oriented images. Shaded graphics, on the other hand, offers a technique for generating pictures that can appear stunningly realistic.

Because the computer performs less work to make a line drawing than a shaded drawing, line drawings are produced much more quickly. Often line drawings are used to test animation of a shaded object. When the line animation shows that the motion is acceptable, the time required to make the shaded pictures is allocated.

STATIC VERSUS DYNAMIC DISPLAY

The name of the game in computer graphics is to draw pictures. One purpose for these pictures may be to produce high-quality graphics for still pictures (slides), or broadcast/film-quality animation. When we make a high-quality computer-generated image, we want it to look as good as possible. The better a picture looks, the longer it takes to draw, so making high-quality images means waiting a long time for each picture to be made. And although there are shortcuts available to make the pictures render faster (such as not worrying about little objects, a problem we will encounter in Chapter 11), they should be avoided. A high-quality picture should look like a photograph. To achieve this kind of quality in the image, the computer must work hard, and the effect of that effort is the time that we must wait for the picture to be drawn. We refer to this kind of operation as producing *static* images, or pictures that take so long to generate that there is no illusion of movement from one picture to the next.

The other popular use of computer graphics is for simulation and testing. An example of simulation is training a pilot to fly a new kind of airplane. The control panel is just as it is in the airplane, but the windows of the cockpit look out onto the screens of computer graphics equipment, tv tubes, or projection-tv displays, as in Fig. 1-1. As the pilot flies the airplane, the view out the windows should look as if the plane really is surrounded by the countryside, buildings, water and other "reality." Here we don't care about the aesthetic purity of the individual images as much as we want the images to come out, one after the other, fast enough to move and react to the pilot's control of the airplane.

You can take shortcuts in making the pictures, since no single image

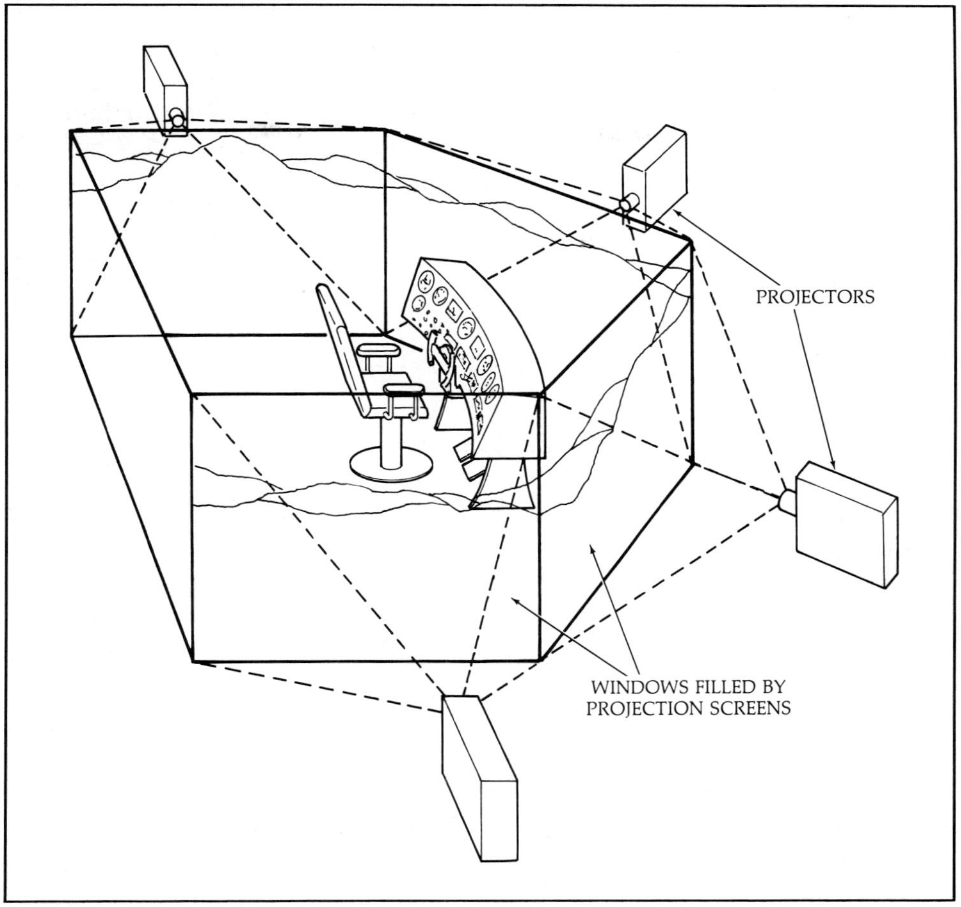

Fig. 1-1. A schematic illustration of a flight simulator.

remains long enough to be examined for small flaws. This kind of operation is called *dynamic*, or moving image generation.

Synonymous with the word *dynamic* when discussing motion, is the term *real time*. This term refers to something happening at a rate consistent with the outside world. Making a movie where each frame requires two minutes to generate is not real time; a simulator is by necessity real time.

STATIC VERSUS DYNAMIC MODELS

Just as a display can be static or dynamic, these words can be used to classify scale models. A model in which there are no moving parts (like a canoe) is called a *static model;* a model with moving parts (like a sailboat with working rudder and moving sail) is a *dynamic model.*

The distinction becomes important if you want to animate with your model. A static model cannot change its shape; because of its mathematical description, it can only be moved about the screen, scaled up and down and photographed from different angles. If you want a sequence of several planets orbiting a sun, then a static model of each planet would be sufficient because the planets do not change in any way (see Fig. 1-2). But a model of the whole solar system would be classified dynamic because of the movement of pieces inside the model.

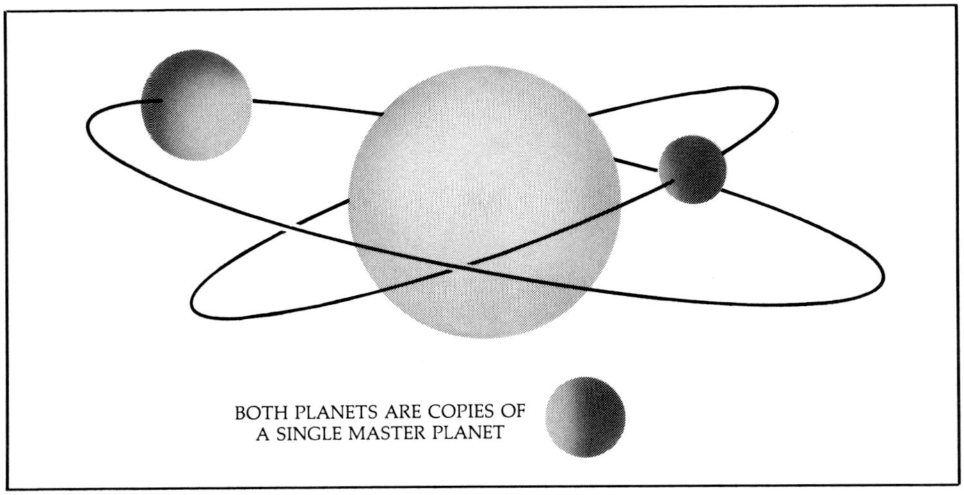

Fig. 1-2. How a single planet is used several times, using scaling.

Although dynamic models require more work to create, they are often necessary. For example, to simulate a pogo stick, the spring must compress when the foot bar comes down (Fig. 1-3). You can tell the computer how to do this compression in many ways (which we will cover later), but the capability of spring compression must be built into the model description when it is entered into the computer. This ability to move or actually change the shape of all or some of the model is what distinguishes a static from a dynamic model.

PHYSICAL SYSTEMS (HARDWARE)

The act of generating computer graphics places the artist in direct contact with the computer. To make this contact as pleasant as possible, a number of techniques have become very common for communication between the computer and artist.

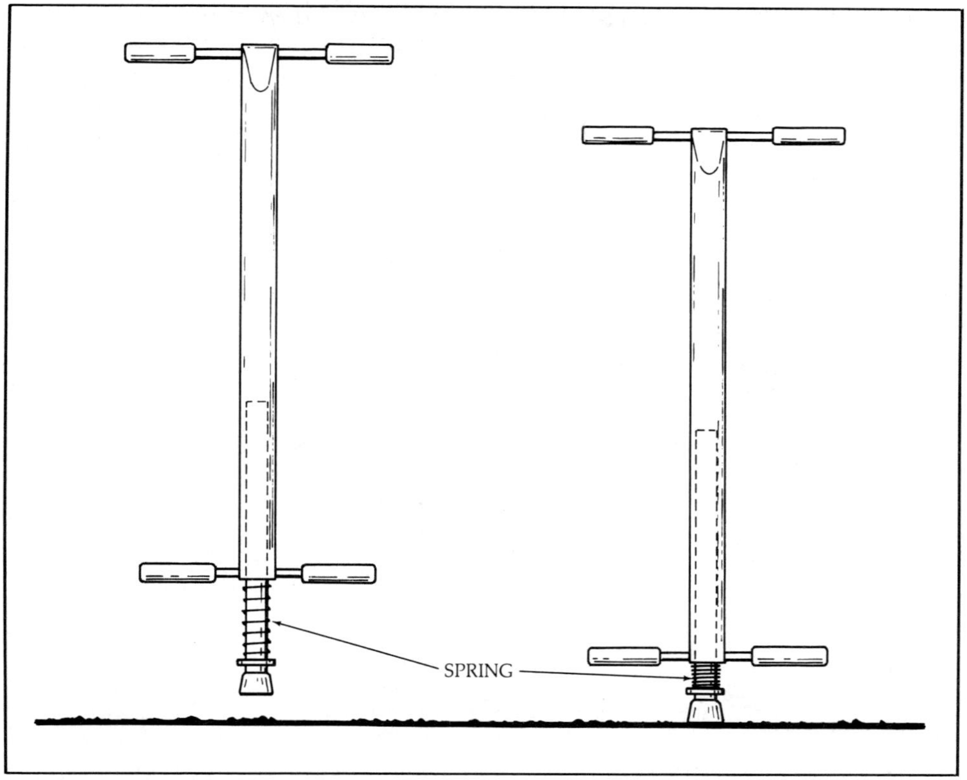

Fig. 1-3. Although its overall shape is the same, the spring compresses when the pogo stick hits the ground.

These techniques are intimately linked with the hardware that the computer offers to the artist, rather than with the programs (software) that the hardware executes. You may think it's bad to be bound by the hardware available to you, but consider that when you drive an automobile, you'll drive differently and interact with your car differently if you have a manual transmission than if you have an automatic transmission. Throughout this book we will see examples of how the computer and artist interact through hardware.

The next few sections of this chapter will be dedicated to discussing the various equipment that you are likely to find around a computer graphics installation. It's not possible to describe all the many kinds of devices possible in just one chapter, nor will every site have all the hardware that we will be able to discuss. But a general idea of the most common hardware can help you feel more comfortable when you sit down to use a new computer for the first time.

The imaginary computer graphics workstation we'll work with is shown in Fig. 1-4. This workstation is completely decked out, so you won't normally find all this equipment in one place. We'll examine each piece individually.

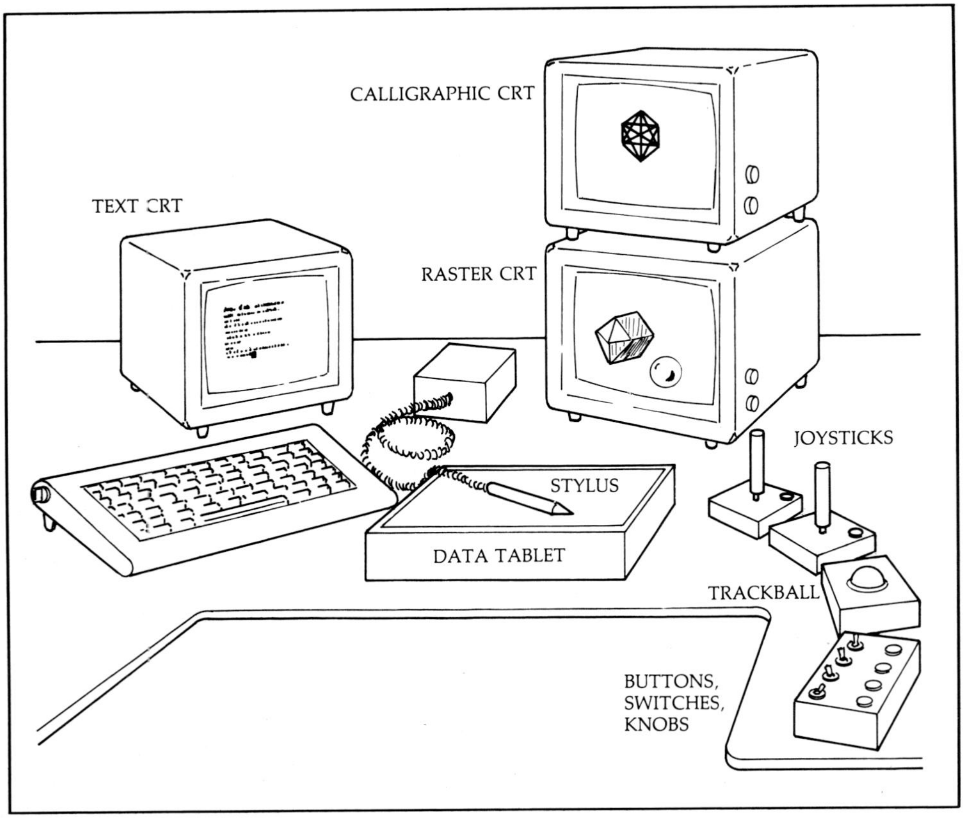

Fig. 1-4. A really complete workstation.

Text CRT and Keyboard

The crt and keyboard make up a standard computer terminal. It has a tv-tube display that can show text (text refers to exclusively letters, numbers, and punctuation; anything that might come out of a standard office typewriter). The display is usually black and white, and the keyboard looks like a regular typewriter keyboard although there are sometimes a few special-purpose keys.

The computer terminal is where you sign or *log on* to the computer, run programs, type in data, and it is what you usually consider home base. The acronym *crt* stands for *cathode ray tube,* a formal name for a television picture tube.

Raster Monitor CRT

The raster monitor crt is another tv-tube affair, but it is much larger, has the ability to display color, and in general is capable of high precision in color intensity and positioning of the image. This monitor is where the computer draws shaded pictures.

Calligraphic CRT

The calligraphic crt is yet another tv tube, but it only draws lines (although sometimes they can be in color). The advantage over a raster crt is that it draws lines with much greater precision. The lines also look smoother and can move about on the screen faster because of its construction. The calligraphic crt is also referred to as a vector crt.

Printer/Plotter

The printer/plotter is a small device that can give text listings of information inside the computer; i.e., name all the pictures you've entered so far and type out documentation on the system. It can also draw relatively crude black-and-white (and sometimes color) pictures for reference, like the "computer portraits" taken at shopping malls and flea markets. Figs. 7-6 and 7-8 show a couple of line drawings produced on a computer plotter.

Data Tablet

This large, flat piece of plastic, and stylus (pen) has two special features: a long wire coming out of the pen body connecting it to the computer, and a small switch in the tip of the pen. You can hold the pen and draw with it as though it were a regular ballpoint pen, but it doesn't leave ink behind. Instead, the computer can always determine just where the pen is electronically (as long as the pen is on or near the plastic surface of the tablet).

The computer will often let you know that it is following you by tracking your movements on one of the crt's. Fig. 1-5 shows a typical tracking display. The computer has drawn a small arrowhead on one of the crt's. The upper-right corner of the tablet corresponds to the upper-right corner of the crt, and the other corners match as well. You can point to any position on the screen by moving the pen to the corresponding place on

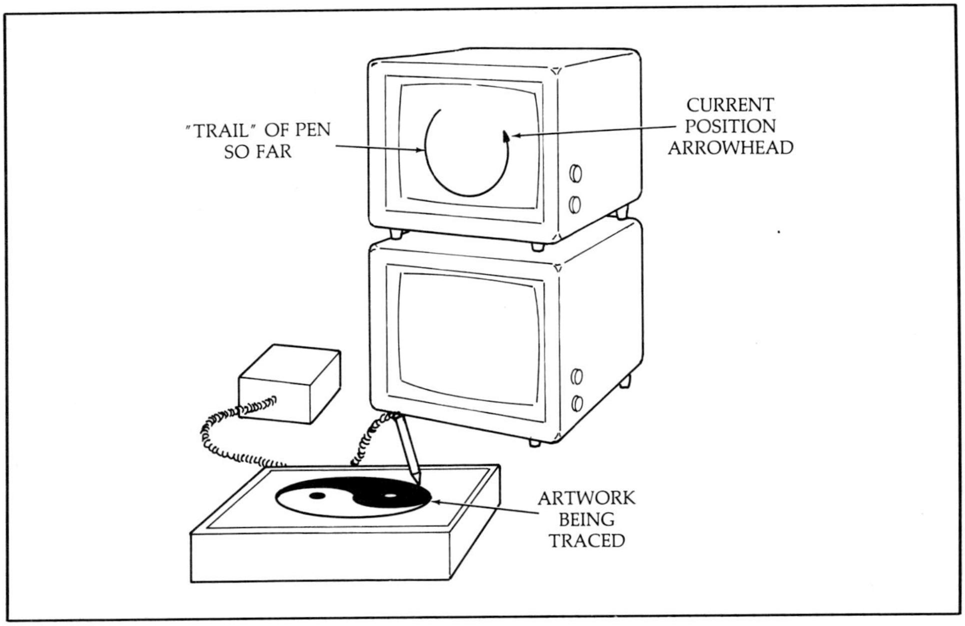

Fig. 1-5. A data tablet may be used for drawing freehand pictures.

the tablet. As you move the pen, the arrowhead on the screen moves with you.

You can tell the computer about a special event it has been programmed to expect (like drawing a line from the center of the screen to the current position of the pen) by pressing down onto the surface of the tablet with the pen. There's a small switch in the tip of the pen that closes when you press the tip of the pen onto the surface. Picking the pen up off of the surface opens the switch.

Since the tablet/stylus combination is very popular and common, when we illustrate particular interactions with the computer in this book, the illustrations will be with the combination just described. There are many variations on the same idea that can enhance your use of the computer and make using the machine more enjoyable.

One variation is for the tablet to be *pressure sensitive,* so it can respond to how hard you're pressing down with the stylus. Another variation is for the stylus to be *tilt sensitive,* so the computer can "know" at what angle you're holding the pen. These enhancements can make using the computer a very intuitive kind of experience, when the computer is running programs that look for this information and use it to help you.

In addition to a stylus with just one button (in the tip), you may sometimes use a *puck* or a similar device called a *mouse;* both are illustrated in Fig. 1-6. The puck is a small box with a little see-through crosshair at the top and several buttons below it. The computer can read the position of the puck or mouse from the tablet, and can respond to the pressing of different buttons as commands.

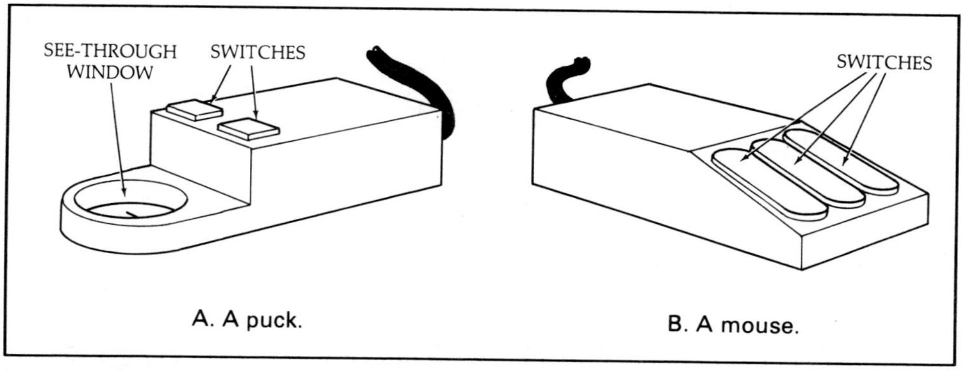

Fig. 1-6. Two input devices that rest on the surface of a tablet; both have switches on top.

Joysticks and Trackballs

Both the joysticks and trackballs, usually used to position something on a screen, can convert physical motion to the numerical input the computer needs. For example, we might say, "Move the chair to the right." The computer would want us to say, "Move the chair 5.33 feet to the right." With these input devices, we can just move the joystick or trackball to the right, and it will give a number to the computer that represents how much and in what direction we've moved.

Joysticks are shafts that freely rotate and swing from left to right and top to bottom, pivoting from the bottom of the shaft. Sometimes you can rotate the handle as well (as in Fig. 1-7). The computer can determine the current position of the joystick and react to it, in the same kind of way that a television set can determine the position of the channel selector and respond to it by tuning into the correct channel.

A *trackball* is usually a hard plastic ball that you can spin with the force of your hand (Fig. 1-8). The computer responds to the trackball in one of two ways. The first way is to monitor how long the ball is spinning, and as long as it spins to the right (for example), an arrow on the crt will track the movement and go right at a constant speed, no matter how fast the trackball is being moved. The other way is for the arrow to move with a speed relative to the speed of rotation of the trackball. For example, spinning the trackball to the right very fast would cause the cursor to move to the right very fast. Spinning the trackball slowly to the right would move the cursor slowly to the right.

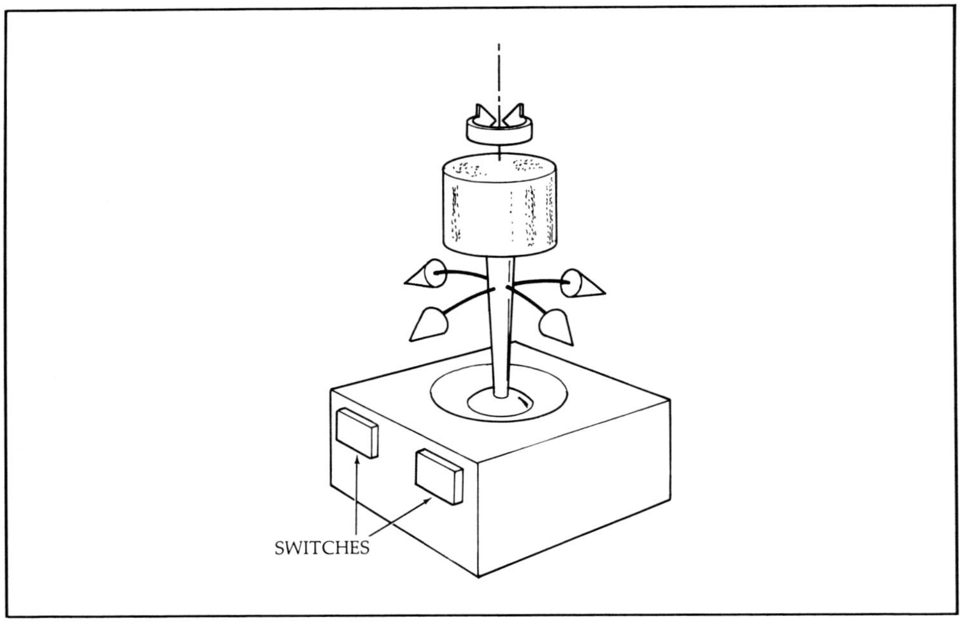

Fig. 1-7. A joystick.

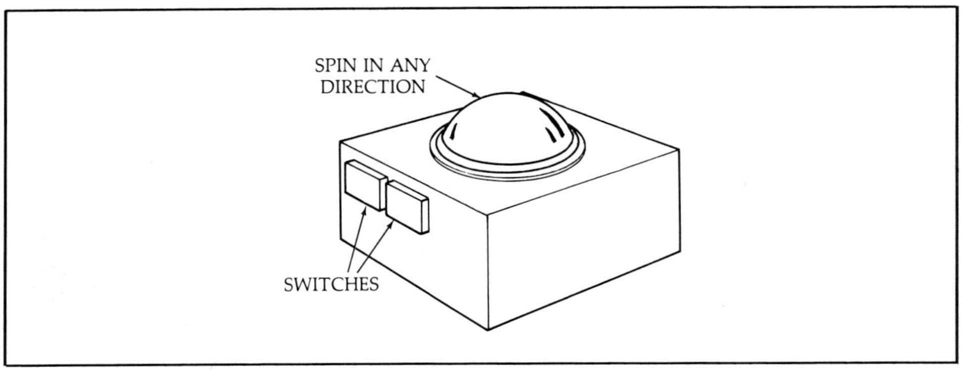

Fig. 1-8. A trackball.

SUMMARY

This chapter was broken up into two main sections: some general ideas about computer graphics and a description of some common hardware used in computer graphics.

The word *model* can be used in two ways: A *scale model* is a copy of some object (usually recreated larger or smaller than the original). A *mathematical model* is a set of equations that describe some physical process, from the movement of a scale model to the future of the economy.

When you want to create models with the computer, you may either come to the computer terminal prepared with engineering drawings that describe your model, or you may interactively build your model, such as assembling an object out of wooden blocks. Generally, most modeling is prepared.

An object may be created by *subtractive modeling*, where you remove chunks of an object to arrive at your desired shape, like carving marble. Or you may build up an object with *additive modeling*, where you add material to the object to make it take form. Sculpting with clay is an example of additive modeling.

When the computer draws the final picture, it may be either as a *line drawing* or as a *shaded drawing*. Generally, line drawings are used for engineering purposes and for quick sketching of an object for examination, and shaded drawings are used for final production of realistic-looking images.

A computer may generate images that are either *static* or *dynamic*. Generally, a static display is a single picture that is displayed for a second or more. We often generate static displays when we generate high-quality stills of shaded drawings. To make the picture high quality means we have to wait a long time for it to be produced, so the last picture drawn generally sits on the screen for a while. *Dynamic* displays are used when we want to create images in *real time*, sort of making a movie on the spot in response to the user's control. Aircraft simulators use dynamic display.

Models also may be static or dynamic. A *static model* is a fixed shape, like a canoe or dining-room chair. A *dynamic model* has properties built into the model description that enable it to change its shape within certain limits created by the modeler. Examples of dynamic models are a sailboat with a moving rudder, or a folding chair.

We then looked at some of the hardware you might find around a computer graphics installation. We covered the different *crt* screens (one for text, one for shaded pictures, and one for line drawings). We mentioned the uses of a *printer/plotter,* which can generate line drawings or crude shaded drawings. We also looked at data tablets, with their associated *stylus, puck,* or *mouse.* We found that the computer could always determine where the stylus or puck is on the tablet, and will often let you know it's following you by *tracking* the stylus on one of the crt's. The computer can also read the status of various switches and buttons that may be associated with the tip of the stylus or on the puck.

We also looked at *joysticks* and *trackballs,* which provide an intuitive and interactive way for us to move things around on the computer screen in addition to the stylus and tablet. By holding a joystick to one side, we can cause the cursor to move at a constant speed in that direction. We also saw that by spinning a trackball we could cause the cursor to move across the screen in the indicated direction. We saw we could choose between having the cursor move in the direction of spinning at a constant rate irrelevant of the speed of the trackball, or have the cursor move at a speed proportional to the speed of the ball's rotation.

Chapter TWO

Geometry

In this chapter we're going to define a few concepts and phrases associated with geometry that are essential to computer graphics. We'll start with a review of basic geometry and move on to discussing how to locate points in space and describe their movements.

We'll also talk about how to measure angles using two different measuring systems. Next, we'll look at curves and curved surfaces and mention a way we can measure the curvature of these objects.

We'll then discuss how to move objects around in space and describe those movements mathematically, and close with a discussion of a new symbol that actually represents three different values at once, which will be vital to understanding how the computer shades three-dimensional objects.

DEFINITIONS

We need to define some concepts and terms associated with them before we can get started. They are the building blocks of geometry, much in the same way as nouns, verbs, and sentences are the building blocks of English. We'll use these basic definitions in different ways to discuss more complicated geometric ideas both later in this chapter and throughout the book.

Dimension

We'll be able to consider the word *dimension* as synonymous with *direction*. For example, a piston has one dimension of travel available to it—up/down (Fig. 2-1). A ball on a pool table may travel in two dimensions—left/right and forward/backward (Fig. 2-2). It is an important fact that the total motion of the ball on the table, whatever its direction and speed, may be represented by breaking down its total motion

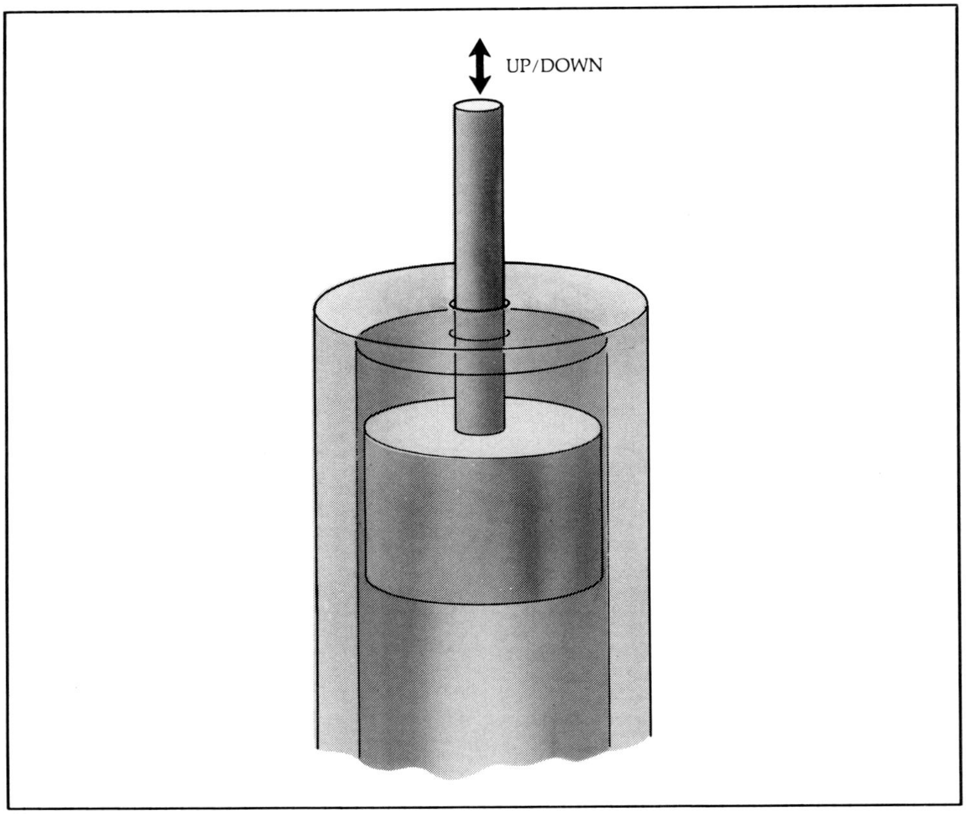

Fig. 2-1. A piston has only one dimension available for movement—up/down.

into its speed along each dimension. For example, Fig. 2-3 shows a ball heading along the table toward a pocket. We can describe the motion of the ball as being partly down the length of the table, and partly across the width of the table. These two motions happening together cause the ball to move at an angle and head in a diagonal toward the pocket. These two independent motions (that together make up the complete motion) are called the *vector components* of the motion. We will cover vectors later in this chapter. The word "component" is synonymous with "part," so the vector components of the ball's motion are the different parts of the total motion. Each vector component is a motion (like down the table or across it), and together they describe the ball's motion. Describing the speed of the ball in each dimension completely describes the motion of the ball. Fig. 2-4 shows a few examples of this.

A kite can fly in any direction within three dimensions (Fig. 2-5). Similarly to the pool ball, its motion in three dimensions may be represented by its motion in each one of the three dimensions listed separately but

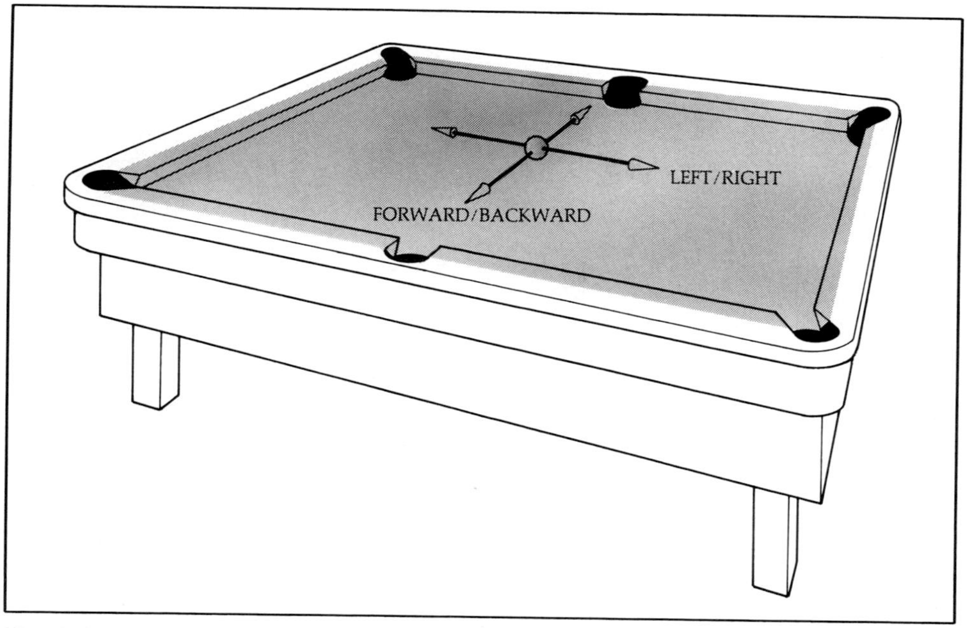

Fig. 2-2. A pool table allows the ball to travel in two dimensions—left/right and backward/forward.

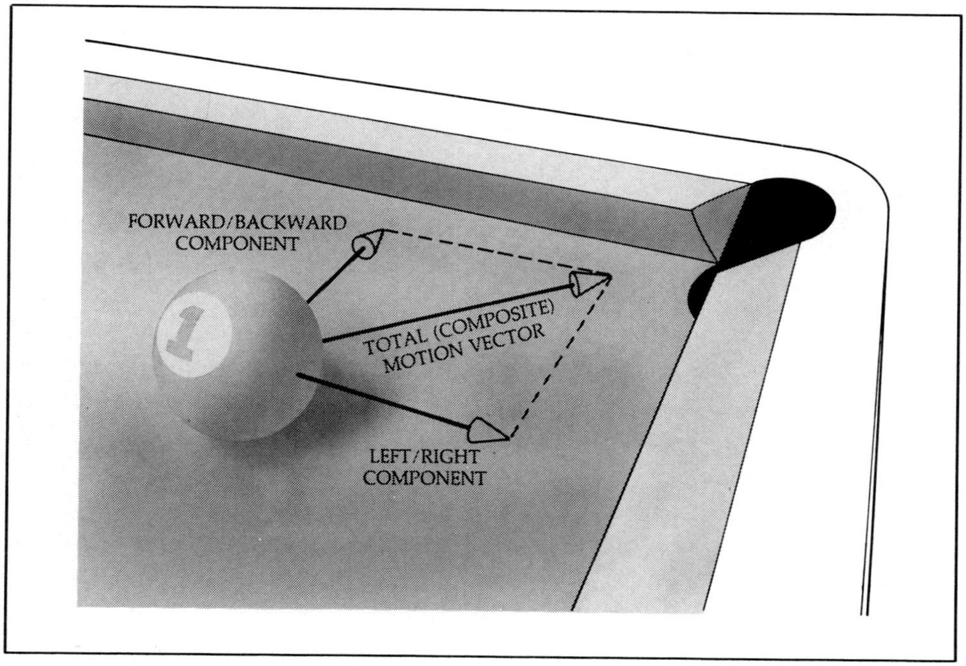

Fig. 2-3. Pool ball moving toward pocket.

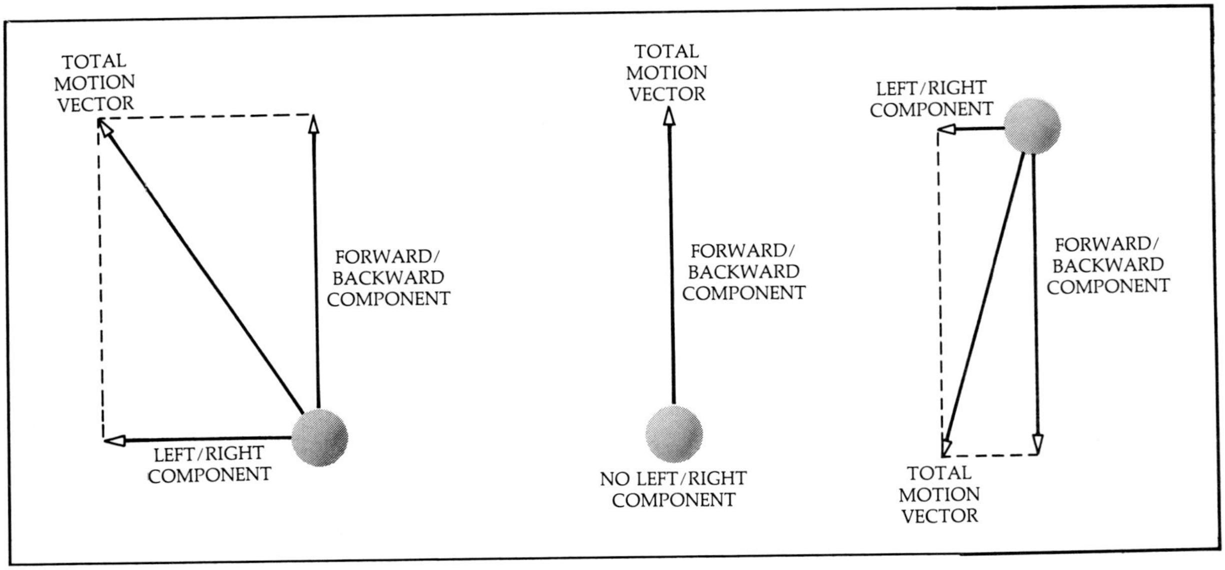

Fig. 2-4. How different components make up a single vector.

taken together (Fig. 2-6). These three separate motions, which taken as a group represent the total motion of the kite, are the three *vector components* of the kite's motion.

Point, Line, Plane, and Space

A set of numbers that describe a location along a set of axes relative to an origin describe a *point*. A point isn't really a thing, rather it's a place where a thing can be.

Imagine two points. They can be anywhere at all and still be connected by a straight *line*. Basically, a line connects two points in the simplest way. A more common definition is that a line describes the shortest distance between two points.

Now if we take a line and place it somewhere, and then place a point (not on the line) somewhere, we can define a *plane* as a flat sheet that passes through both the line and the point. Fig. 2-7 shows a couple of line/point combinations and the planes that join them.

Lastly, if we imagine a point not on the plane, we can say that everything belongs to *space*, and that's as far as we'll go along this train of thought. Space requires three dimensions, so we say that space is three dimensional.

So space is three dimensional, a plane (like a pool table) is two dimensional, a line (like the motion of a piston) is one dimensional, and (surprise!) a point is zero dimensional.

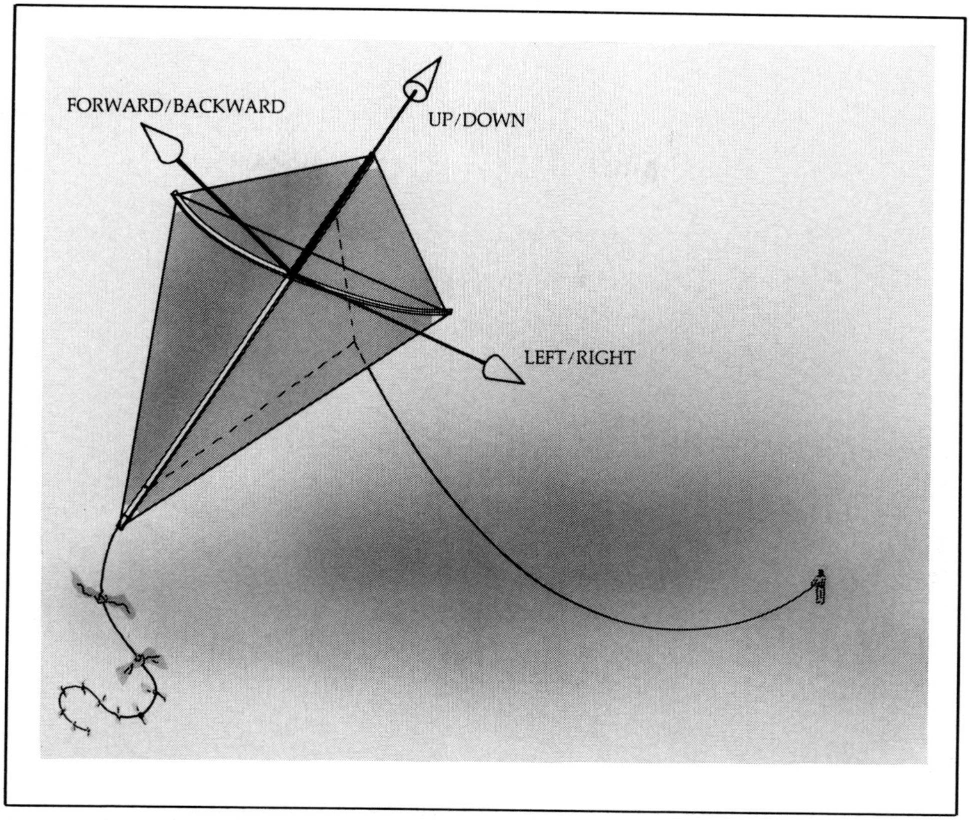

Fig. 2-5. A kite has three dimensions available for movement.

Coordinate System, Origin, and Axis

Let's say you're flying the kite of Fig. 2-5. We have stated that you can describe its motion in three dimensions by specifying its speed in each direction separately, and then taking the three values as a group. This idea may not seem particularly useful right now, but it will become important when we consider animating three-dimensional objects.

So we know how to describe the motion of the kite but that still doesn't describe it completely. We know how it's moving, but where is it? To tell someone else how to locate your kite from a swarm of theirs, you'd have to describe its position relative to a *reference point*. For example, in Fig. 2-8, you might say "My kite is the one immediately left of the kite with the long tail." In this case the kite with the long tail is the reference point. This use of another kite is a poor choice for a reference point, though, because the kite is moving. Another problem with this reference point is that everyone has to stand where you're standing for "left" to mean the same

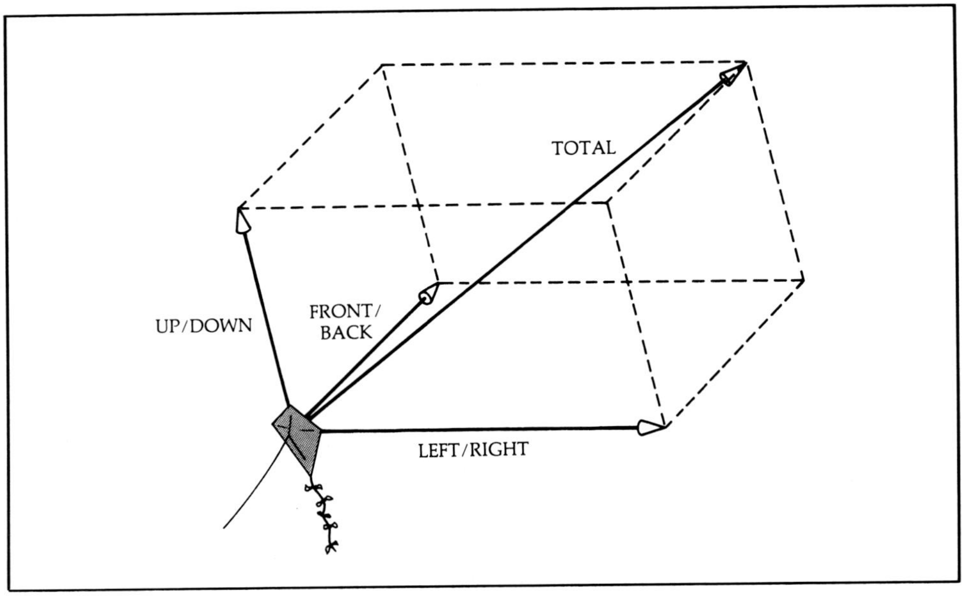

Fig. 2-6. A three-dimensional vector and its components.

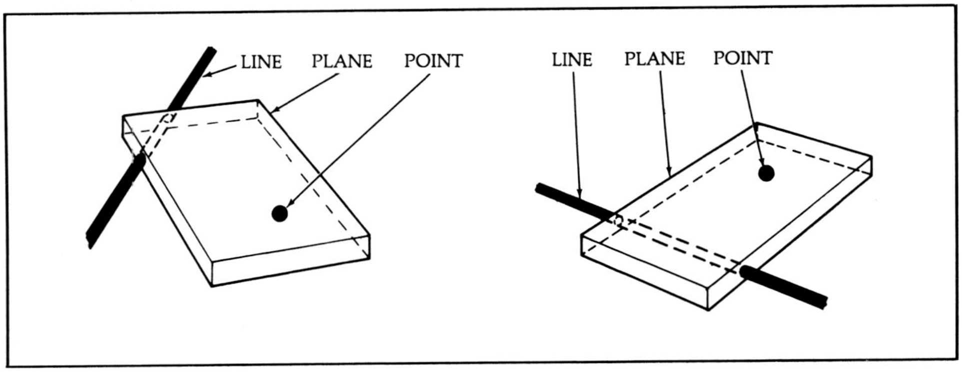

Fig. 2-7. A plane is defined by a line and a point.

thing for everyone. A better reference point is one that is not involved with the thing being measured. A big rock on the ground might do in this case.

We can measure something precisely from such a nonmoving reference point, commonly called an *origin*. We might find, for example, that the kite is 20 feet south, 15 feet west, and 25 feet above the white rock. This description of the kite's position is better than the previous one because it is true for all observers: I don't have to be standing where you are for your west to be my west, as I do if my left is to be your left.

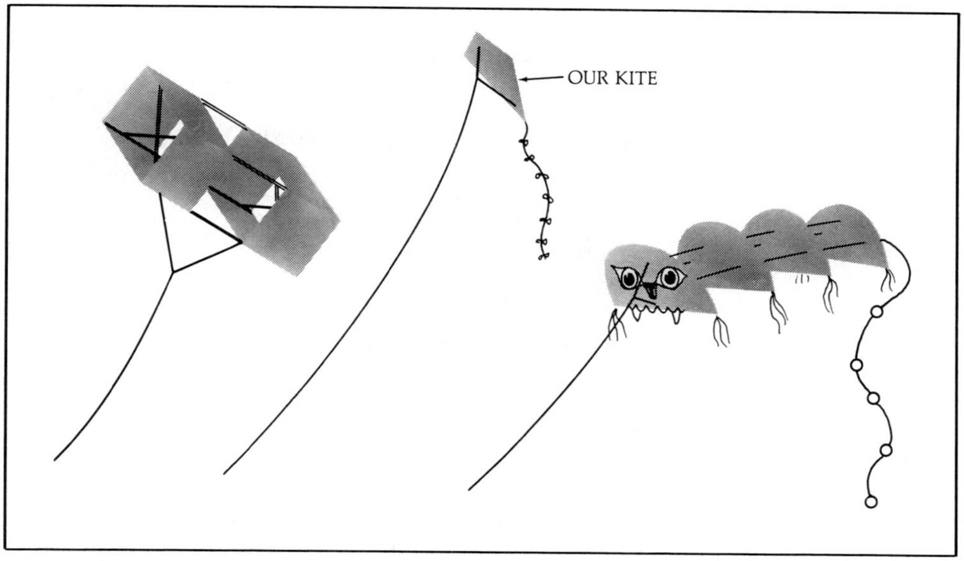

Fig. 2-8. Identifying "our kite" in relation to another kite.

We just located the kite by stating its distance from the origin in three dimensions. The directions were north/south, east/west, and up/down, and each direction had a distance associated with it. When we measure along a line (for example the line of north/south) we call that line an *axis*. If we measure something with a yardstick, then we say we are measuring along the axis of the yardstick, or the yardstick is the axis of measurement. The plural of axis is *axes*.

To specify the kite's location we needed more than just three distances. The distances had to be chosen along axes that gave us the most amount of information. The way these axes were aligned is shown in Fig. 2-9. A combination of axes like this is called a *coordinate system*. Most of the coordinate systems we will use in this book will have either two or three dimensions, or axes, in addition to the origin. The origin is in fact defined as the point where the three axes intersect.

Remember when we discussed the pool ball and the kite, we said that we could describe the motion of these objects completely with the vector components of their motion. We have to choose these vector components in a very particular way if we want to really describe the complete motion of the object. The coordinate system we're using, commonly called the *Cartesian coordinate system*, has proven to be a useful and complete system when we describe the motion of an object as a certain amount along each axis. This system isn't the only one that works; but besides being very

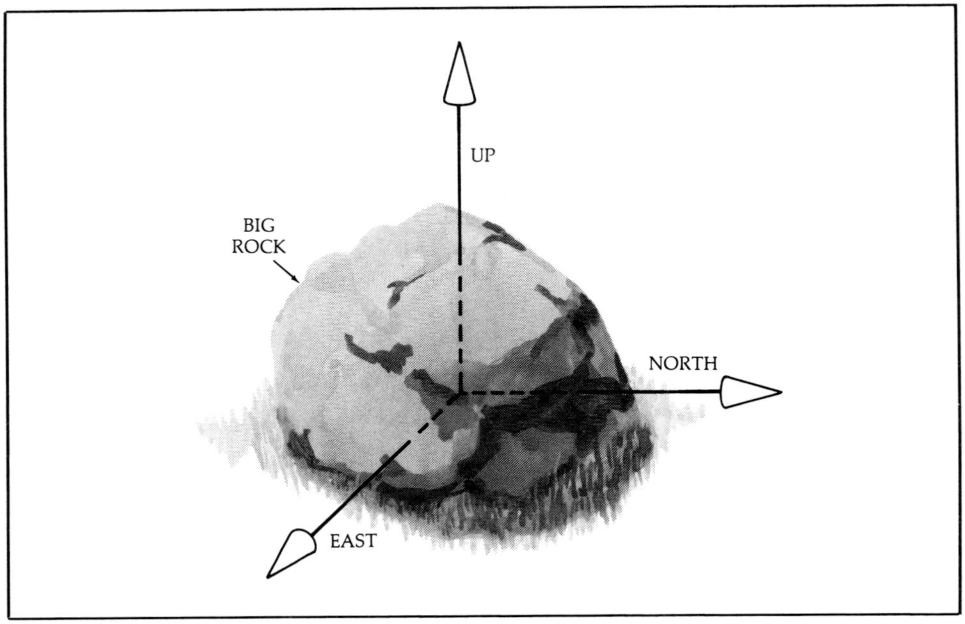

Fig. 2-9. Using the big rock as an origin.

easy to use, it's the one used most often in computer graphics, and the only one we will consider.

Mathematicians are fond of using abstract names for things. Coordinate systems are used so often that it has become inconvenient to label the axes north/south, east/west, and so on. Instead we label the axes with completely arbitrary letters. These letters have evolved by convention to be X, Y, and Z. Fig. 2-10 shows a coordinate system with the axes labeled with these letters. The letters may be lower or upper case although usually they are written in lower case. Also, the units on these axes are also completely arbitrary. We usually mark off distances of one, two, three, and so on, without any mention of whether we're marking off feet, yards, inches, or whatever. We also mark off the units in the other direction (on the other side of the origin), calling them negative one, negative two, negative three, and so on.

The coordinate system allows us to precisely locate a point within it. Fig. 2-11 shows a point called "R" (an arbitrary name). We can find this point by going 3 units along the X axis, 4 units along the Y axis, and then 2 units along the Z axis. We usually represent this point in shorthand by naming the distances that must be traveled between parentheses and separated by commas, and always in the order (X,Y,Z). For example, "R"

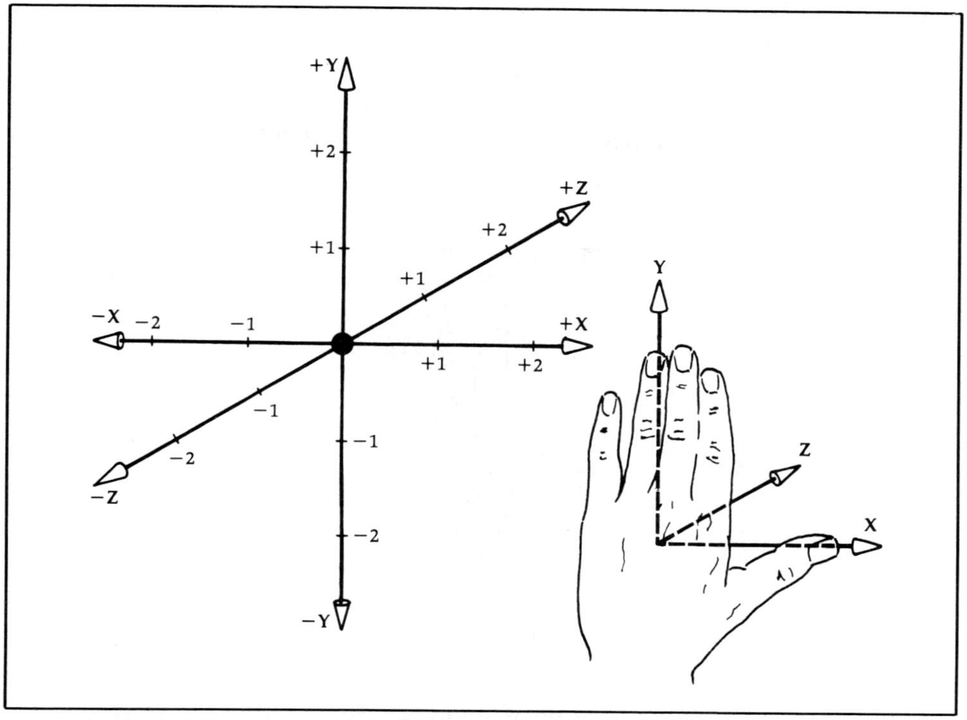

Fig. 2-10. Marking the three-dimensional axes with distance from the origin.

is at (3,4,2). Note that it doesn't matter where you're standing when you measure to find point "R"; it's in the same place for everyone.

ORIENTATION OF COORDINATE SYSTEMS

Recall that in the previous section we pointed out that it was important for everyone to agree on the coordinate system being used and where the origin is located.

The naming of the three axes can be done in many different ways, but there is one that has become the most popular in computer graphics. It is called the *left-handed coordinate system.* It is called "left" because if you hold out your left hand, thumb extended, your thumb points in the direction of positive X, your fingers point in positive Y, and your palm pushes along positive Z. This system is pictured in Fig. 2-10. The origin, as always, is (0,0,0). What the left-handed coordinate system really tells us is which direction to start labeling positive numbers in; we then label negative numbers in the other direction.

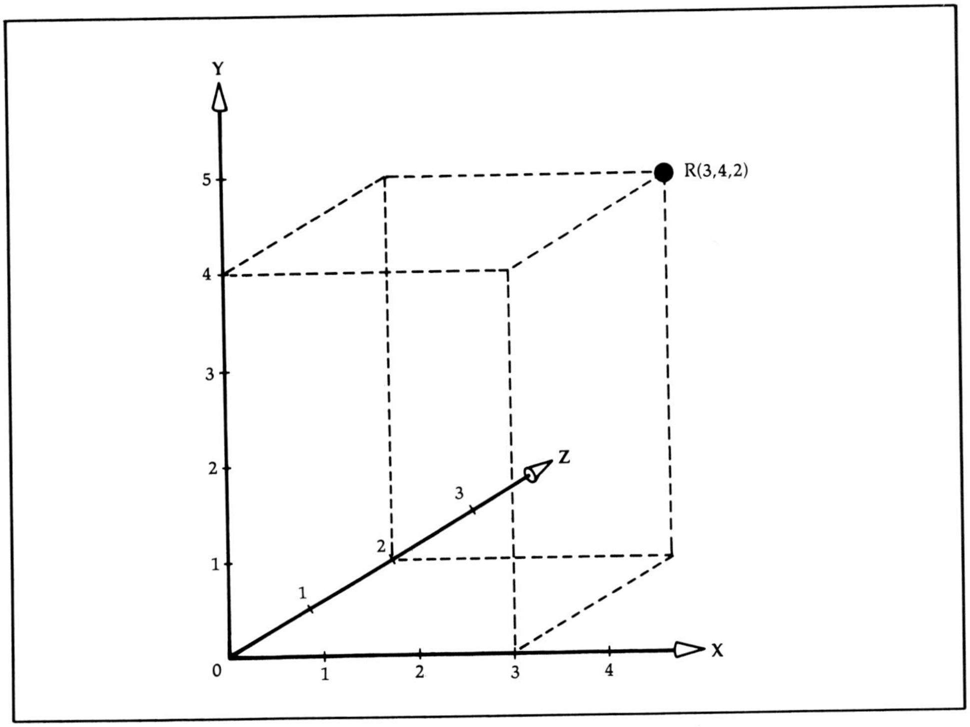

Fig. 2-11. Finding the three-dimensional point "R" at (3,4,2).

We will want to talk about rotating things around the various axes. For example, a child in a swing is rotating about the axis of the top bar in the swing set (Fig. 2-12). We know that the swing is going around the axis, but we want to be able to define the direction of its motion and the amount of rotation. We will call rotation in one direction *positive*, and rotation in the other direction *negative*. We need a scheme that will allow us to uniquely define positive and negative directions of rotation for any axis.

The name of this technique is the *right-handed rotation rule*. Fig. 2-13 gives an example. To find the direction that we will call *positive rotation*, point your right thumb along the axis toward the origin. Curl your fingers around, and they point in the direction of positive rotation. An angle measured in this direction is a positive angle (i.e., 45 degrees), an angle in the other direction is negative (i.e., −45 degrees). Fig. 2-14 shows some examples. Note that the positive angles are in the direction of positive rotation given by the right-hand rule. These positive and negative directions are easy to remember if you think of driving a screw into a piece of wood. The measuring axis is down the length of the screw. Turning the

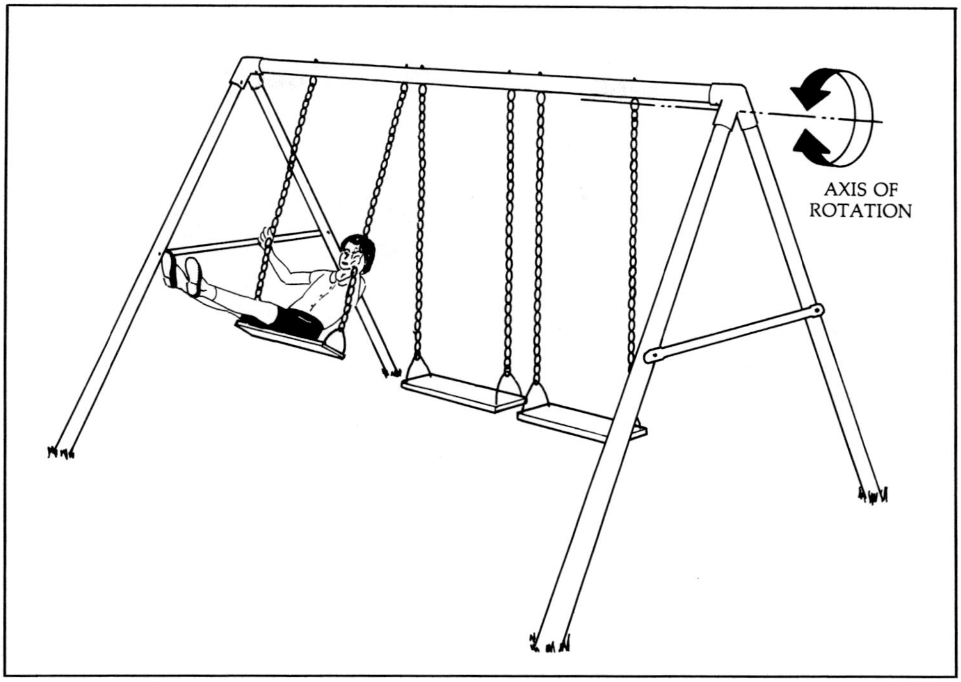

Fig. 2-12. The top bar of the swing is the axis of rotation.

screw to make it go in is positive rotation; turning the screw to make it come out is negative rotation.

ANGLES, RADIANS, AND DEGREES

We often want to compare two things and find out to what degree they are the same, like comparing the pictures my camera takes with the pictures you get from yours. In the case of lines, the only thing that seems to separate two lines from each other is the direction the two lines point in. Fig. 2-15 shows several lines. We might describe these lines as one that's almost horizontal, one almost vertical, and one in between but we haven't assigned a numerical value to the degree in which they line up.

If you examine the point of intersection between two lines, you can measure the amount to which they line up by measuring the angle between them. Our most common system of measuring angles is to cut up a circle into 360 pieces, or degrees, as in Fig. 2-16. If you measure the two intersecting lines in Fig. 2-17, you can find that they meet at an angle of about 26 degrees.

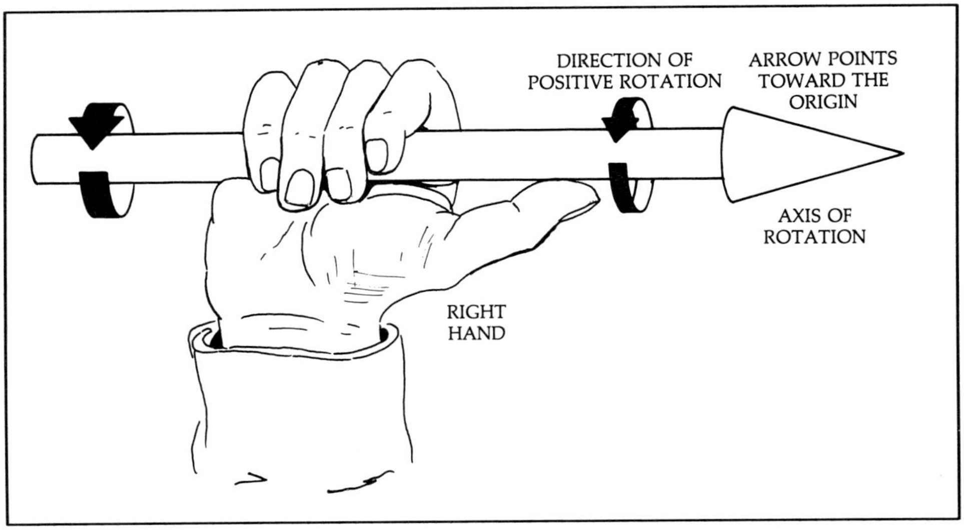

Fig. 2-13. The right-hand rotation rule.

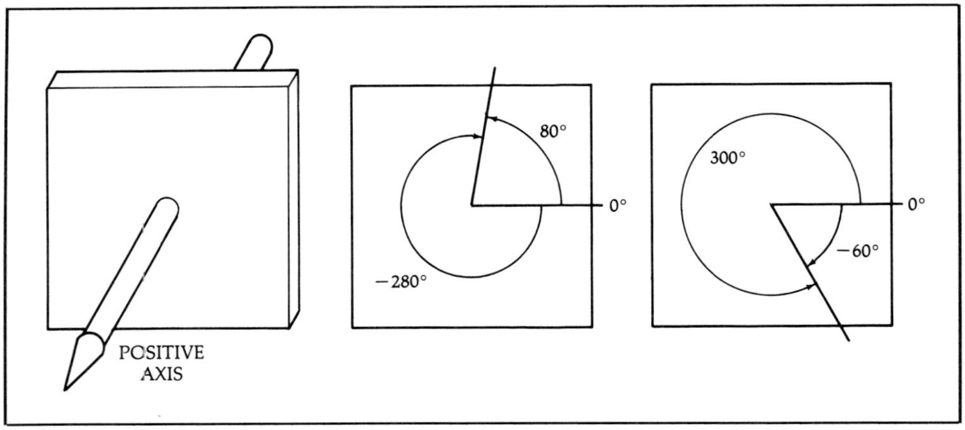

Fig. 2-14. Measuring angles.

The smaller the angle between the two lines, the more they line up or are said to *converge*. As the angle increases, the lines line up less and less, or *diverge*. At 90 degrees, the two lines are as unlined up as they get. We call an angle of 90 degrees a *right angle*.

An alternative way of measuring angles is to use *radians*. We start by defining the number pi. Pi is a Greek letter (π—pronounced "pie"), that works out to about 3.14 (the ratio of the circumference of a circle to its diameter). We say that there are pi radians (or 3.14 of them) in 180

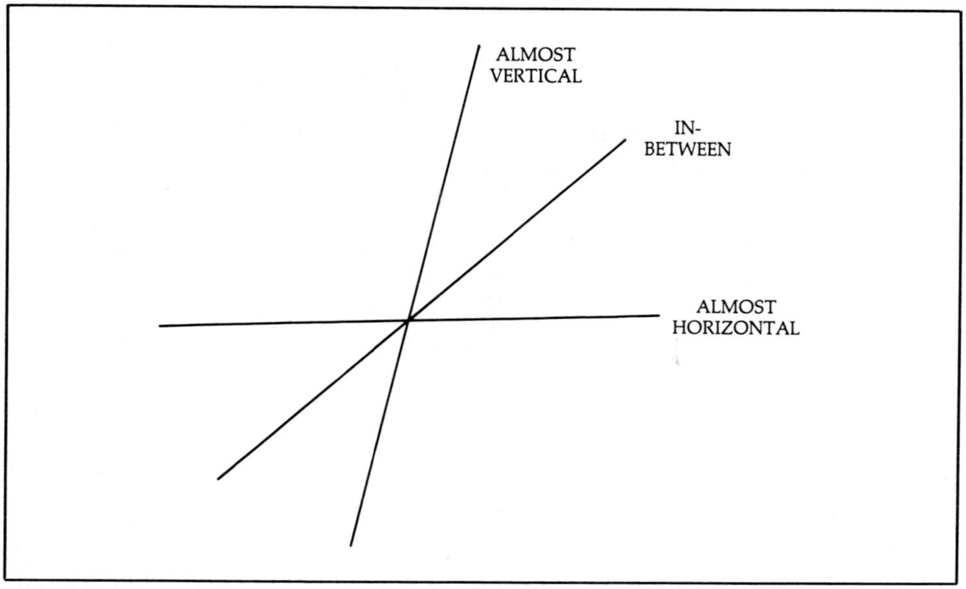

Fig. 2-15. Some lines— how can we describe how well they line up?

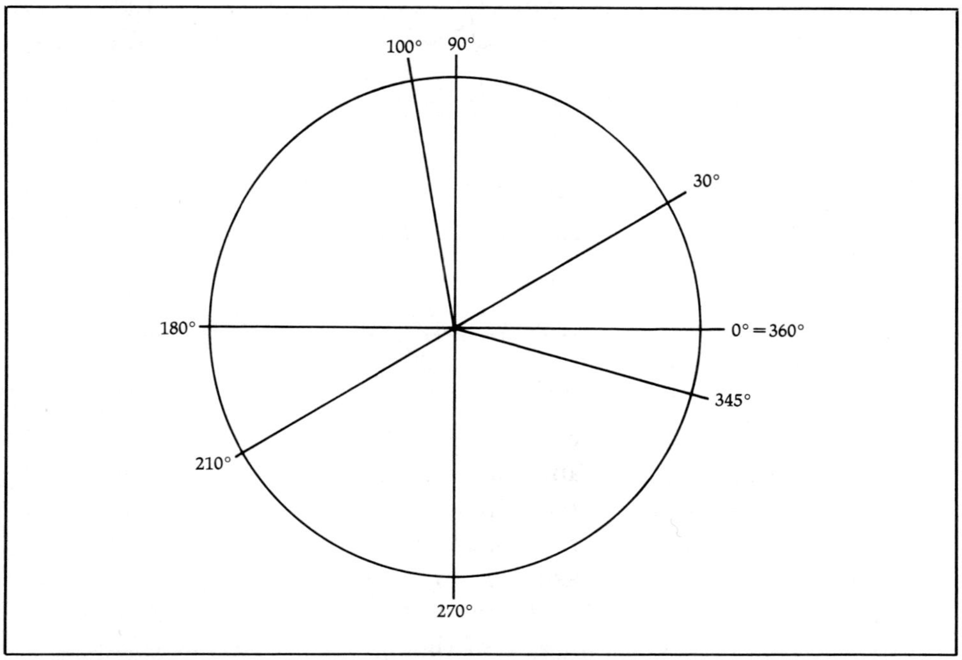

Fig. 2-16. A circle is usually divided into 360°, with 0° going to the right.

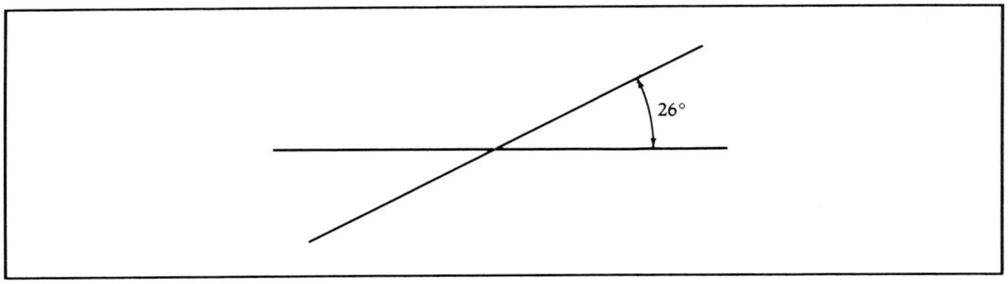

Fig. 2-17. Two lines meeting at an angle of 26°.

degrees. Therefore, a right angle (90 degrees) is equivalent to one-half times pi radians (½ × π or $\pi/2$).

If you're not curious about where these numbers (360 and π) came from, you can skip on to the next section. We're going to briefly see why 360 degrees and pi radians are useful values.

Actually, the number 360 was chosen for the same reason there are 60 minutes in an hour and 60 seconds in a minute. It's a number that's easily broken up into many smaller, equal pieces that are easy to work with because they are whole numbers. Fig. 2-18 shows a circle with the various divisions marked off. For example, we can divide 360 degrees into two pieces (180 degrees each), three pieces (120 degrees each), four pieces (90 degrees each), five pieces (72 degrees each), and so on. Few numbers are

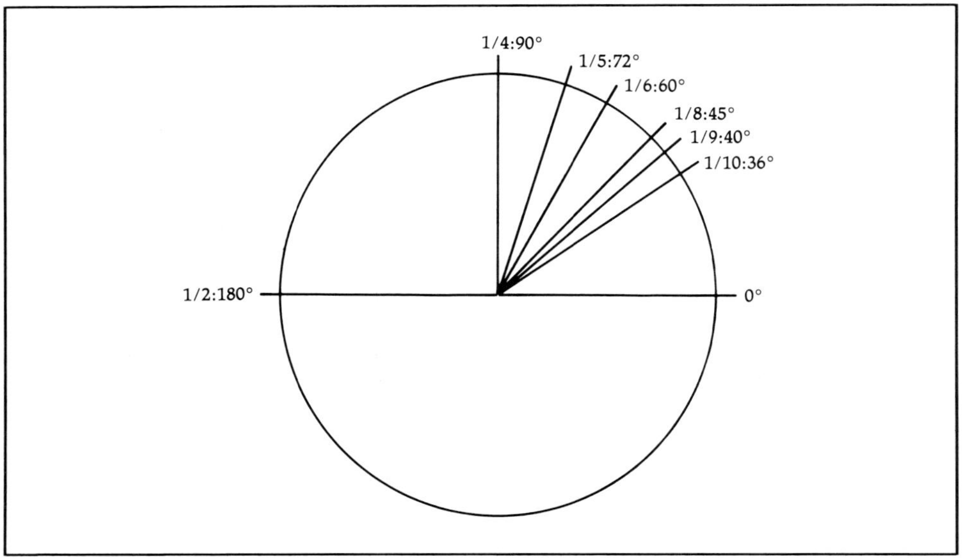

Fig. 2-18. We can divide 360 by many small numbers and still avoid fractions.

as easily divisible by so many small numbers and still avoid fractions. Note that each of these "pieces" of the divided-up circle is a whole number of degrees.

Pi is defined as the ratio of a circle's circumference (the length of the circle if you straightened it out) to its diameter. It turns out that every circle, no matter how large or small, has exactly the same ratio of circumference to diameter. That ratio has been given the name pi. But why do we say there are two times pi ($2 \times \pi$) radians in a circle? Fig. 2-19 may help us see why. Let's pick a circle with a radius of 1 (the units are arbitrary; you may imagine the word "foot" or "inch" after every number if you like). Then, its diameter is two times the radius, or two. We said pi is equal to circumference over diameter ($\pi = c/d$), so circumference is equal to diameter times pi ($c = d \times \pi$), which in this case is $2 \times \pi$. So if we say we have an angle of $\pi/2$ radians, and there are $2 \times \pi$ radians in the whole circumference, the length of the circle that the angle isolates is equal to $\pi/2$. It turns out that in working with these numbers in mathematics, it's very convenient to have the size of the angle tell you exactly the length of the circle it contains. The scheme we just examined does just that, so it has become the other common way of discussing angles, along with degrees.

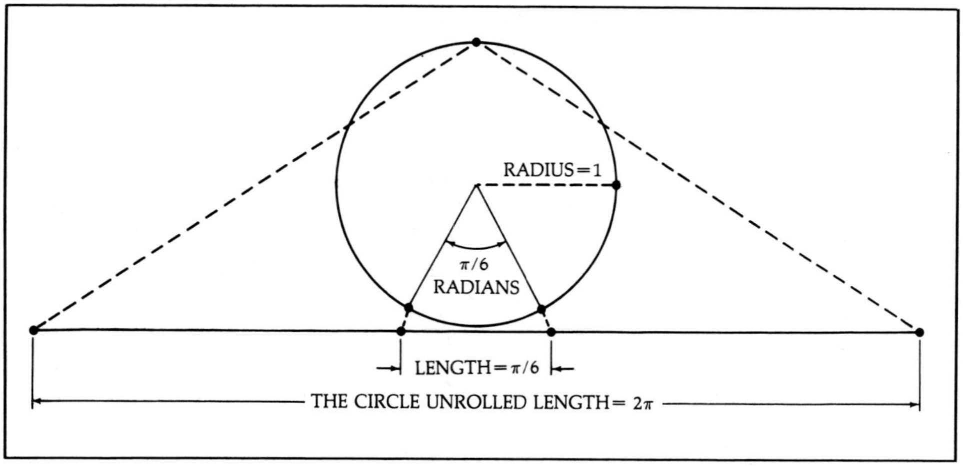

Fig. 2-19. The angle measure is equal to the length of the circle it isolates.

DERIVATIVES AND TANGENCY

We have been discussing mostly straight lines so far, but in practice we use curved lines as often (if not more) to describe all sorts of information to the computer. There are a couple of ideas associated with curved lines that are important to our applications.

Fig. 2-20 shows several curvy lines. We would like to know how the line is curving at different points along its length. We could tell by looking at it, but the computer doesn't have eyes and needs some kind of formal concept for "how the line curves." One very useful technique is to draw a straight line that just "grazes" the point we are interested in. It doesn't matter if this line intersects the curve in other places, and we don't want it

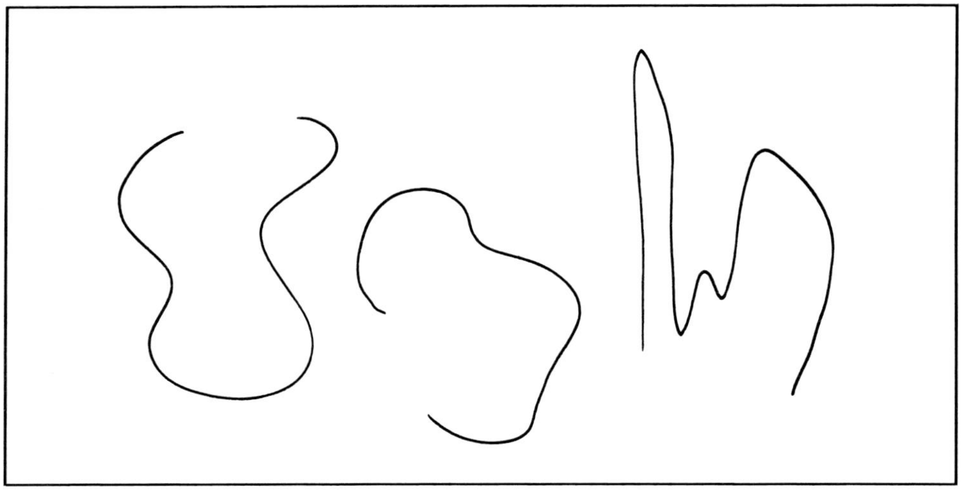

Fig. 2-20. Some curvy lines.

to actually cross the line at our point of interest. The key idea here is that the straight line is drawn so that it just touches the curve. We can then measure the direction, or slope, of the straight line and that tells us how the curve is curving at that point. Fig. 2-21 shows how this technique can tell us about the curvature of the line at different points. The advantage of this technique is that it is relatively easy for the computer to find the straight line that just grazes the curve at a point.

These straight lines are called *tangents*, and they meet the curve at the *point of tangency*. (We also say that the straight line is tangent to the curve.) The slope of the line is called the *derivative* of the curve at that point. It tells us how much (and in what direction) the curve is curving at the point we are inspecting.

Surfaces also have derivatives. At a given point we draw a plane that just grazes the surface, analogous to the line that grazes the curve in the

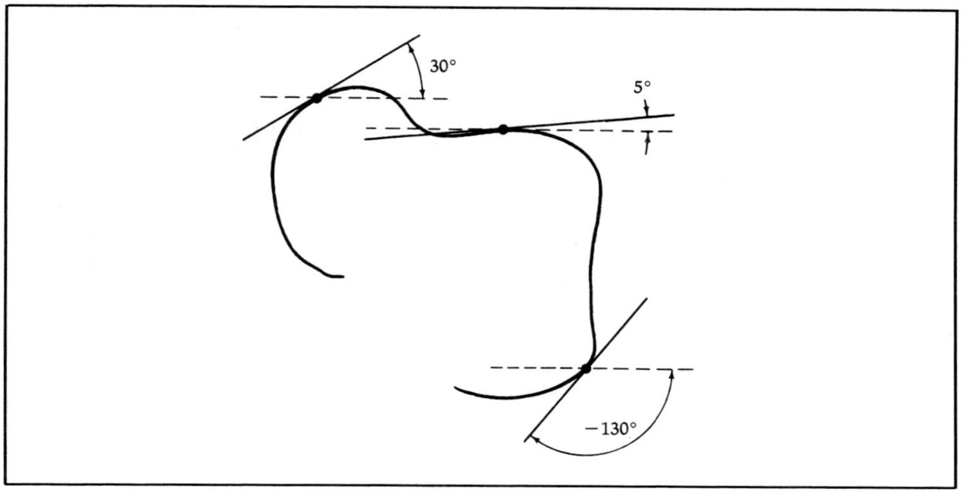

Fig. 2-21. One of the curvy lines from Fig. 2-20 with straight lines just grazing the curves to measure their slopes.

previous discussion. Fig. 2-22 shows such a surface and associated plane. The plane is also said to be tangent to the surface and is called a *tangent plane*. Every point on the surface, just like every point on the line, has its own derivative (or slope of the tangent), and thus, its own tangent (plane or line).

TRANSLATION, ROTATION, AND SCALING (TRANSFORMATIONS)

In computer graphics we generally have no use for points as things in themselves. Rather, they are more like placeholders. A point is usually used to indicate where something is. For example, to describe the flight of a baseball, we could state its three-dimensional location at various instants along its flight. By describing this point so that it moves with time, we're actually moving the location of the center of the baseball, not the baseball itself.

This method is convenient, because it gives us the ability to manipulate entire objects by manipulating only a single point. This procedure is usually done by associating with every object a coordinate system, in effect a new copy of the left-handed coordinate system we just defined. If we have an object that is modeled in this coordinate system, then by moving the point that is the origin of this system, we are moving the whole object

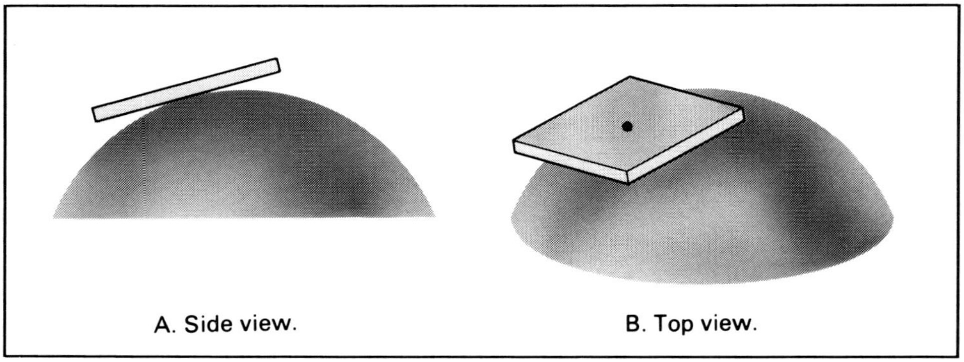

Fig. 2-22. The tangent plane grazes a surface at a particular point.

relative to the original position of the coordinate system. We'll cover this idea in more detail later, but the general idea is all we need right now.

Moving the object along any straight line is called *translating* that object. We might translate an object 5 units along the X axis and 3 units along the Y axis, for example (Fig. 2-23).

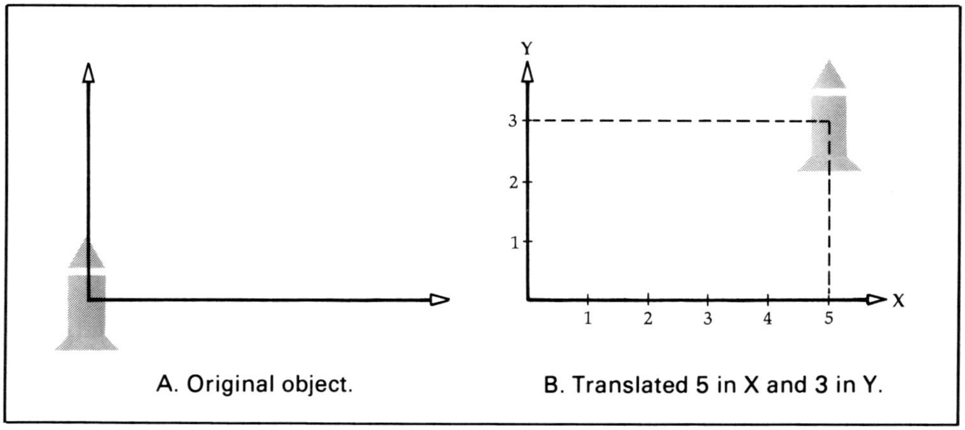

Fig. 2-23. The effect of translation.

Actually, of course, we are not moving the object itself at all, merely its origin and hence its coordinate system. This smaller, moving coordinate system is, however, always positioned relative to a larger, or *global*, coordinate system that serves as our stationary point of reference.

Another common manipulation of an object is *rotation*. Given an axis (or line) in space (perhaps even one of the coordinate system axes) and an angle, we can spin an object around that axis by the given amount, and produce a new copy of it at the new location. Fig. 2-24 illustrates this concept. We can rotate in either the positive or negative direction. The right-handed rotation rule tells which way rotations go around an axis.

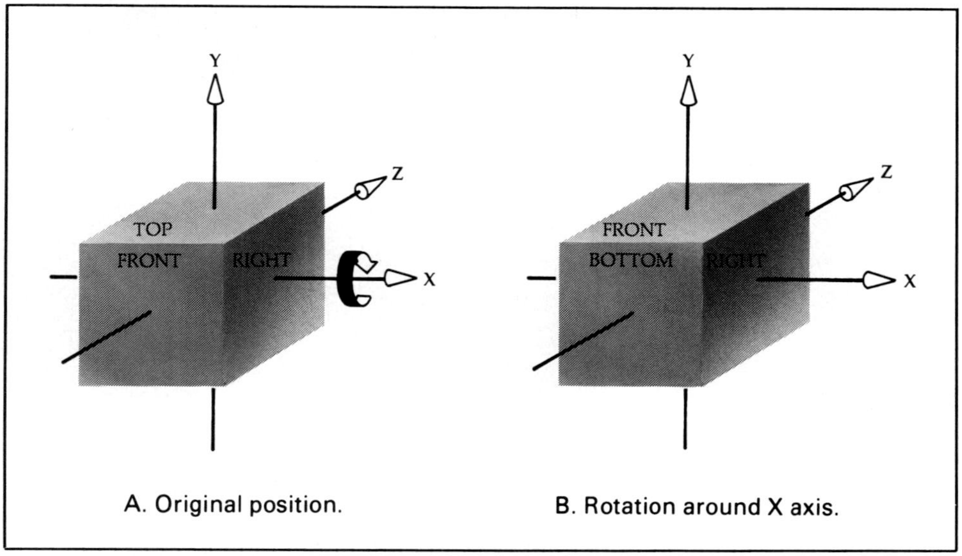

Fig. 2-24. The effect of rotating -90° around X. Note that we did not move; the coordinates stayed in place and the box moved.

Another useful manipulation is called *scaling*. To scale a coordinate system is to stretch it or compress it by different amounts along different axes. The effect of scaling by a number greater than 1 is to make it larger, by pushing every point away from the origin. Scaling by an amount less than 1 shrinks the object, pulling every point in toward the origin. Fig. 2-25 shows different effects of scaling.

These three manipulations of a coordinate system are called *transformations*. These aren't all the transformations that may be applied to a coordinate system, but they are the most common.

It's not worth going too far into detail right now, but note that the order of applying these transformations makes a great deal of difference in the final orientation and location of the object. For example, translation followed by scaling produces a very different result from scaling followed by translation. Fig. 2-26 shows scaling by 2 and translating by 2 in X.

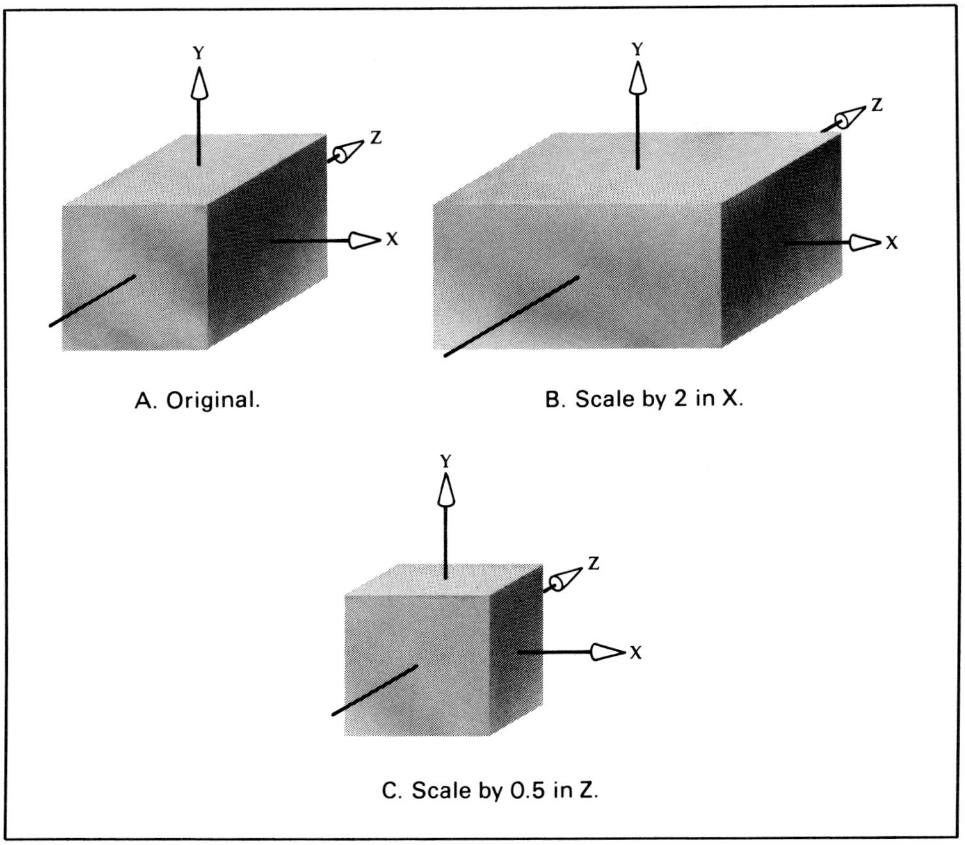

Fig. 2-25. The effect of scaling in different directions.

VECTORS

Points are very good for describing the location of something in space, but they are best for things that are not moving. A point can tell you where a leaf in a river is at a particular time, but not which direction it's headed in nor how fast it's moving.

Since these pieces of information (location, direction of movement, and speed of movement) are all very common and often used together, a new kind of symbol has been invented to carry around all three of them at once. It's called a *vector.*

A vector is symbolized by an arrow. An arrow begins at some point (location), points in some direction (direction of movement), and has

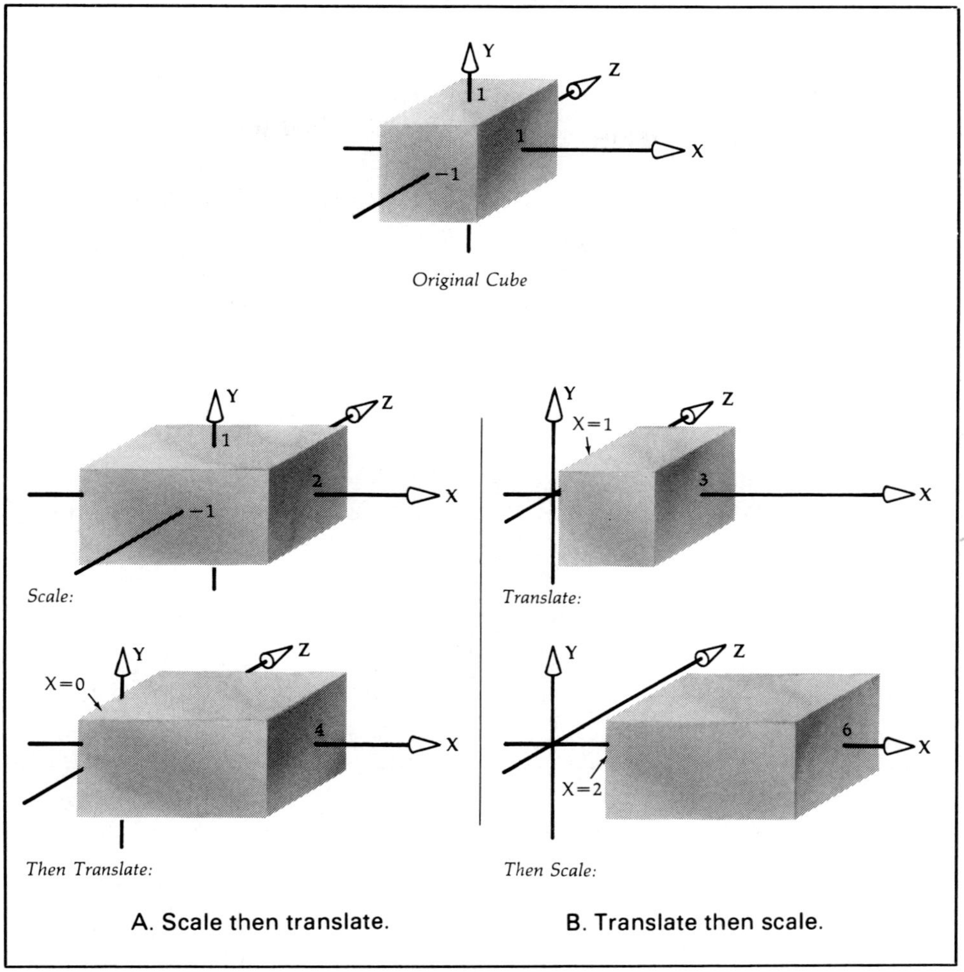

Fig. 2-26. The order of operations is important. Scaling before translating is quite different from translating before scaling.

some length (speed of movement). A long arrow denotes a large speed, a short arrow means a small speed. Some vectors are shown in Fig. 2-27. The idea of a vector is that one symbol can carry around all three pieces of information, like a little suitcase. This is why we use vectors; they are convenient. Note that the velocity is tangent to the track in the roller coaster in Fig. 2-27C.

Vectors find applications throughout computer graphics for the programs that actually render pictures. We won't consider how they're used in those procedures, but we will want to use vectors all the time in repre-

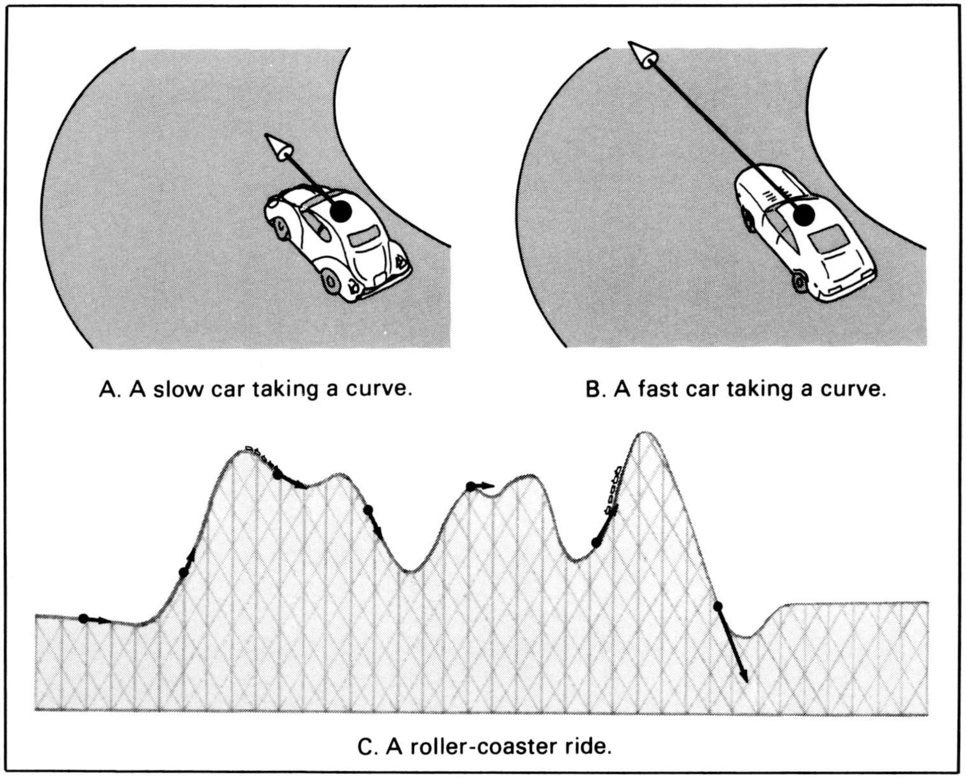

Fig. 2-27. Vectors are arrows that indicate a point, a direction, and a quantity.

senting attributes of a point. Although vectors are usually used to represent the direction and speed of movement of the point they are associated with, they can represent other features of that point as well. They can be any three pieces of information. For example, a vector could represent a tiger. The point of the vector is the position of the tiger, but the length of the vector indicates how hungry the tiger is, and the direction of the vector indicates where the sun is at the time of measurement.

SUMMARY

In this chapter we first reviewed some basic geometry. We defined the word *dimension* to mean something a lot like direction, saying that a piston has one dimension of travel available to it (up/down), while a pool ball has two (left/right, forward/back), and a kite has three (east/west, north/south, up/down). The labels we use on the different directions are totally arbitrary.

We then talked about *points*, *lines*, *planes*, and *space*. We saw that we can move in three dimensions within space, so space is three dimensional. We have two directions to move in a plane (like a pool table), so a plane is two dimensional. The piston that moves in a line has only one dimension available to it, making a line one dimensional, and a point is zero dimensional.

We then said that if we take a line and mark off different lengths upon it and measure with it, we call it an *axis*. A set of axes taken together make up a *coordinate system*, which has an *origin* defined as the place where the axes intersect.

We drew a picture of a *left-handed coordinate system*, which lets us all agree on which directions should be positive and which should be negative for a three-dimensional coordinate system.

We then looked at the different ways we can measure an *angle*. One way was with *degrees*, which we defined there to be 360 of in a complete circle. The other measure was with *radians*, which we defined there to be $2 \times \pi$ of in a complete circle. We saw that 360 degrees and $2 \times \pi$ radians were convenient numbers to use.

Given a curvy line, how much is it curving at any given point and in what direction is it curving? The *tangent line* gave us some idea of the answers to this question by drawing a line that just grazes the curve at the point in question. We saw that we could also draw *tangent planes* to curved surfaces to find out what direction they are curving in.

We then talked about three different *transformations: translation* (moving along a straight line), *rotation* (spinning about an axis), and *scaling* (either pulling an object in or pushing it away from the origin). We found that if we want to perform a series of transformations on a single object, one after the other, it was very important to get them in the right order. In other words, scaling an object and then rotating it gives us a different result from rotating it and then scaling it.

We then mentioned the idea of *vectors*. Vectors are symbolized by an arrow with a starting point, a length, and a direction. This economy of description (three ideas in one arrow) makes vectors very useful for computer graphics where we often have several pieces of information associated with a point. We can then associate a vector with that point where the vector begins at the point on a surface we are interested in, and the length and direction of the vector represent some characteristics of the surface. These characteristics might be anything from the curvature of the surface at that point to the glossiness and color of paint that point is covered with.

The ideas covered in this chapter will all prove valuable to us as we get further into the methods of computer graphics. The better we understand the underlying concepts behind the methods, the better we will understand the methods themselves. And when a method is well understood, it can be used creatively and correctly.

Chapter THREE

Computer and Mathematical Concepts

In this chapter we're going to cover some of the basic ideas associated with using and discussing computers, and then talk about a couple of things that we're going to want the computer to be able to do for us when we do animation.

The discussion will be general, so there won't be any problem with trying specific commands on specific machines. What we're going to cover are the concepts that are common to every computer system that you may come across. The exact names and forms of the commands will vary from machine to machine, so to actually name a command for a given computer would probably cause more confusion than provide explanation.

Armed with the knowledge from this chapter and later in the book, you should be able to ask the right questions of people who know the computer in order to learn the specifics for your machine.

BITS, BYTES, AND WORDS

A computer memory is made up of a great many small locations, each of which can hold only a small amount of information. It's important to understand some of the terminology and workings of a computer's memory, so let's start with a look at a typical computer memory with the help of an analogy.

Imagine the stockroom of the world's biggest shoe store. A small wall of shelves is shown in Fig. 3-1. Every pair of shoes that is or may be in stock has its own storage place on the wall. We are taking inventory, and all we are interested in is whether there is a box of shoes in a given place or not.

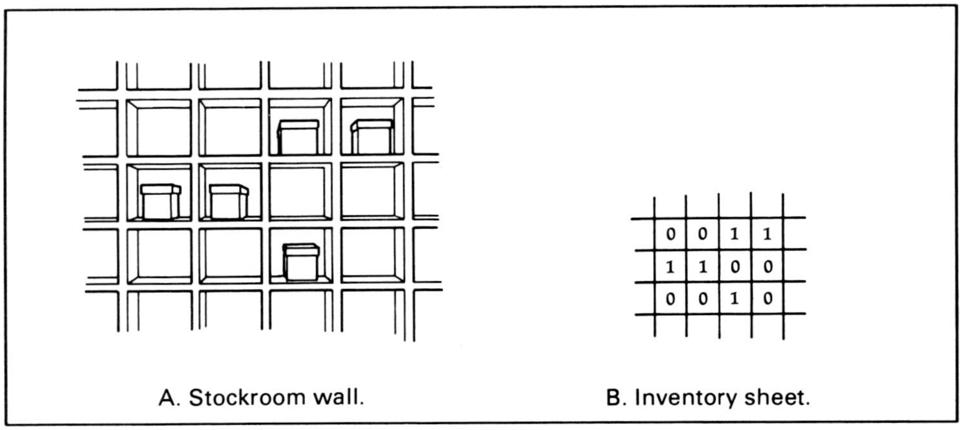

Fig. 3-1. Shelves from a shoe store stockroom wall and the corresponding inventory sheet.

We don't care about style, color, or anything else; just, is there a box in the corresponding place on the wall or is there not?

As we look at every possible place for a box of shoes to be, we ask this question again, "Are there shoes here?" If there are, then the answer is true. If not, the answer is false. We might write down "T" for true and "F" for false. We might also write down a "1" for true and a "0" for false. In this way we can represent the entire wall as a sequence of zeros and ones, which would tell us exactly where there are shoes and where there are not.

Fig. 3-1A resembles how a computer's memory looks—just a big list of ones and zeros, no more! It is a very simple scheme that might appear impractical or even useless for storing information on a routine basis, but that is exactly what a computer memory is. With this simple structure, we can store everything from checkbook-balancing programs, to the data those programs use, to pictures, and anything and everything else that you've ever seen in a computer store.

These ones and zeros are stored in different ways for different uses. Some are stored internally in the computer as immediate information for it; for example, the program it is executing. Sometimes this data is stored on magnetic tapes where it can be safely stored for long periods of time.

We should make sure we keep track of what we mean when we say *memory storage location* because that term can either mean the location where we store the memory itself (like the plastic box where we keep floppy disks), or a spot inside a memory itself where information may be placed. Usually, the meaning of a phrase like "memory storage location" will be clear from the context in which it appears.

We call each storage location in memory (where we may store exactly one "0" or one "1") a *bit*. We call groups of eight bits taken together a *byte*. Groups of bytes then make up *words*. The number of bytes in a word varies but it's usually a multiple of two.

These terms are used so that we can compare the sizes of different computer memories, find out how much room a computer has left to store new information, and otherwise discuss memory sizes.

Often the single unit of a bit is inconvenient. Computer memories usually contain hundreds of thousands of bits, and the numbers describing the size of the memory become unwieldy. It is more common to talk about bytes. But even bytes are too small, and we often refer to thousands of bytes (*kilobytes*), and millions of bytes (*megabytes*), as in "This is a 20-megabyte memory, " meaning it has 20 million bytes of storage. To get a handle on what this means we can usually consider a single byte as just the right amount of room to store one character of text (a letter, number, or punctuation mark). For example, this book (without captions on the illustrations) contains about a quarter of a million characters, so 250 kilobytes of memory is enough to hold the text of this book.

MEMORY TYPES

There are many different technologies for memory storage. The subject can quickly become very complex, but we can make one broad kind of generalization about types of memories and remain unconcerned about the technological details of how they're manufactured and used.

We can approach the distinction with an analogy. When close friends tell us of their birthdays, we generally think of filing that away as information to be remembered over a long span of time; we don't want to forget it right away. Psychologists say we store this kind of information in our *long-term memory*.

On the other hand, say, when driving down a freeway and you see the sign for your exit, you want to remember for the next minute or so that your exit is coming up, but you don't want to retain this information any longer. After you take the turnoff, the memory "My exit is coming up" is useless and need never be remembered again. This kind of information is stored in *short-term memory*.

Computers also have long- and short-term memories. A short-term memory is used by the computer for its own work and any temporary data it may need. When the power is shut off, all information in the short-term memory is lost.

On the other hand, long-term memory is usually external to the computer, and is mediated by human users. This memory will not lose its information when the power is shut off. Such memories consist of magnetic tapes, magnetic cards, floppy disks, "bubble memories," and so forth.

NUMBERS AS ATTRIBUTES

Programmers make an effort to enable users to communicate with computers in languages that the user understands and is familiar with. But natural languages are usually not sufficient for specifying actual values for the computer to process; the computer works with numbers, and often the user must supply input to the computer as numbers.

For example, you might be interested in telling the computer how bright a light source ought to be, or how red you would like a table to be. We will be concerned less with the *qualitative*, or verbal, description (it is very red), and more with the *quantitative*, or numerical description (for example, it is position six on the color wheel) in such cases. We could say that such numbers are characteristics of the models they are applied to. Synonyms for characteristic in this context are attribute and parameter.

An example would be to say, on a scale from 0 to 10, with 0 as dark and 10 as bright, how bright should a light be? Instead of "fairly bright" (a qualitative description the computer cannot work with), we say 3.4 or 7.1, quantitative answers that are understood directly by the computer.

INTERPOLATION

One of the advantages of using a computer for animation is that we can let the computer do a lot of the tedious, uncreative jobs associated with animation that would otherwise have to be done by people. One such job is called *interpolation*, and we will describe what it is and how the computer can help do it for us. We should note, however, that skilled animators are still a vital part of the in-between process when they set it up.

We will give the computer two *extremes*, or *endpoints*, and ask it to fill in the in-between spots with new values.

For example, look at Fig. 3-2. On May 1 it was 30 degrees outside, and

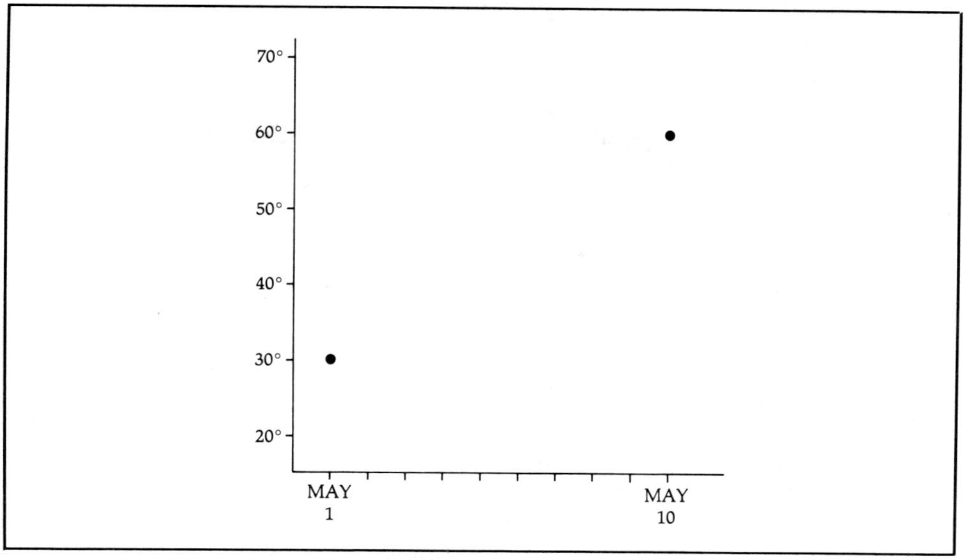

Fig. 3-2. A couple of recorded temperatures.

on May 10 it was 60 degrees. These are the endpoints, and now we may ask what the temperature was on May 5.

We find the temperature at any point in the given range by interpolating between the two extremes. If we perform a *linear interpolation*, it means we connect the two extremes with a straight line (Fig. 3-3). This linear interpolation tells us that on May 5 (halfway between May 1 and May 10) the temperature was 45 degrees.

We might, however, choose to perform a *nonlinear interpolation*, which literally means interpolating with anything other than a straight line. This curve may be created in a great number of ways. Fig. 3-4 shows some nonlinear interpolation curves and how they affect the value of the graph we are interested in. We often do nonlinear interpolations in computer-assisted animation to make movement look smoother.

A special type of nonlinear interpolation is to fit a smooth curve to the available data. There are many ways of fitting a smooth curve to available points. One of the most popular methods is called *spline interpolation*. A *spline* is a curved line that goes through all the data points we have to offer. There is a large body of theory on the different kinds of splines there are and how they work, but they are really all for the same purpose: somehow getting a curvy line to "fit" some data points in a reasonable way.

Fig. 3-5 shows some data points that we would like to have joined in the

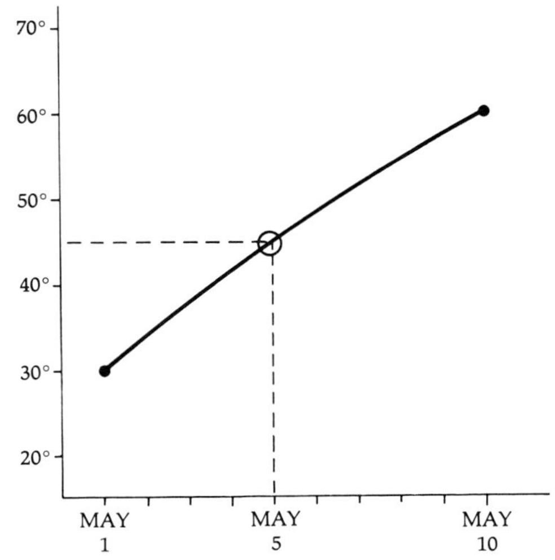

Fig. 3-3. Performing linear interpolation to find the temperature on May 5.

indicated order. When a spline is used to join data points, these points have historically come to be called *knots*. The figure shows how one kind of spline interpolates this set of knots. The best way to understand the splines that are implemented at your computer graphics site is to play with different arrangements of knots and see what happens.

Another common way of saying "draw a spline to connect this data," is to say, "fit a spline to this data."

RANDOM NUMBERS

Often when we simulate some natural phenomenon, we want the results to have some kind of "randomness" in them. For example, we might want the computer to simulate the rolling of a pair of dice in a backgammon program, so of course we want the dice to be as unpredictable, or random, as possible. Randomness appears everywhere in the kind of objects we might want to model with computer graphics: the texture on a tree's bark, the location of "goose bumps" on cold skin, the placement of leaves on a tree, etc.

It isn't really possible for the computer to make truly random numbers, but there are some good techniques for "faking" them. The different techniques generate random numbers in different ways. Usually, there are

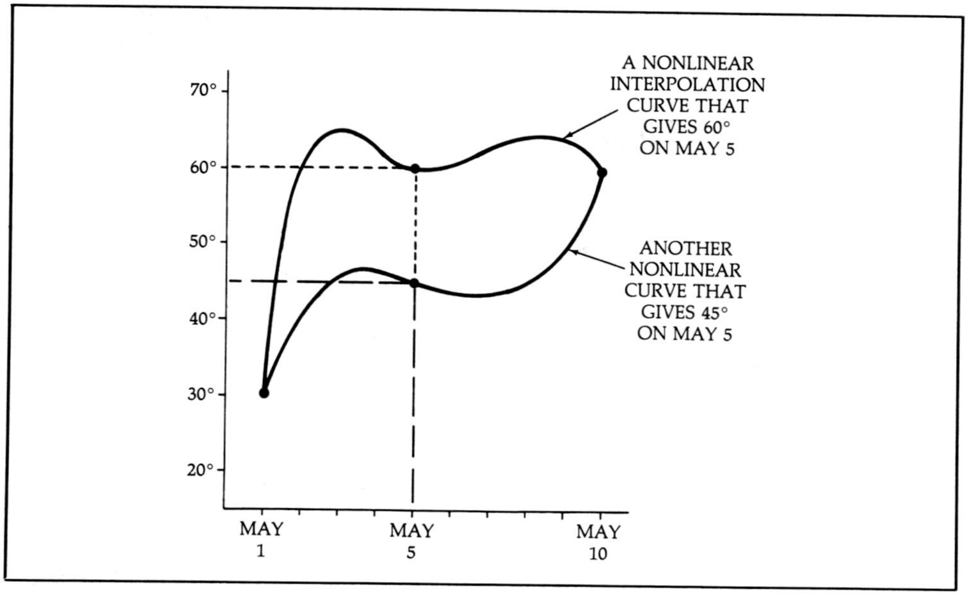

Fig. 3-4. Nonlinear interpolation gives very different results.

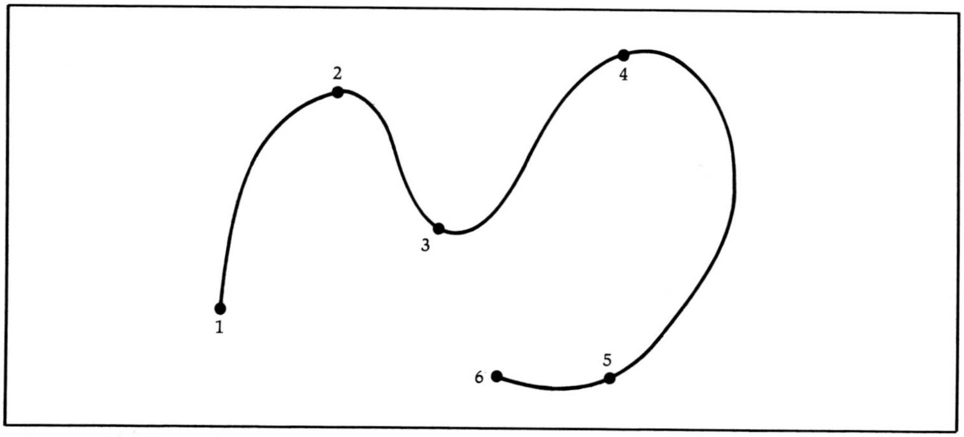

Fig. 3-5. Some points connected by a spline.

some very large-scale patterns to the kinds of numbers that come out of a random number generator. We sometimes find that numbers seem to "group" around a particular average value instead of being spread across a wide range smoothly. We say that different random number generators produce numbers with different *distributions*. When modeling some natural phenomena like the ones just discussed, using different distributions will usually yield different pictures. Fig. 3-6 shows some possible distributions. In particular, the distribution in Fig. 3-6A is called a *bell curve* or a *Gaussian* (pronounced Gow'-see-in) *distribution*. The Gaussian distribution is closely related to the "student curve" used by many teachers when determining a final grade for a course or test.

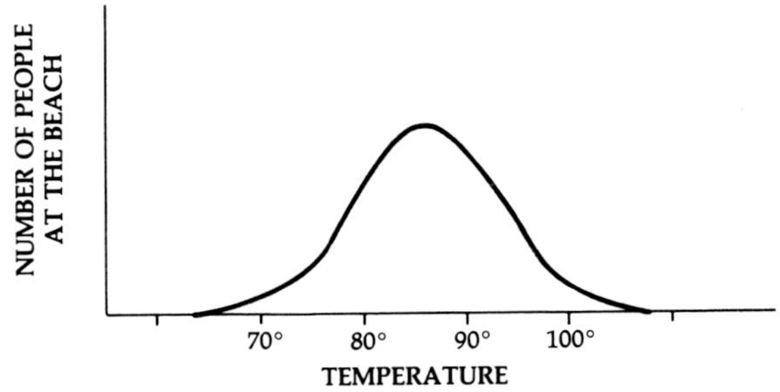

A. Number of people at the beach represented with a bell curve, also called *Gaussian distribution*.

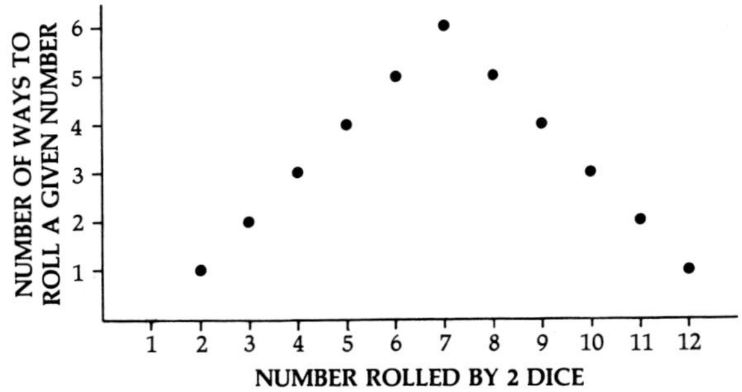

B. Number of ways to roll a given number represented with a linear graph.

Fig. 3-6. A pair of graphs.

SUMMARY

In this chapter we discussed some of the most common ideas associated with computers, and a couple of things that the computer can do for us.

We started by defining a *bit* as a storage location in a computer memory where we can put exactly a zero or a one. We said that a computer memory is nothing more than many of these bits all strung together. It's the task of the computer's hardware and programming (software) to understand what all these ones and zeros mean, not ours.

We defined a *byte* as a group of eight bits, and a *word* as two or more bytes taken as a group. We mentioned that it is often convenient to talk about memory sizes in multiples of thousands of bytes, which we called a *kilobyte*. A million bytes we called a *megabyte*.

We then saw that some memories may be classified as *short-term* memories, which means that they hold temporary data for the computer. That data is often erased by the computer to make room for new temporary data, and is always completely lost whenever we turn off power to the computer. On the other hand, we saw that *long-term* memories can hold information indefinitely. Long-term memories consist of such devices as floppy disks, magnetic bubble memories, magnetic tapes, and so on.

We then considered actually using the computer to do useful work for us, and saw that it can't understand *qualitative* descriptions ("I haven't eaten in a long time"), but needed *quantitative* descriptions ("I haven't eaten in 6.3 hours"). We found that when we want to describe something with a number, we sometimes call that number an attribute or parameter of the item.

We then considered *interpolation*, or finding a value between two *extremes*. We saw that *linear interpolation* would draw a straight line between two extremes and give us the value in between where that line happened to fall. Other schemes are collectively known as *nonlinear interpolation* techniques. One particular nonlinear interpolation technique we looked at was *spline interpolation*, where we fitted a spline, or a curvy line, through the points. The advantage of spline interpolation is that for some computer animation, it looks much better than linear interpolation.

We then briefly considered that we often have a need for *random numbers* to be generated for us by the computer. We mentioned that different schemes for generating random numbers give us numbers that tend to follow some kind of pattern on a very large scale. One pattern is for the numbers to seem to "cluster" around particular values. We can draw pictures of the different *distributions* of these numbers. In particular we looked at the *bell curve*, or *Gaussian distribution*, a very useful kind of way of choosing random numbers.

Chapter FOUR

Surfaces in Space and Lighting

In this chapter we will start talking about three-dimensional shaded graphics. We'll begin by making an initial, broad generalization about the kinds of surfaces you might encounter or want to use in making models.

We'll then talk about those surfaces that get hidden behind other surfaces when we actually draw the picture. We'll go on to defining a piece of information at every point on the surface that helps us determine in what direction that surface is pointing.

We'll then see how that information helps us get started on shading by seeing how the computer treats light sources and their effect on surfaces.

SURFACES

In computer graphics we usually describe scenes we want the computer to render by supplying models of the different objects. These models are actually groupings of simpler surfaces, like spheres, cylinders, and cones. We will call all these shapes *surfaces*. A surface may have many attributes beyond its shape, such as color, texture, transparency, reflectance, and more.

It is helpful, however, to make a broad distinction between two types of surfaces. Fig. 4-1 shows some surfaces that have edges, and we can refer to them as having a top and bottom, front and back, and so on. This kind of surface is called an *open surface*.

Now consider Fig. 4-2. The surfaces here can only be considered overall as having an inside and an outside. We call this kind of surface a *closed surface*. It may be helpful to note that any closed surface may be made with a collection of smaller open surfaces, correctly shaped and placed.

Fig. 4-1. Surfaces with a top and a bottom.

Fig. 4-2. Surfaces with an inside and an outside.

For example, an inner tube is a closed surface, but when it breaks, we patch it with a small patch of rubber, which is an open surface. If the inner tube had been patched many times, then we might find that nothing remained of the original rubber. In that case the closed surface of the inner tube would be completely made up of smaller, open surfaces (the patches).

The idea of combining surfaces to make a more complicated one is a central concept in computer model making. The fundamental simple surfaces that any system provides are called the *primitive surfaces,* and any new objects made from them are called *complex surfaces.* A set of primitive surfaces is shown in Fig. 4-3.

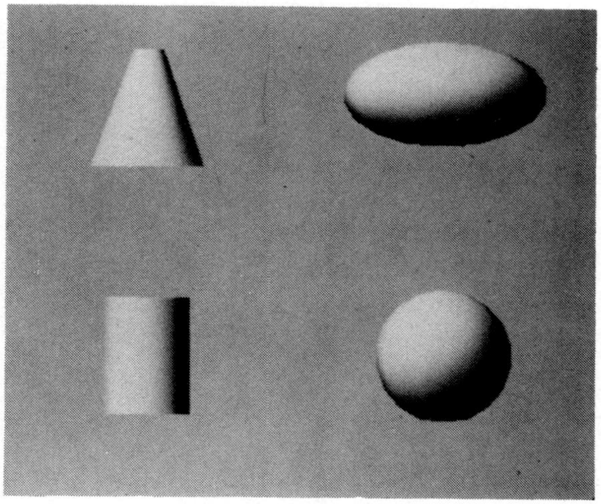

Fig. 4-3. Some primitive surfaces that may be created with one command.

HIDDEN SURFACES

Whenever several opaque surfaces are brought together, some may be closer to the eye and in the direct line of sight of other surfaces. The surfaces that are blocked are referred to as *hidden surfaces.*

It is very important to the overall realism of a picture that these surfaces are removed when they are not wanted. Many techniques have been developed for this purpose, and they are considered solutions to the hidden surface problem.

For example, see Fig. 4-4. Here is a line drawing of a cube, but it is difficult to tell the orientation of the cube. With the hidden surfaces (or lines) removed (Fig. 4-5), the ambiguity is resolved.

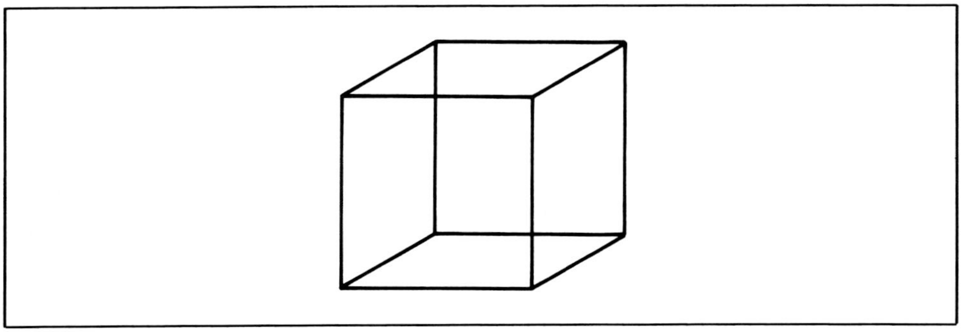

Fig. 4-4. It's hard to tell which face of the cube is closer to you.

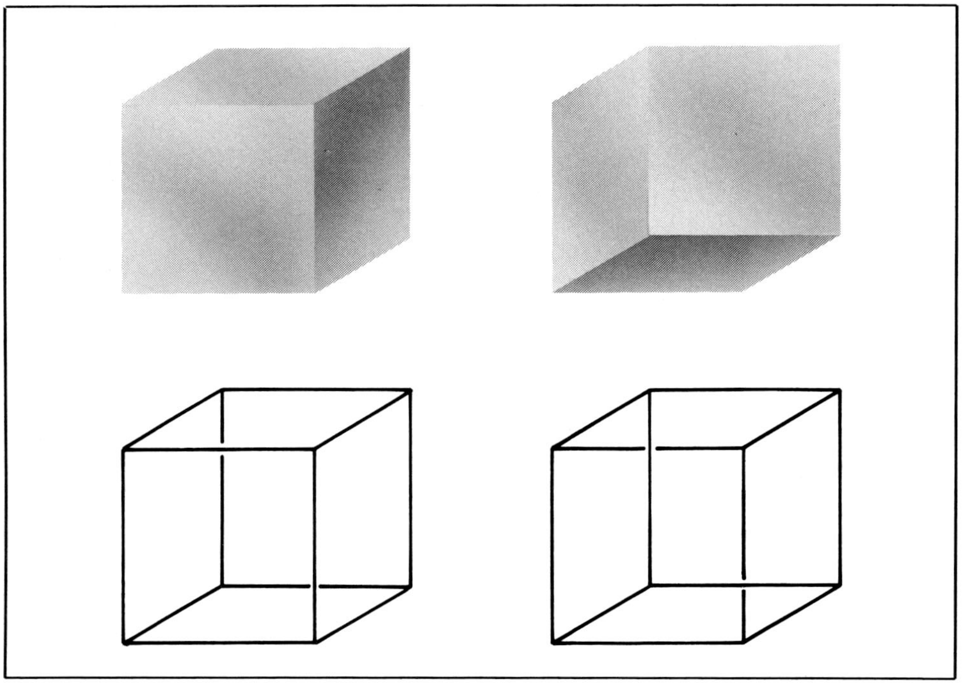

Fig. 4-5. We can draw the cube with either face closer, and there is no ambiguity.

SURFACE NORMALS

When the computer has a surface ready to be shaded, there are several pieces of information it must have to do the job of shading correctly. Some of this information consists of the orientation of the light sources, how bright they are, and the texture of the surface. Another important attribute of a surface is usually not defined by the modeler directly but is automatically derived by the computer. But since it plays a very important role in understanding shading, we will consider it now in some detail.

This piece of information is called the *surface normal*. The word *normal* is key to the meaning of the name. A normal is usually a line perpendicular to a plane. See Fig. 4-6 for some examples. Even if we are dealing with a curved surface, we can find the normal at any point by finding the normal to the tangent plane to the surface at that point.

The surface normal is a vector. That is, it has a starting point (usually somewhere on the surface), a length, and a direction. We usually draw a vector (as in Fig. 4-7) as a line with an arrowhead. We will see later that

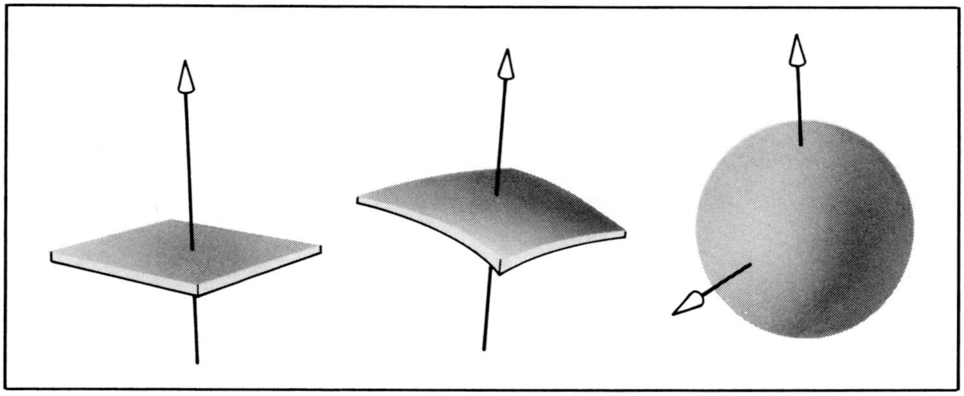

Fig. 4-6. A *normal* is a line (more usually a vector) perpendicular to the tangent plane.

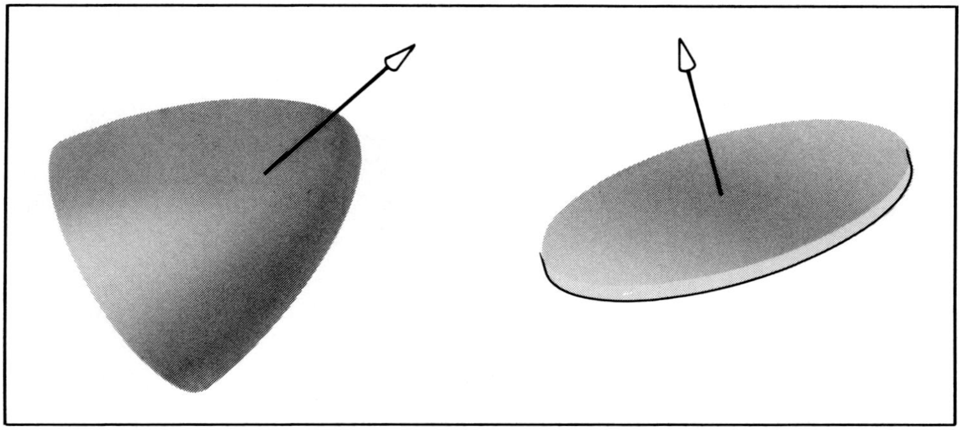

Fig. 4-7. Normals are often represented as vectors (note a starting point and direction).

the direction of the surface normal controls the shading at that point. Its length is unimportant in this application.

There are some other important attributes of a surface that the modeler gets to specify. We would like to describe the texture of the surface in some general ways.

There are two values that are used to describe how well the surface reflects light, and the two values generally interact with each other when the surface is actually drawn. The two values are measurements of the *diffuse reflection* and *specular reflection* of the surface.

The *diffuse value* (or *diffuse coefficient*), describes how "matte," or "flat," the object is. A high degree of diffuse reflection means that the light hitting the surface is scattered in all directions. Some very diffuse surfaces are yarn, cork, and chalk.

The *specular coefficient* describes how much light can be reflected off the surface back into the observer's eye, making a highlight. A lot of specular reflection causes a large highlight. Some very specular surfaces are polished brass, still water, and a mirror.

A set of spheres with different amounts of specular and diffuse reflection is shown in Fig. 4-8.

LIGHTING MODELS

Another important piece of information that computers must have to render a scene is a description of the light sources; where they are, what color they are, how intense they are, where they are pointed, and so on. We supply this information with a lighting model. Here we are using the word *model* to mean a mathematical system that mimics a real system. We build up a mathematical description of the light sources; we don't actually create surfaces of them.

One attribute of the light on a scene is the amount of *ambient* light cast upon it. Ambient light doesn't come from any one source, it's just a kind of overall illumination that comes from reflectances off the walls of the room, off of other objects, and the like. Most scenes look good with some ambient light. If you don't want any in your scene, you can set the ambient light coefficient in your lighting model to zero. Higher values mean more ambient light.

Individual light sources themselves have a location, a color, a direction, and an intensity. This might suggest to you that light sources can be described as vectors, where the start of the vector is the position of the light source, the direction of the vector is the direction of the light source,

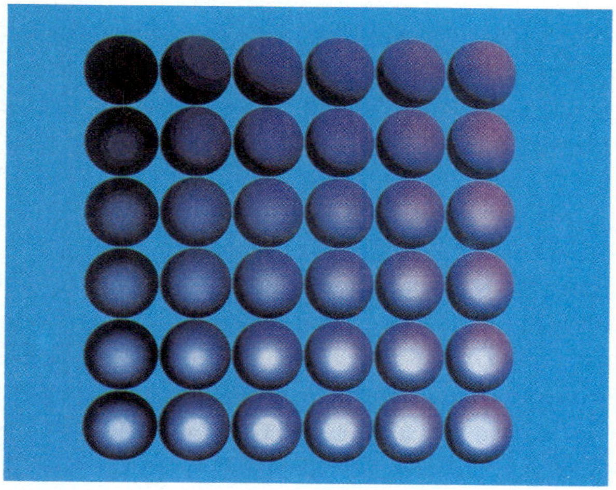

Fig. 4-8. **As we travel to the right, we increase the diffuse reflection of the surface; as we travel down, we increase the specular reflection.**

and the length of the vector is the intensity, which is often the case. The color must be carried along separately, or you can model the light as three vectors, one for each primary color. We haven't discussed color systems yet, but one set of primary colors for computer graphics is red, green, and blue, implying we can model a light source as three vectors, each of which represents one of the three colors, as in Fig. 4-9.

Additionally, there is another attribute that is not a model of real light

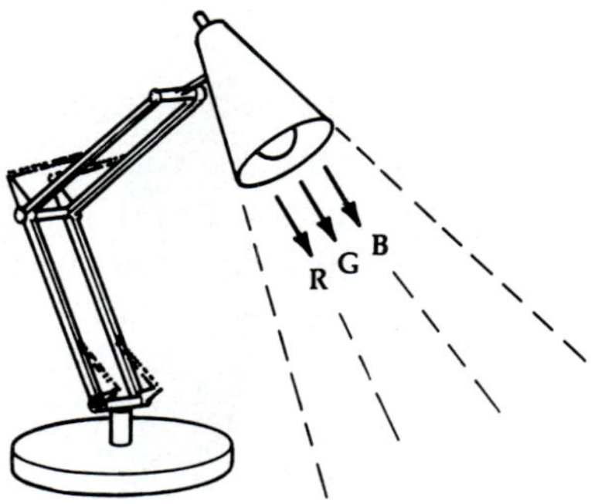

Fig. 4-9. **We model a light source as having three independent colors: red, green, and blue.**

sources but is a requirement because of how the computer actually performs the shading.

We may think of garden-variety light sources illuminating from a point just out of view. For example, a photographer usually does not include a picture of the strobe light in a photograph. We can think of lights outside the picture, and lights both inside the picture and inside an object. A light inside an object will illuminate it from the inside, and perhaps that object will glow.

The light from the sun is very far away, so far that we sometimes consider it "infinitely" far, compared with a strobe light, for example, which is a clue to that additional piece of information we must supply about a light source; we declare it to be *local* or *infinite*. The first difference is how much time the computer must take to shade the object. Local light sources often cause pictures to be drawn much more slowly than a picture made up of exclusively infinite light sources. So why pay for the extra time it takes? The answer is in the second difference between the two light sources: they illuminate objects differently!

Fig. 4-10 shows an infinite light source lighting a scene of four spheres resting on a plane. Note that all the light is coming from one direction and all the objects are shaded in the same way relative to that light source. Fig. 4-11 shows the same scene illuminated by a local light source. The difference is that the local source shades different objects differently, based on their location relative to it.

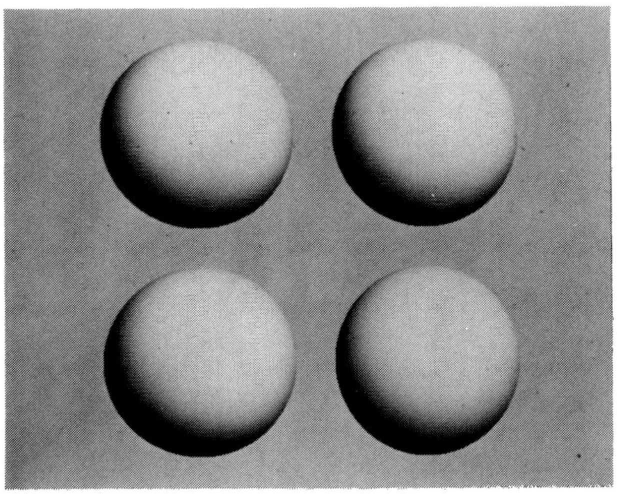

Fig. 4-10. Four spheres lit by an infinite light source.

Of course, several light sources may be used to illuminate a scene, with any combination of local and infinite. Fig. 4-12 shows a single scene illuminated with a combination of the local and infinite sources of Figs. 4-10 and 4-11. Fig. 4-13 shows a single model lit by three different lighting schemes.

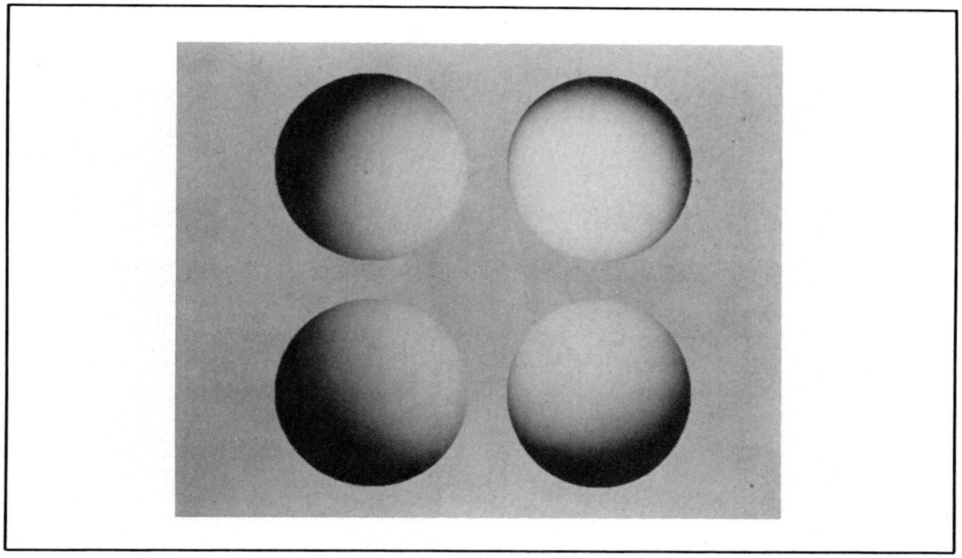

Fig. 4-11. Four spheres lit by a local light source.

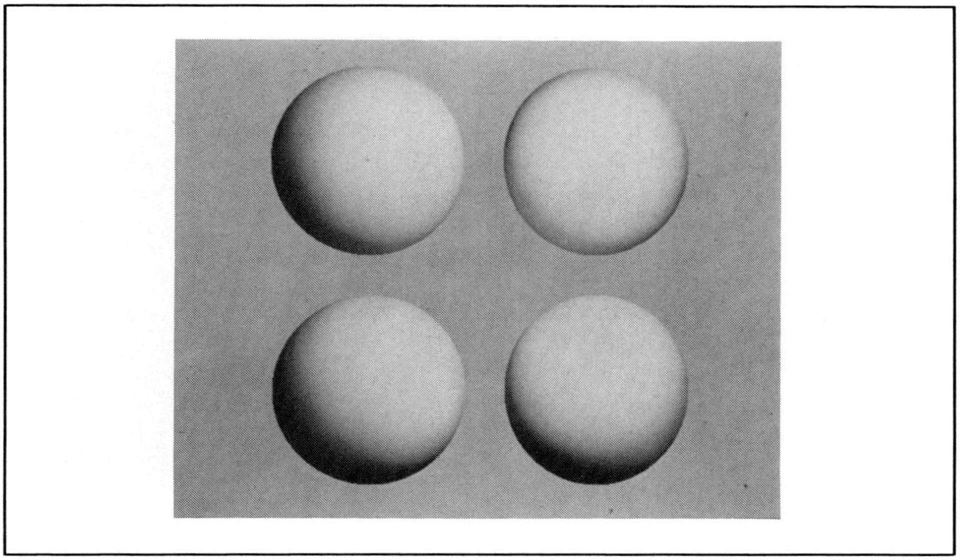

Fig. 4-12. Four spheres lit by both a local and an infinite light source.

SUMMARY

In this chapter we took a broad look at generalizing surfaces. We said that there are basically two types of surfaces: *open surfaces* and *closed surfaces*. A surface is open if both sides of it can be touched at once like a

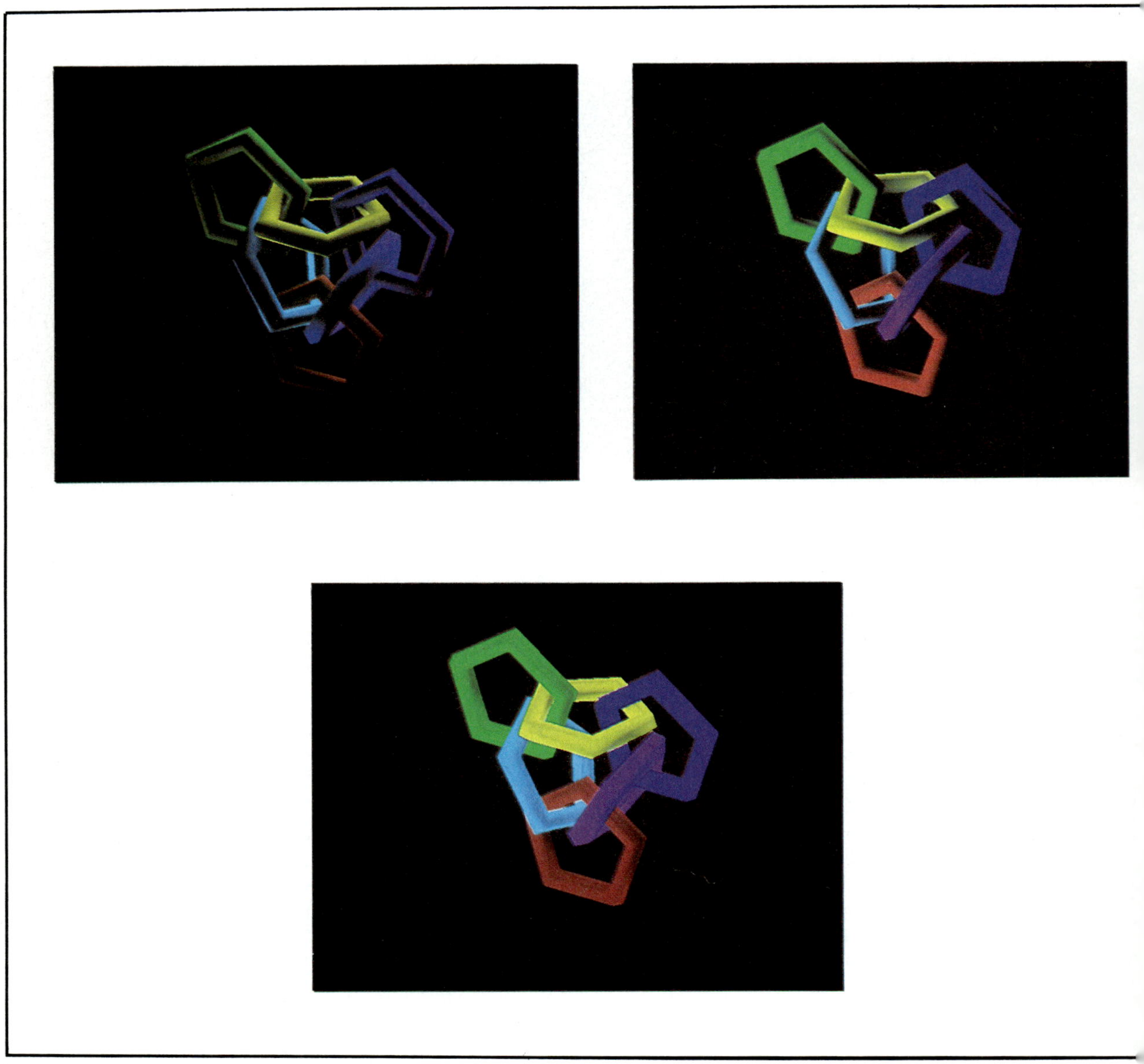

Fig. 4-13. The same scene lit with different light placements and intensities.

piece of paper. A surface is closed if both sides of it cannot be touched at once, like a hollow sphere.

We then saw that if a surface is hidden behind another in a final image, we say that the surface that is covered up is called a *hidden surface.*

We then defined the *surface normal* for a point on a surface, which is a vector perpendicular to the tangent plane to the surface at that point. We saw that the more the surface normal pointed in the direction the light was coming from, the brighter the surface is at that point. We said that there were two kinds of reflection we would want to model: *diffuse* and *specular*, which correspond to how matte the surface is at that point and how glossy it is, respectively. We defined how much diffuse and specular reflection there was off a given surface by assigning each kind of reflection a number, or coefficient.

We then looked at the two different kinds of lighting models that we work with in computer graphics. The first is the *infinite light source.* This lighting source shades all objects in the scene the same way. The other kind of light is the *local light source.* This might shade different objects in a scene differently, because it's close enough to the scene that some objects might be on one side of it, and some objects might be on the other.

We said that the computer could draw a scene with a lot of infinite light sources almost as fast as it could draw that scene with just one infinite light source, but that each local light source slows it down noticeably.

This chapter was our first plunge into three-dimensional shaded graphics, and sets us up with enough knowledge that we can look at how complete objects are shaded in the next chapter.

Chapter FIVE

Polygons And Surface Shading

This chapter is perhaps the most difficult and the most important in the book. In this chapter we will look at how the computer goes about shading three-dimensional objects.

We will concentrate on the shading of a particular class of objects called *polygons*, but the ideas and techniques are the same for all surfaces. Later chapters will show how to use the ideas presented here for other kinds of surfaces.

We will start by defining what polygons are, and we'll briefly discuss some possible variations on our definition that you may be able to get away with on your particular system. We'll then take a broad overview of computer shading before considering a number of different techniques in detail.

We'll talk about several different ways of shading three-dimensional objects. Each will have its advantages and disadvantages, but generally the ones that produce the best (or most realistic) pictures are the ones that take the longest. After we look at how the different shading techniques work on polygons, we'll look at some of the problems inherent in using polygons to make up models.

I suggest that you go slowly on this chapter—it contains a lot of material that is key to the whole idea of computer graphics and should be understood. It should also be enjoyable, though. To approach the various ideas here in the same spirit as the people that developed them might be helpful. You want to make pictures, and you want them to look real. So you ask yourself, "What rules can I invent that I can make so definite and simple that even a computer can understand them?" These rules control how the computer makes the shaded images we see on the screen.

Some people had some very clever answers to this question, and this chapter is a description of their answers and why they work.

POLYGONS: A WORKING DEFINITION

We will define a *polygon* as a set of noncrossing straight lines joining points that all lie in the same plane and enclose some single area. This definition is really only useful once you already know what it means, so we will examine it piece by piece.

Drawing a polygon is like playing a connect-the-dots game. The idea is to draw straight lines from one dot to another in a specified sequence. Most connect-the-dots games are played on a sheet of paper. Perhaps it is obvious that all the points must then lie "flat" on the sheet of paper. We say that these points are *planar*, and it's what the previous definition is getting at by saying that all lines must " . . . lie in the same plane." The part about enclosing some single area is best shown by example, as in Fig. 5-1. Additionally, lines that make up a polygon are not allowed to cross each other in our definition.

Fig. 5-1 shows that a set of less than three points cannot enclose an area, so we need at least three points to make a polygon. This rule holds true for all polygons discussed here: A polygon must have three or more points. Each line in a polygon is called a *side*, or *edge*. Each corner is called a *vertex*, for which the plural is *vertices*.

A polygon is like a cut-out piece of cardboard. As such it can have all kinds of attributes that describe its surface, like color, shinyness, transparency, and more, that we will cover in later chapters.

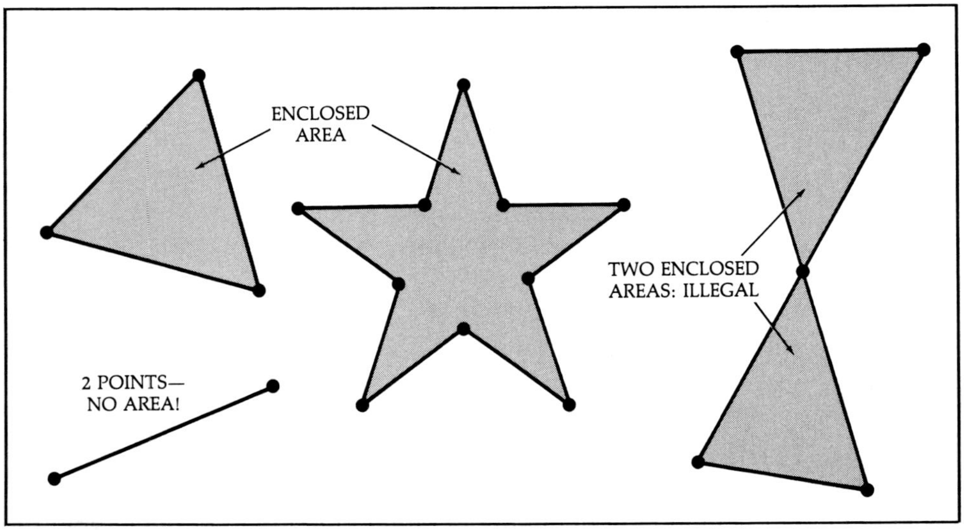

Fig. 5-1. Some polygons and nonpolygons.

HOW TO MODEL A POLYGON

Let's say that we have drawn a polygon on a sheet of paper and measured all the points, so we know the coordinates of each vertex. How do we describe this polygon to the computer so that we can use it in pictures? The answer is to type in the points in exactly the order we want them joined to produce the polygon. Listing the points in the correct order is very important: Fig. 5-2 shows that from a given set of points, an incorrect numbering can violate our definition of a polygon and lead to trouble, not to mention lack of the shape we were trying to draw in the first place. We want to adhere to the definition we have (and perhaps the variants to come) because computers will always assume you typed in what you meant, and if it's not what the computer expects, then the results will not be what you wanted.

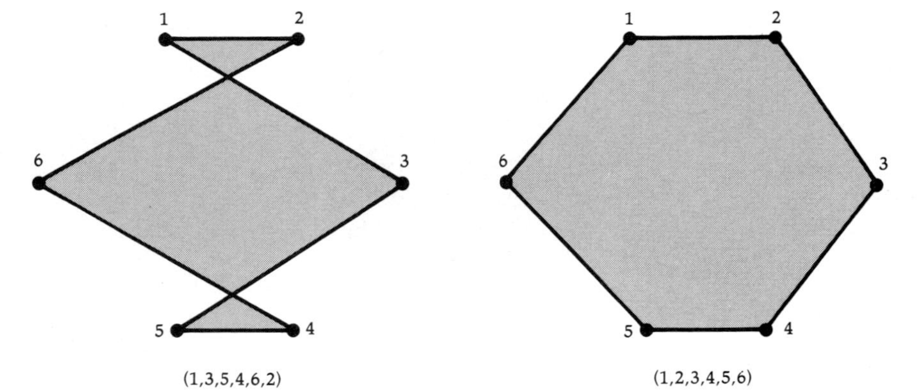

A. This numbering encloses three areas and makes an illegal polygon.

B. This is a legal numbering, or listing of the vertices.

Fig. 5-2. The points of the polygons should be listed in the right order.

A polygon has two sides, which we might call front and back. These sides are also called *faces.* If you curl the fingers of your right hand in the direction of successive points in your point list (as in Fig. 5-3), your thumb will point out away from the *front face* of the polygon. The heel of your hand points to the *back face.* The definition of which face is the front and which is the back is completely dependent on the order in which you name the points. When the polygons are drawn on the screen, you may very well see a mixture of front and back faces among the polygons there.

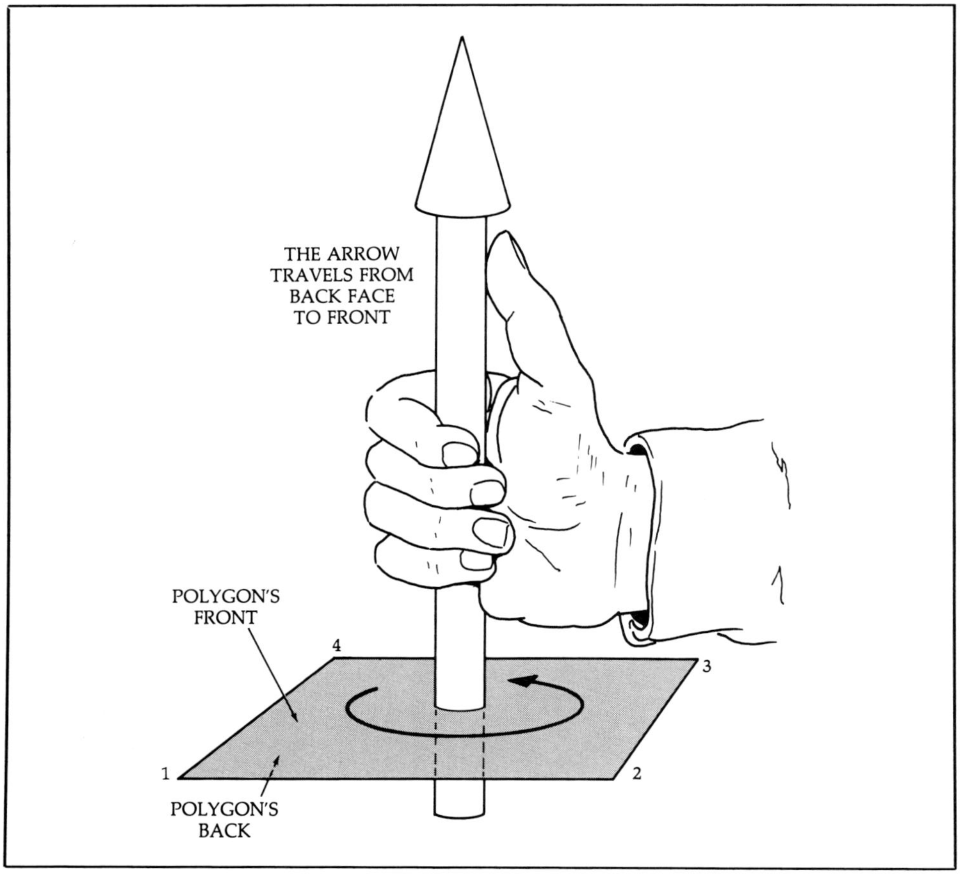

Fig. 5-3. Using a right-hand rule to find the front face of a polygon.

We mention the distinction between the two faces because some polygon rendering systems treat back-facing polygons in a special way to speed up the rendering of an image.

When we compute the surface normal for a polygon, we define it to point in the same direction as your thumb points according to the previous procedure. This formalism helps us shade polygons, as we will see later.

Almost all polygon rendering systems will accept and correctly render polygons that meet our working definition. Some different pieces of the definition may be relaxed for different systems, and the polygons will still be drawn correctly. This kind of special capability differs from system to system, so we'll just take a quick look at some nonstandard kinds of polygons.

Variation 1: Nonplanar Polygons

Part of our definition of a polygon was that the points must all lie in the same plane. If we remove that requirement, then polygons may be *nonplanar*. Fig. 5-4 shows a planar polygon being lifted out of the plane it was defined in. Sometimes a computer will correctly render a nonplanar polygon, and sometimes it will not; it all depends on your particular pro-

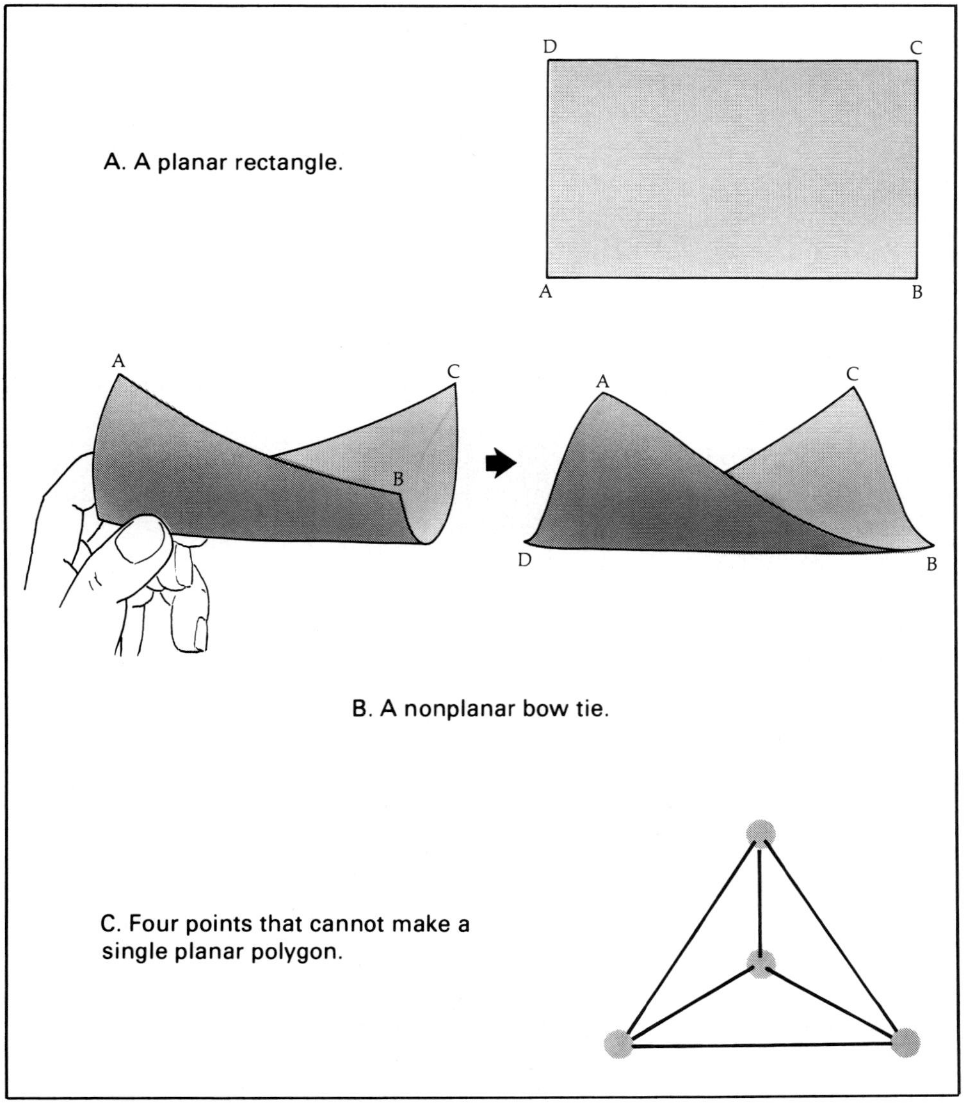

Fig. 5-4. All polygons must normally be planar.

gram. It's worth experimenting with on your system, but don't expect the results to be universal, or even consistent, unless the program was specifically designed to handle such a variant. The reason is that the mathematics most programs use to shade the polygon assume that it is planar! A program must be written with special mathematics to handle nonplanar polygons. Without the special programming, the results of shading will often be unpredictable.

Variation 2: Self-Intersecting Polygons

We now return to our original definition of a polygon, but this time we'll let the polygon enclose more than one area, which is the same as letting lines cross. Such a polygon is called *self-intersecting.*

Self-intersecting polygons can always be considered a collection of our "standard" polygons, as Fig. 5-5 suggests. Any self-intersecting polygon can be remade out of nonintersecting polygons but you may need to define a few new points. Self-intersecting polygons are primarily useful for saving computer time and storage, at the expense of making things a bit more difficult for the modeler. So although you may run across them, the human time needed to work them out properly versus the computer resources saved usually makes them a bad deal. They are also much less versatile when you decide to change your model and move some of the polygons about. We won't discuss them anymore; they're best avoided. This section was just to expose you to the idea so you'll understand what people are talking about when they say, "Avoid self-intersecting polygons!"

Variation 3: Polygons With Holes

Some systems allow you to define a polygon within a polygon. In this case the inner polygon is defined to be a "cut-out" of the outer polygon, effectively creating a hole in the outer polygon. Fig. 5-6 shows a couple of examples. Usually this act of cutting holes must be explicitly indicated to the computer with a special command.

Not all polygon-rendering systems are sophisticated enough to deal with holes, however. Fig. 5-7 shows that although it can be a hassle, holes can always be "faked" by building up other smaller polygons around them.

Some systems allow many holes in a single polygon. And, of course, once a hole has been cut out, objects behind the polygon may be seen, and other polygons may be placed inside the hole, which is often helpful for detail work and special effects.

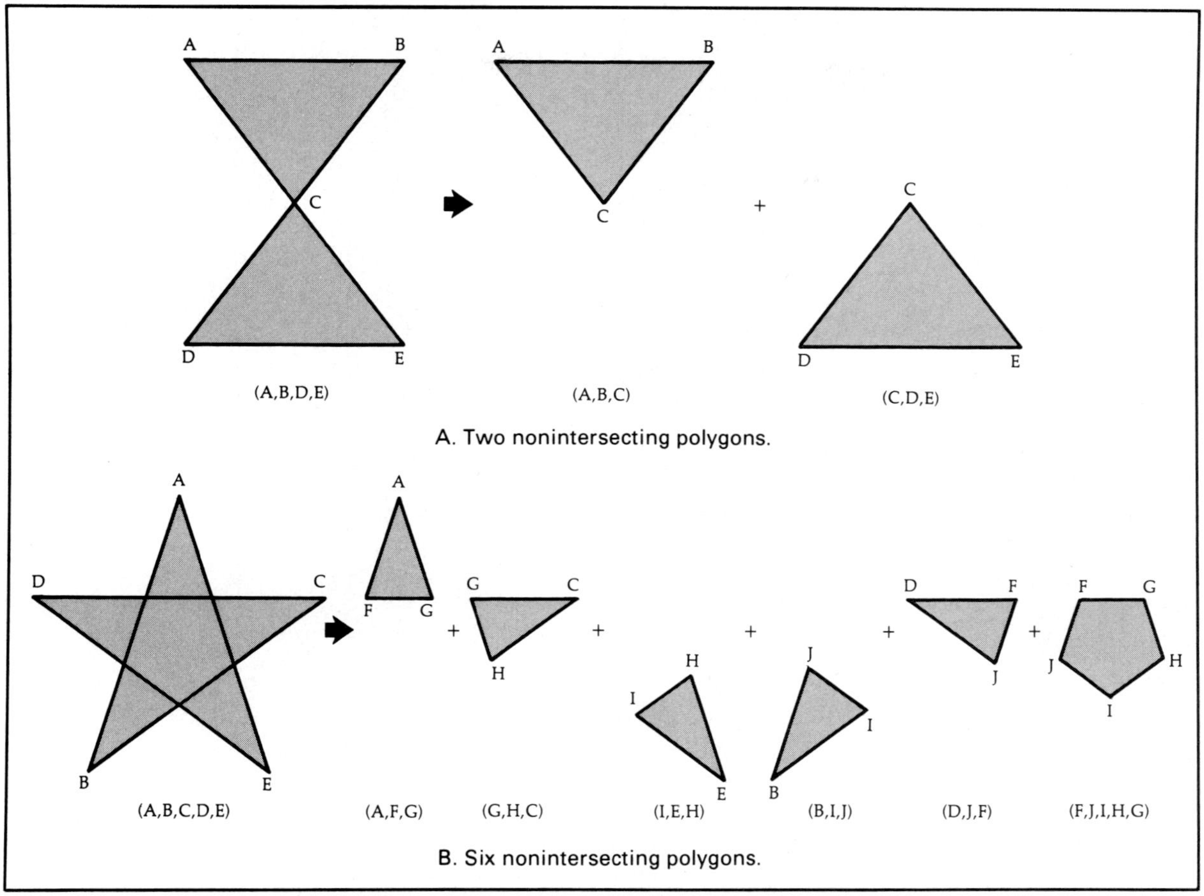

Fig. 5-5. Self-intersecting polygons can be remade out of nonintersecting polygons.

SHADING: AN OVERVIEW

Let's say that you've entered a collection of polygons into the computer in the proper way for your computer system. Using the ideas we will cover later and the mechanics of your system, you have specified information about the light sources, color and texture of the polygons, and other information about the surfaces and the lights illuminating them. For the computer to draw a picture of these polygons on the screen, it must mathematically project the lights onto the surfaces of the polygons and see

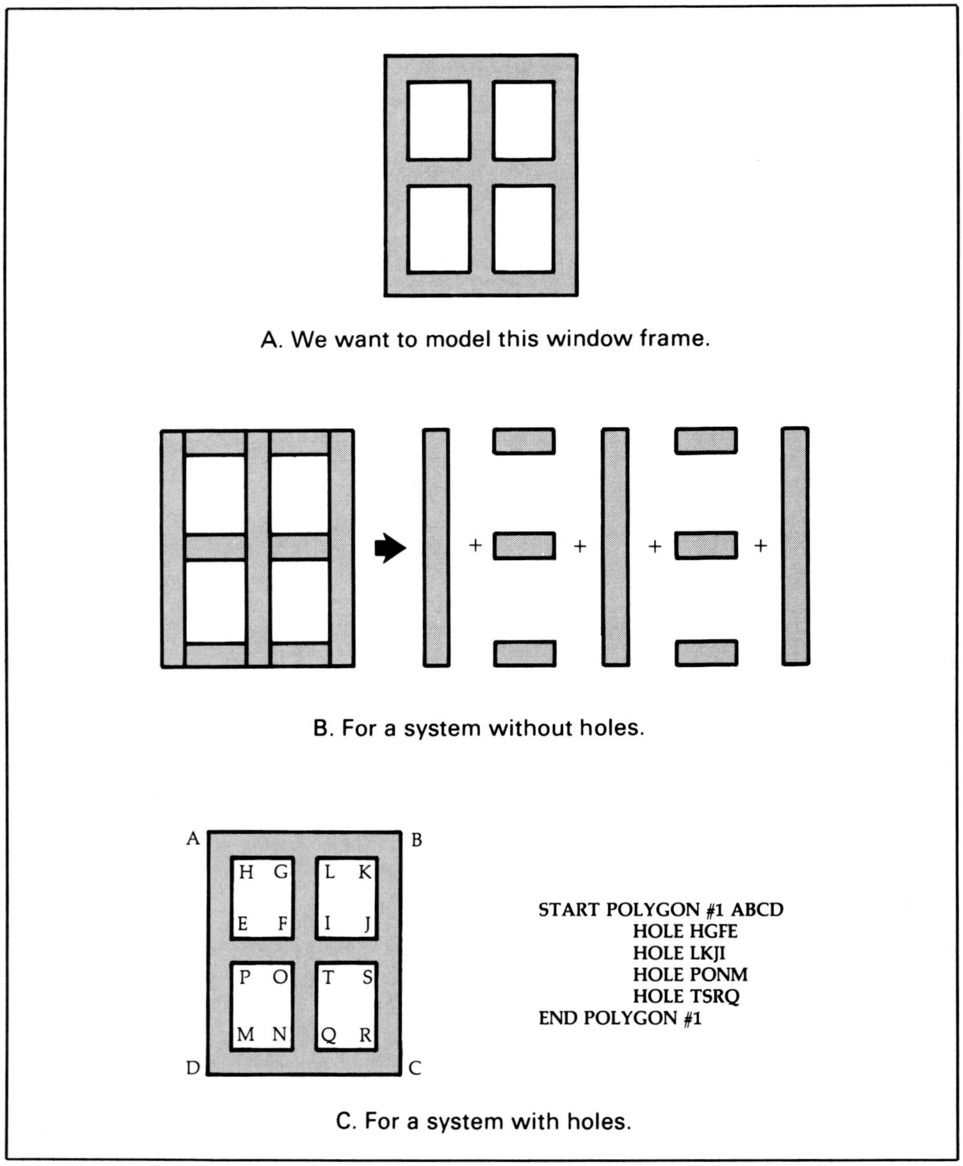

A. We want to model this window frame.

B. For a system without holes.

C. For a system with holes.

Fig. 5-6. Modeling a window.

how they are illuminated. Once the computer knows how much light is falling on a particular point in a polygon, it can adjust the color at that point to simulate the reflection of the light. That point can then be drawn on the screen.

The computer can take one of at least two popular routes to do this, with variations on each one (as usual!). The first method is to treat each polygon as an independent surface to be shaded and drawn irrespective of the rest of the scene. The other method is to somehow use the other polygons that are nearby to help shade points on the polygon of interest. We'll consider each method and the advantages and disadvantages of each.

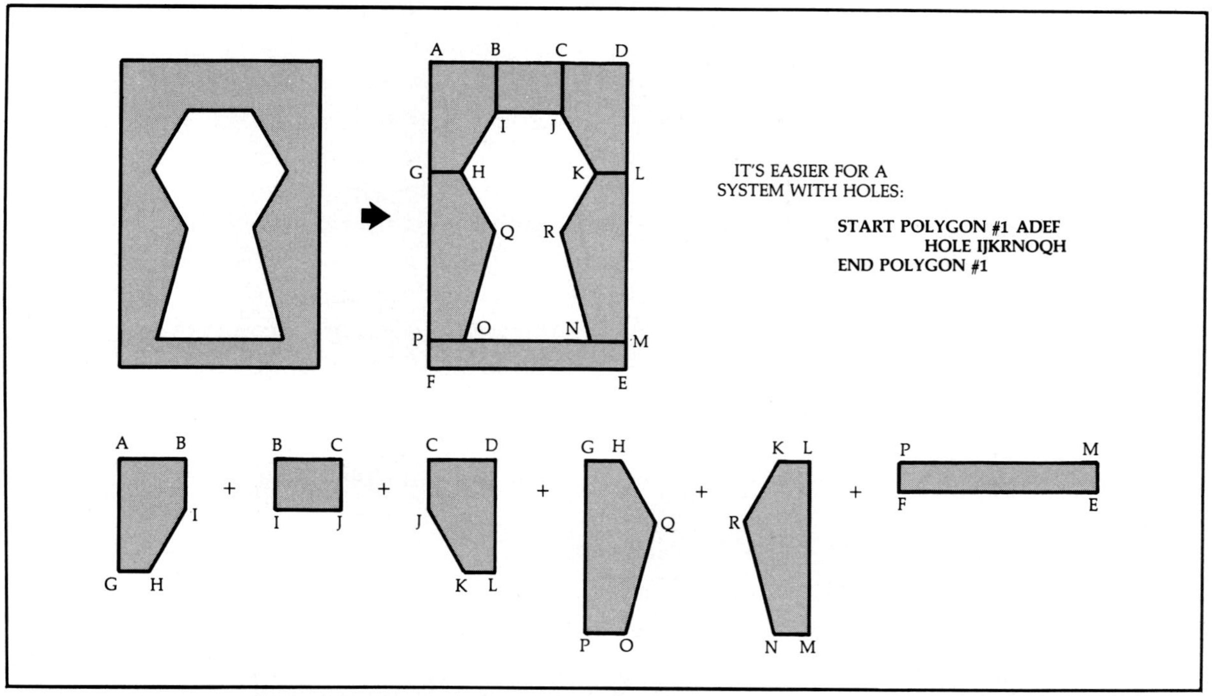

Fig. 5-7. Another example of modeling a polygon with holes.

Generally, the different shading schemes have two names. One name is descriptive of the process, and usually has something to do with the mathematics of the shading. The other name associates the name of a person who had ideas fundamental to that shading process, and is honored in the discipline through the association of his name with the technique. This is standard practice in science; consider the volt (Count Alessandro Volta), Maxwell's Equations (James Clerk Maxwell), Einstein's Theory of Relativity, and Murphy's Law.

Lambert (Faceted) Shading

Lambert (or *faceted*) *shading* considers a single polygon from the complete scene description, shades it irrelevant of the rest of the scene (except perhaps for shadows and reflections), and moves on to the next polygon when the current one is completely shaded. The term *faceted shading* is associated with this technique because objects shaded according to this scheme usually appear to be made up out of many little tiles, or facets.

Lambert shading is the simplest of the shading techniques we will discuss. It restricts its attention to how much light is hitting a particular point (on a polygon or other surface). It then modifies the color of the surface appropriately for the reflected light.

Consider Fig. 5-8. It shows several polygons in different orientations to a light source. Note that when a polygon is edge-on to the light source, no light is reflected from the surface. As the polygon faces more and more towards the light it is hit by more light, and therefore reflects more light and appears brighter.

The computer needs an exact method for determining how much a polygon "points towards" a light source. The method is to compare the surface normal of the polygon with a vector that describes the direction of the light source. In Fig. 5-9 both vectors have been drawn. Note that the more parallel the two vectors are (a simple operation for the computer to

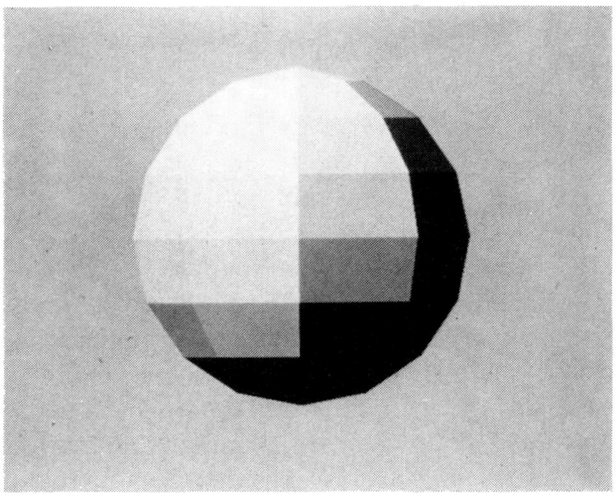

Fig. 5-8. Polygons get brighter as they present more of their face to a light source.

Fig. 5-9. The direction of the light source is blue. The polygon normals are magenta.

check), the more the polygon faces the light source, and hence, the brighter it is. Since the entire polygon is shaded with the shade computed by the comparison of the surface normal and the light vector, the shading across the entire polygon is constant, which is what gives rise to the characteristic faceted appearance of Lambert shading.

This comparison of a vector on the object's surface (usually the surface normal at a given point) with the light source vector is at the heart of all the shading techniques we will discuss.

We will note in passing that although the computer usually automatically computes the surface normal for the polygon, the modeler may specify it when entering the polygon into the computer.

Lambert shading is the quickest and (from the computer's point of view) the easiest of the shading techniques in popular use in computer graphics. It is usually used when a modeler or animator wants to check a model's shape or movement but doesn't need a lot of realism and wants results fast. For final production, usually a more sophisticated shading model is used.

Recall that the surface normal of a polygon is defined to point away from the front face. It is often useful to only shade those polygons whose front or back face points toward the light source, leaving the opposite face black, transparent, or unshaded.

Smooth-Shading Techniques

The other shading techniques we will consider try to get away from the faceted appearance of Lambert-shaded objects by pretending that the polygonal model that is being shaded is just an approximation of a smoother object. For example, a sphere can be approximated polygonally, as illustrated in Fig. 5-10. The polygonal appearance can be reduced in this case by adding more polygons, but the problem is only diminished at the cost of more computer expense. The problem is not resolved. Furthermore, in many models it is very difficult to just arbitrarily add more polygons where it doesn't look just right. Notice that in Fig. 5-10 as we move to the right, we have more polygons running from east to west ; as we move down, we have more running north to south.

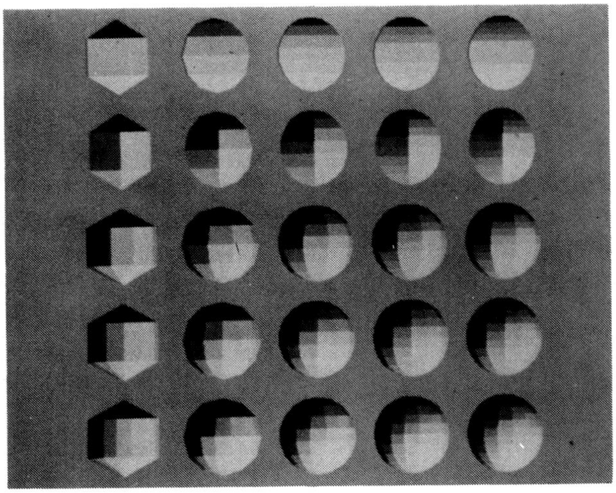

Fig. 5-10. The effect of using different numbers of polygons to approximate a sphere.

Smooth shading techniques try to remove the faceted appearance by smoothing the surface of the object. It would be very expensive for the computer to actually create a new, smoother model, so another approach is taken. The computer attempts to shade the model as if it were smoother. Some more discussion may help make the distinction clearer.

Lambert shaded objects look faceted because each entire polygon is shaded with the amount of light reflected from the surface at one point (where the surface normal is). We might try to make it look better by

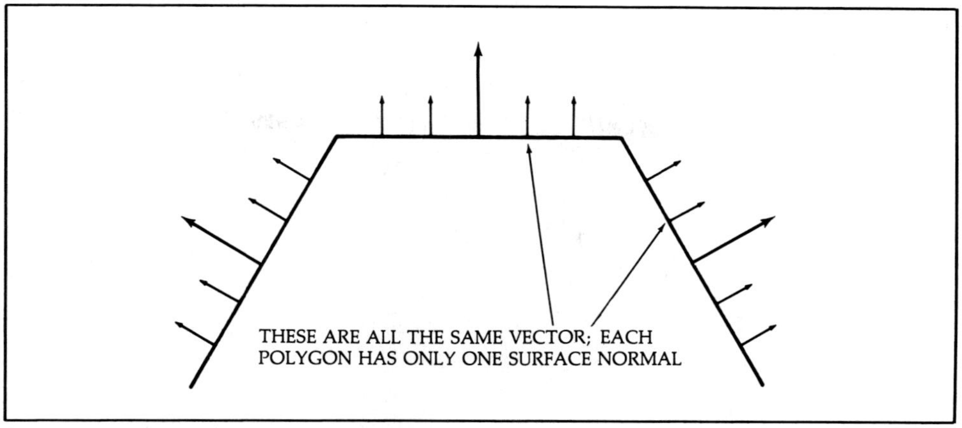

Fig. 5-11. It doesn't help to look at more points on a polygon since the whole polygon has only one surface normal.

computing the shade at more points on the surface, but since a polygon is planar, these values would all be the same (Fig. 5-11). Smooth shading techniques actually do compute the surface shading at many points on the surface of the polygon, but they modify the surface so that it appears to be a small surface of a larger, smoother surface. Fig. 5-12 shows what these models do. In both parts of Fig. 5-12, the objects share exactly the same surface description. Note the straight edges where the cones meet in Fig. 5-12B. The surfaces are still flat polygons, they just *look* smooth.

The different techniques produce pictures with varying amounts of realism, based on the amount of work the computer must do, and consequently, the time the user must wait to receive a completed picture. These are the models we will consider now.

Gouraud (Smooth) Shading

Gouraud (pronounced Guh-ŕoe), or *smooth, shading* is one technique for smoothing a polygonal model before shading it. The basic idea behind Gouraud shading is that light reflection is computed at every vertex, instead of at the center of every polygon. The shades at the vertices of a polygon are smoothed and blended across its surface, which effectively smooths the polygonal model! Fig. 5-13 shows conceptually what Gouraud shading does to shade a polygon.

Let's look more closely at what we just said. Perhaps the most strange idea is that this new shading of polygons causes the entire model to look smoothed. Note that the surface itself is not changed in any way, it's still

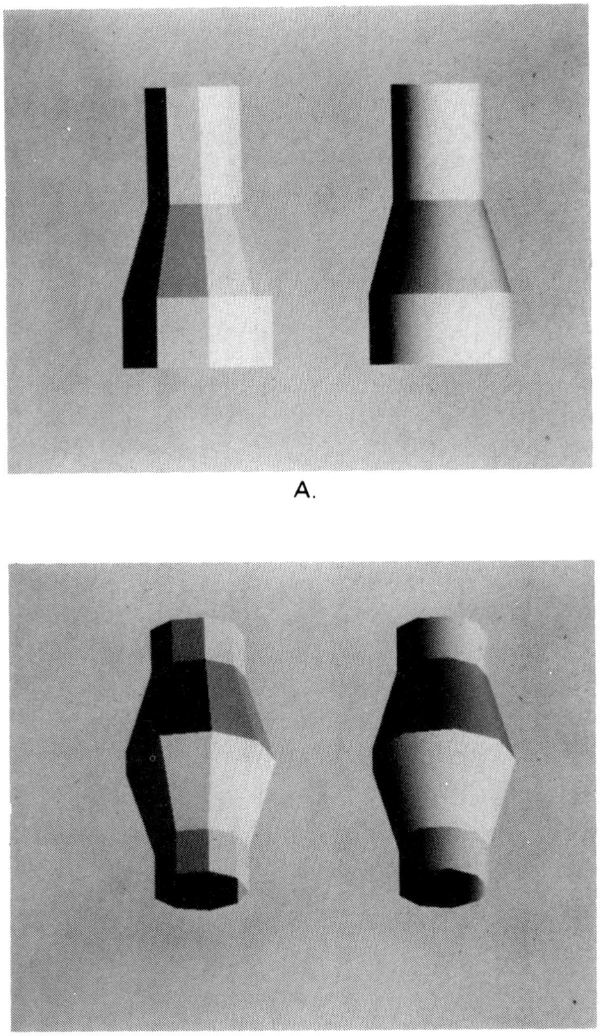

A.

B.

Fig. 5-12. Smooth shading can help polygonal objects appear smoother.

just a bunch of polygons. But by blending the shading across the surface of each polygon, Gouraud shading creates the illusion of a smooth object.

The other new idea is that Gouraud shading computes the shading at each vertex. How does one compute the shade at a vertex? It can't be done

Fig. 5-13. Gouraud shading finds the shading at vertices, and blends those shades across the surface of the polygon.

by finding a vector perpendicular to a surface; a vertex is where several surfaces meet. How would you decide which one to use? The answer is not to choose any one, but to average the surface normals of all polygons that share that vertex, as illustrated in Fig. 5-14. Once this averaged surface normal has been found, it is compared against the light source as before to determine a shading at that point.

Gouraud shading relieves most of the crisp borders around polygons so evident in Lambert-shaded pictures. It is not much more expensive from the computer's standpoint, so it is relatively fast. This is a rather attractive shading scheme, but it still isn't perfect.

Phong (Normal Interpolating) Shading

Gouraud shading is an improvement over Lambert (or faceted) shading, but it still has its problems. Although less noticeable, there are often definite contours around the outside of polygons. And in certain cases (especially in regions of high curvature, like the end of a fishhook), the smooth blending of shade does not look very good, or can be very "wrong" from the sense of how it would look if a real model had been illuminated. A much more time-consuming method is available to circumvent these problems and add even more realism to an image. Before we

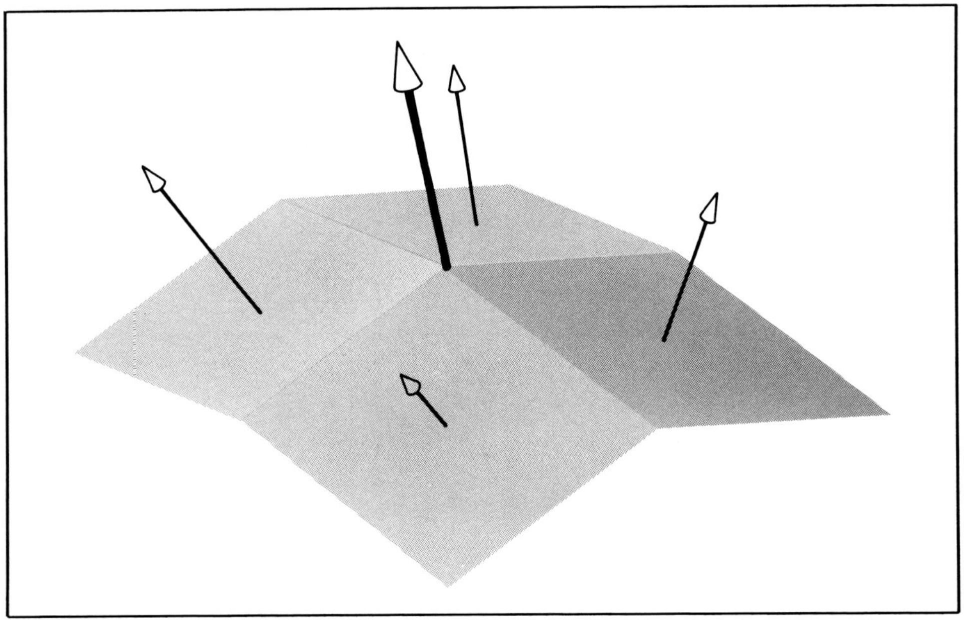

Fig. 5-14. The surface normal at a vertex is found by averaging the surface normals of all polygons that share that vertex.

consider this technique, however, let's look at a significant problem with Lambert and Gouraud shading.

Consider Fig. 5-15. In this illustration we will assume that the sphere in the picture is painted with a glossy paint, giving it a reflective surface. If the shading is to be completely accurate compared with the real world, there should be highlights where the image of the light is bounced back to the observer. Highlights are usually the color of the light source, with some room for discoloration due to the pigment on the object.

In the illustration the highlight is supposed to be in the center of a particular polygon. If we compute the intensity of light at each vertex and then blend as Gouraud shading instructs us, we get the shading shown in Fig. 5-16, which obviously lacks the highlight.

In this situation Lambert shading will also completely miss the highlight.

So Gouraud shading can only give us highlights when they happen to fall on a vertex. Even then, highlights often come out blurred or distorted, as shown in Figs. 5-15 and 5-16, which have been contrived so that a vertex picks up the highlight. Another problem of Gouraud shading is that it does not work well with local light sources. Fig. 5-17 shows how we would like a sphere lit with a local light source to look. Fig. 5-18 shows how Gouraud

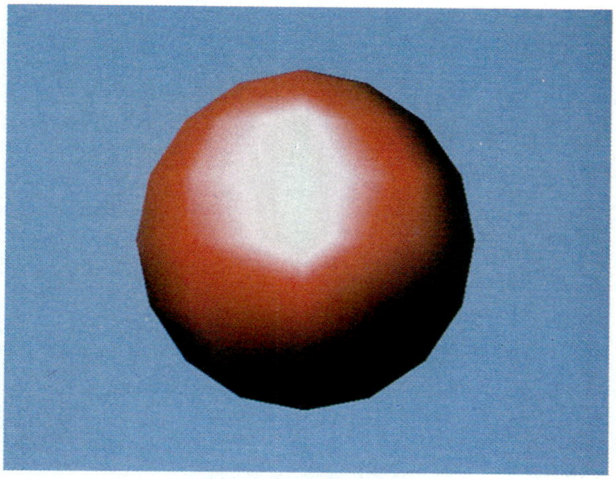

Fig. 5-15. A glossy red sphere lit by a white light. Notice how poorly Gouraud shading handles the highlight.

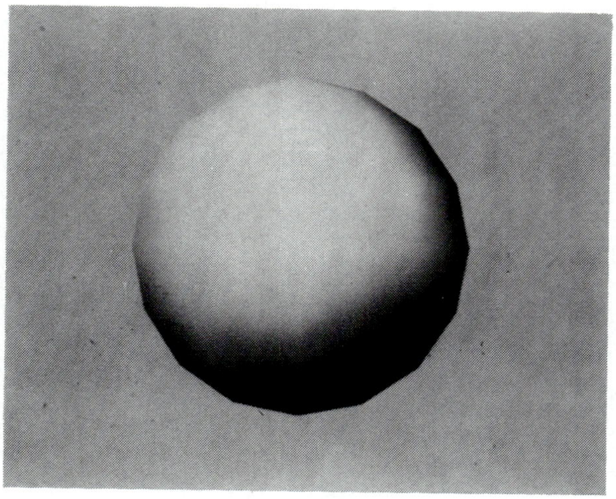

Fig. 5-16. Gouraud shading of a sphere with highlights.

shading would shade the sphere. Again, this is not what we want, and we can see that Gouraud shading is not the ultimate shading model.

So although Gouraud shading is more realistic than Lambert shading, it is slightly slower and thus more expensive as well as having some serious

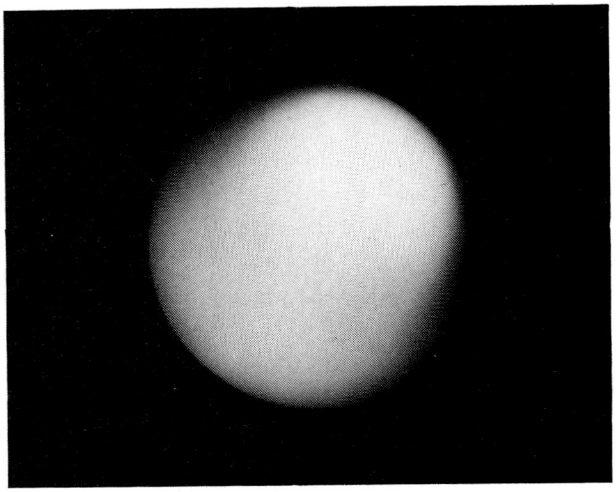

Fig. 5-17. An "ideally" shaded sphere with a highlight.

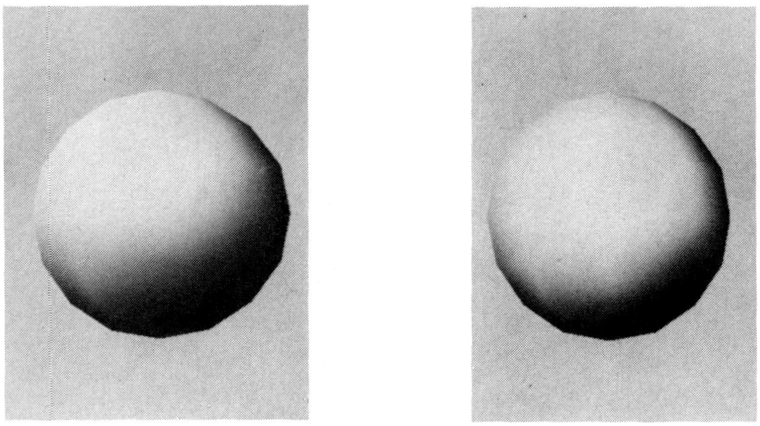

A. The effect of a local light source on Gouraud shading.

B. The same sphere lit with an infinite source, for comparison.

Fig. 5-18. Spheres shown with local and infinite light sources.

problems. A new scheme of shading that can handle local light sources and highlights in a more convincing manner sounds worthwhile. Such a scheme exists, and is called *Phong* (pronounced Fong), or *normal interpolating, shading*.

Gouraud shading found the surface normal at each vertex, shaded that vertex, and then blended the shades across the polygon. Phong shading finds the surface normal at each vertex, and then blends the surface normal over the face of the polygon, comparing it to the light vector and computing a new shade for every point on the screen as shown in Fig. 5-19. This increased complexity makes Phong shading a much slower process, but results in superior-looking pictures that don't suffer from the effects noted previously for Gouraud and Lambert shading.

Fig. 5-20 shows how well Phong shading works. For every point on the polygon the surface normal is found by interpolating all the vertices in the polygon. This surface normal is then compared to the light source vector, and the more parallel they are, the brighter that point is. This new normal is compared to the vector representing the observer's eye, and if a highlight exists at that point for that observer, it is added. Although it is the slowest method we have discussed so far, Phong shading is often the standard shading model employed in realistic three-dimensional rendering today.

PROBLEMS WITH POLYGONAL MODELS

Polygonal models are an excellent technique for three-dimensional modeling. They allow exact surface descriptions (of polygonal objects!),

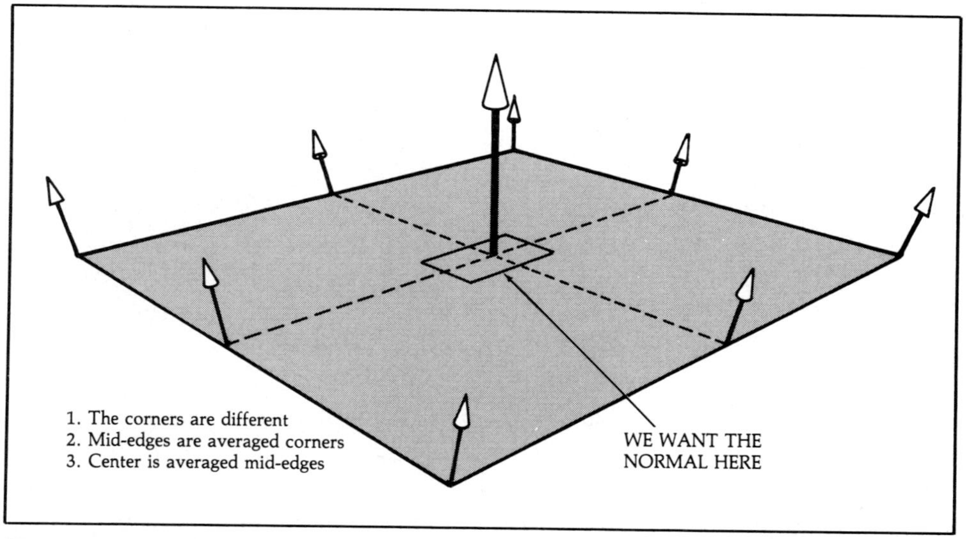

Fig. 5-19. Phong shading interpolates the surface normal across the polygon and computes the shading at each point.

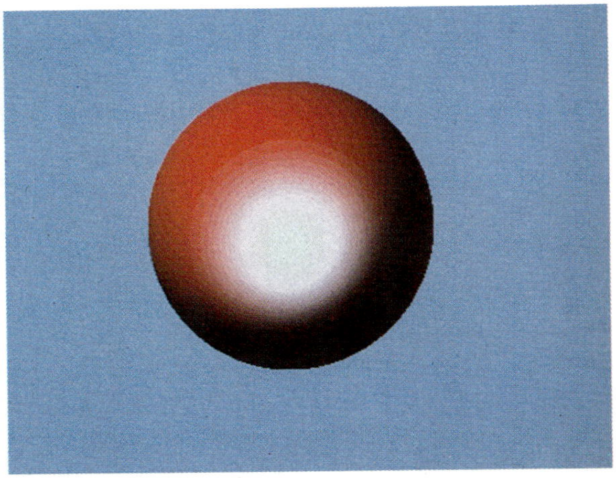

Fig. 5-20. Phong shading, showing a highlight and a local light source.

are easy to define and manipulate, are easy to change, and offer a high level of realism when appropriate shading technique is used. There are, however, some problems with polygonal modeling. Some of these problems are inherent in the shading techniques, some are a result of the fact that polygons are by definition bounded by straight lines, and some are a result of the mechanisms of the human eye.

Silhouettes are a fundamental problem with polygonal models. Consider an object rendered with Phong shading. It may look quite smooth and acceptable on the surface, but there is a problem at the outside edges. Look at the silhouette of Fig. 5-12. Note that the edges are not really round. Objects in high contrast or in extreme close-up will exhibit this effect, which can ruin the illusion of reality. The only way to alleviate this problem is to add more polygons to the object description before rendering, or somehow carefully blur the edges of the polygons before or after rendering. Both solutions present their own difficulties.

This problem leads us to another type of problem with polygons. The human eye is particularly sensitive to contrast. Given a scene of smoothly changing colors, the eye will search for an area of rapid brightness change, which gives rise to an effect called *Mach bands* illustrated in Fig. 5-21. The line at the right in the figure shows the intensity. Mach bands are areas where the color perceived by an observer is not really the color in the

Fig. 5-21. The shading of the square varies continuously from top to bottom. The line at the right shows the intensity. Note where the amount of change from one line to the next suddenly changes. These are Mach bands.

picture; it is an artifact of the perception process. Mach bands can occur when a smoothly shaded object changes curvature quickly. It is an effect that is most noticeable in Gouraud-shaded objects though it is also perceptible in some Phong-shaded images. It's not a fault in the process of modeling with polygons; Mach bands are present in the "real world" as well. For instance, the next time you see a rainbow, note how easy it is to find places where the colors appear to change quickly, even though you know they change smoothly across the bow.

Mach bands should be suppressed in computer-generated images. They cause the picture to look badly shaded and distorted, and care should be taken to alleviate them. Mach bands can be alleviated somewhat by adding more polygons to the object description, so that the changes in curvature are not so extreme.

There is another problem that we have not covered yet. It is a result of the averaging of surface normals of polygons to compute a surface normal at a vertex as in Phong and Gouraud shading. Consider Fig. 5-22. This figure shows a bunch of polygons that clearly point in different directions. The surface normal at each polygon is indicated in the figure. Also indicated are the surface normals at each vertex. Note that all the vertices have the same surface normal. Thus, Gouraud shading would assign the same

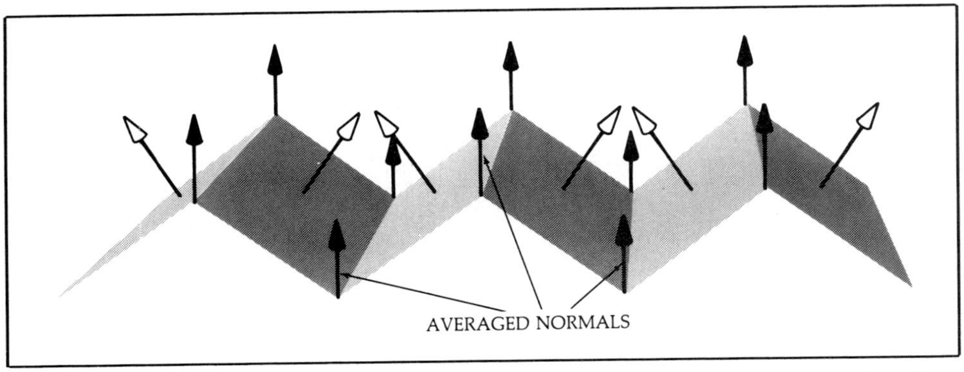

Fig. 5-22. Observe that all the averaged surface normals point in the same direction.

shade to each vertex, causing the whole object to have one shade! Phong shading does no better; since all the surface normals at the vertices are the same, interpolating between two equal surface normals always gives the same surface normal, so the shade assigned to that every point will also always be the same!

This problem can be corrected as in Fig. 5-23 by adding some smaller polygons at the edges where the big polygons meet. As a modeler you'll have to watch out for situations where you want a sharp contrast between polygons. To keep a sharp edge you'll have to insert three small polygons between the two previously adjoining polygons just like we did here.

SUMMARY

In this chapter, we mentioned a working definition of a polygon and then discussed some variations. We said that a *polygon* is a set of noncrossing straight lines that all lie in the same plane and enclose some single area.

Fig. 5-23. Adding more polygons helps get the normals pointing the way we want them to go.

A polygon is modeled by naming the points that make it up in the order in which they are to be joined. For an object to be considered a polygon here, we stated that it must consist of at least three points.

Surface normals were defined to point out of the *front face* of a polygon. The front face is pointed to by the thumb when the fingers are curled around the points in the order in which they are named.

We then discussed shading techniques. The first one was *Lambert* (or *faceted*) *shading* that covers an entire polygon with the shade that corresponds to the shading of the surface normal placed at its center. Objects rendered this way have a faceted or crystalline look, and depending on the light source under consideration, are either *front-facing* or *back-facing*.

The second technique discussed was *Gouraud* (or *smooth*) *shading* that blends the shade from the vertices across the polygon for shading. Both Gouraud and Lambert shading have difficulties with areas of high curvature, local light sources, and highlights.

The third technique, *Phong* (or *normal interpolating*) *shading*, can handle these objects at the cost of more computer time. It interpolates the surface normal at each vertex to find the surface normal at every point, then computes the shade directly for that point.

Following the discussion on shading, we considered problems of polygonal models: silhouettes, unlucky vertex averaging, and *Mach bands*.

Polygons are a friendly and versatile modeling technique, which when used with care, can create very good-looking pictures. Although we will discuss more sophisticated types of surfaces later, the power of polygons to convert realistic-looking objects and scenes should not be underestimated.

Incidentally, most of the images in this book (including the cover) were made with a Phong-shading polygon system.

Chapter SIX

Mapping

In the real world most objects are textured. Most objects that we want to model in computer graphics are not smooth and a single color on the outside, but have some coloration and texture on them. For example, an orange can be considered a sphere with bumps pasted (or drawn) onto it. Or you might want to draw a globe of the Earth, with political boundaries (each country a different color) and mountain ranges (which would look bumpy).

It would be very difficult to directly model this kind of detail onto a surface. An alternative method of coloring or distorting a surface is to use a *map*. A map in this context can be thought of as a picture, where the picture can be considered as some information that is to be applied to a surface. The *map* is commonly called the *surface texture*, the surface it is applied to is called the *mapping* (or *mapped*) *surface*.

PICTURE AND BUMP MAPPING

There are two ways (at least) of using a map to alter the texture of a surface. The first is to paint a picture directly on the surface, like applying wallpaper. To do this, the desired image to be painted is placed in the surface texture (or is specified as the surface texture). An example of this kind of texturing is shown in Fig. 6-6. It is usually called *picture mapping*, because it maps a picture onto a surface.

There's another kind of mapping that not only can enhance surfaces, but actually save some modeling time in generating small details on a larger surface. Imagine modeling a golf ball. It's basically a sphere, but has a lot of dimples on the surface. If you were to model this golf ball as a collection of polygons (for example), unless you had a program to generate the polygons, there would be a lot of typing to be done.

If we wanted to model this object directly with almost any kind of surface, it would be very difficult. However, we can make a realistic-looking golf ball with relative ease using a different mapping technique.

The idea is called *bump mapping* or *normal perturbation*. The idea is to use a surface texture to modify the surface it is applied to, causing the computer to distort the surface before it is drawn.

Recall that the way the computer shaded an object was to compare the various light source vectors with the surface normal (Chapter 5). We stated that the surface normal was usually computed automatically, but that it could be supplied by the modeler. One way to supply that surface normal is to encode it into a picture (or surface texture) and have the computer consult that texture at every point for the surface normal you put there. This kind of "coding" information into a picture is rather complex mathematically, and we will not discuss exactly how it's usually done. Rather, we'll just state that an image (called a texture) can somehow supply us with vectors that we can then use to modify a surface normal.

Refer to Fig. 6-1 for the following discussion. We will assume the role of the computer, and we will say that we are drawing a sphere, with the texture to be "bump mapped" onto it.

We want to render a point on the sphere. Normally, we compare the surface normal at that point to the different light vectors, and compute a shading from the results. Then, we fill in that spot on the screen with the appropriate shade.

With bump mapping, once we have determined what spot on the sphere we wish to work with, we don't immediately calculate its surface normals and compare them to the light sources. First, we calculate the surface normal. Then, we find the point in the surface texture that corresponds to that point on the object. Which point in the map we choose is a subject we will consider in the next section. The value we get from the texture map is actually a vector itself, and we use it to perturb, or "wiggle," the surface normal to cause it to point in a different direction. We then compare this new normal to the light sources and shade as usual.

We wiggle the surface normal at every point according to the information stored in the texture map for that point. This information actually describes a vector to be used to modify the surface normal on the object to which we are applying the texture. There are many ways of encoding this information into the texture map, so we'll pick a straightforward one for example. We'll say that each point in the texture represents the height of a bump at that point on the surface. If the number is a zero, there is no bump at all, or if it is maximum (say 255), then the bump is of some given maximum height.

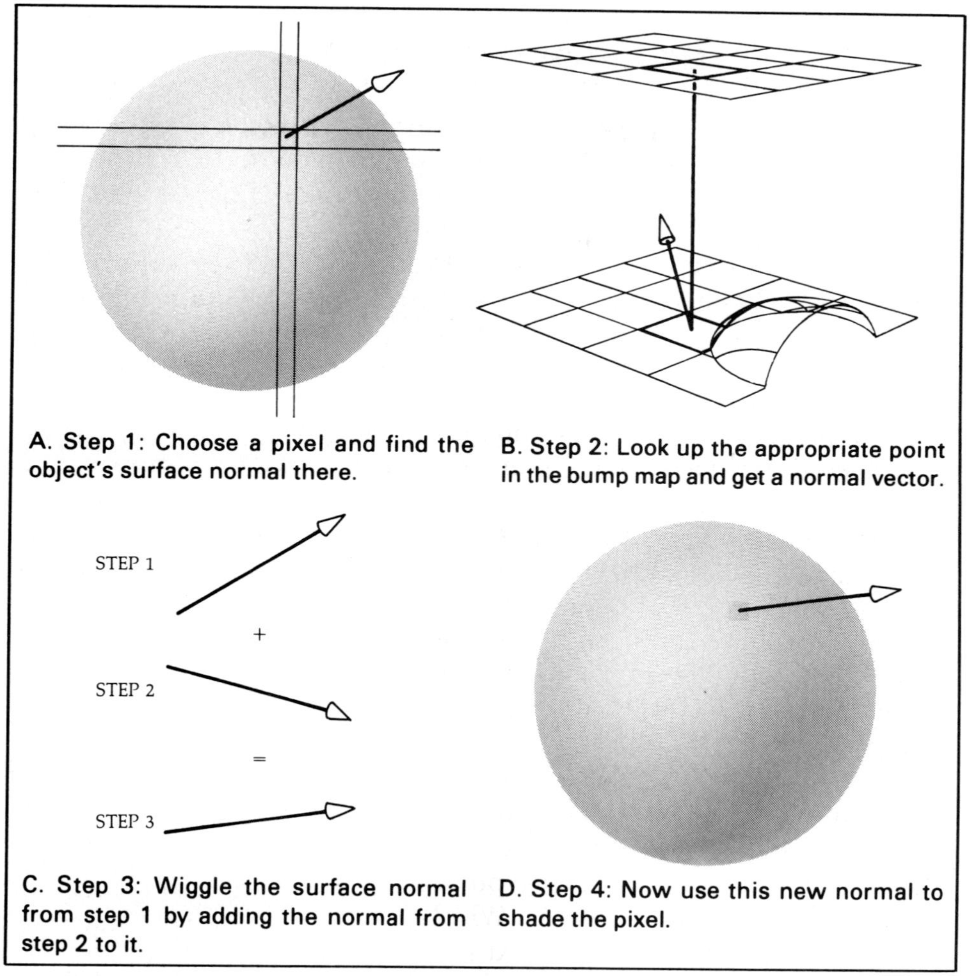

A. Step 1: Choose a pixel and find the object's surface normal there.

B. Step 2: Look up the appropriate point in the bump map and get a normal vector.

C. Step 3: Wiggle the surface normal from step 1 by adding the normal from step 2 to it.

D. Step 4: Now use this new normal to shade the pixel.

Fig. 6-1. The technique of bump mapping.

It's as if we distort the surface being rendered by some shape encoded in the bump map. But the shape really isn't being distorted, it's just being shaded as if it were, which results in a great savings of modeling effort and computer rendering time.

Bump mapping is very useful for putting the rinds on oranges, the treads on tires, grilles on speakers, and the like. Any subtle variation of the shape of the surface of an object is a good application of bump mapping. Bump mapping suffers from a limitation in its inability to correctly distort the shape around the perimeter of an object, as we will see later.

SHADING MAPPED SURFACES

A picture-mapped surface is shaded exactly as if there had been no mapping involved. The intensity of light hitting the surface is determined, the coloration at the surface (derived from the map) is adjusted, and the shading is complete.

Shading bump-mapped surfaces, however, is a different story. The entire trick of bump mapping is, of course, the shading itself, and the calculation of a new surface normal at every point. You can combine maps if you want; i.e., apply several maps, one after the other, to a single surface but the process becomes very, very slow.

Bump mapping suffers from a deficiency that is sometimes negligible and sometimes quite a problem. Recall that the surface isn't really distorted; it just looks that way. So the silhouette of an object will not change if it is bump mapped. That is, a golf ball in profile has the silhouette of a sphere, not a puckered sphere. If you must have a correct silhouette, then bump mapping, although potentially a great time saver for both you and the computer, will not do.

APPLYING TEXTURE

We have seen that texture mapping can greatly enhance the apparent reality of a surface without requiring the modeler to do much more work. If we want to use this technique regularly, we need to have some kind of useful system for determining how to apply the texture to the surface.

For example, take the surface texture in Fig. 6-2. How do we find the "correct" point in the texture for a given point on a surface, say a sphere or cylinder?

The most common scheme for identifying the correspondence between points on the surface and those in the texture map is called *surface parameterization*. The idea is that we think of various points in a texture map as identified by a distance along two axes, as in Fig. 6-3. We call these two values parameters. As Fig. 6-3 shows, these axes are often referred to as the U and V axes, to distinguish them from the X and Y axes that we use when modeling. These names are just common notation, though; you may label the axes with any letter or name you like.

So a given pair of U and V values identifies a particular point on the texture. If every point on the surface is assigned a pair of U and V values,

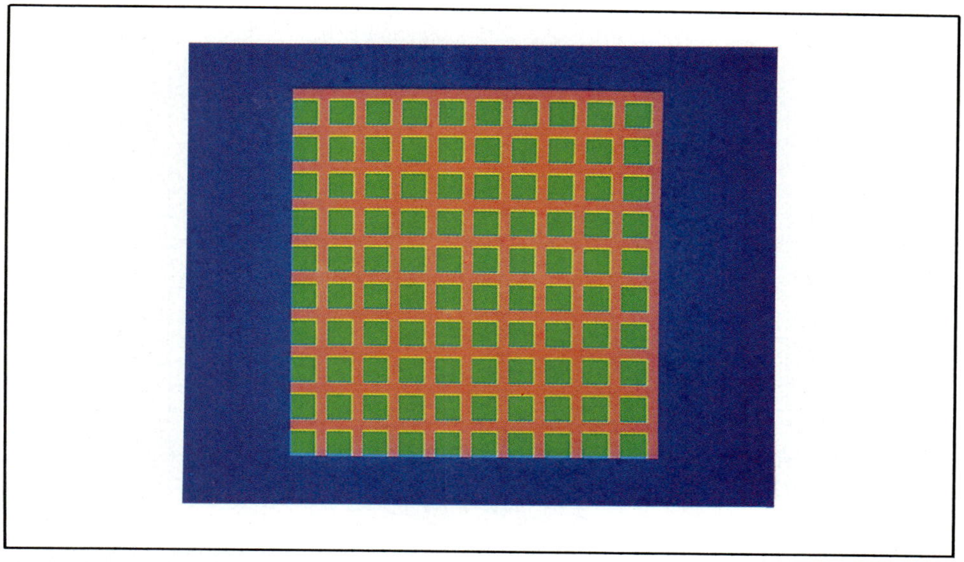

Fig. 6-2. An example texture.

then we have a complete and versatile scheme for getting back and forth between points on the surface and points in the texture map.

Some surfaces seem to have a "natural" kind of parameterization. Fig. 6-4 shows our checkerboard texture mapped onto a sphere. We can see that U and V run like lines of latitude and longitude.

Fig. 6-5 shows our checkerboard texture on a cylinder, where we can see the lines of U and V run around the cylinder and up and down. Fig. 6-6 shows the checkerboard on a cone, where the parameterization is much the same.

These parameterizations are typical of most systems. They seem to be easy to get used to, and more importantly, when you're designing a texture, it's easy to see how that texture will eventually look on the surface.

But, the parameterization may be done any way you or a programmer would like to have it done. Fig. 6-7 shows the same cone and the same checkerboard as in Fig. 6-6, but we have changed the U and V coordinates on the surface of the cone. Neither the cone itself nor the texture was changed, just the coordinates on the surface of the cone.

We can map any kind of texture; we don't need to stick with checkerboards. Fig. 6-8 shows a red heart on a green background mapped onto a sphere, and Fig. 6-9 shows the same heart mapped onto the same cone with two different parameterizations.

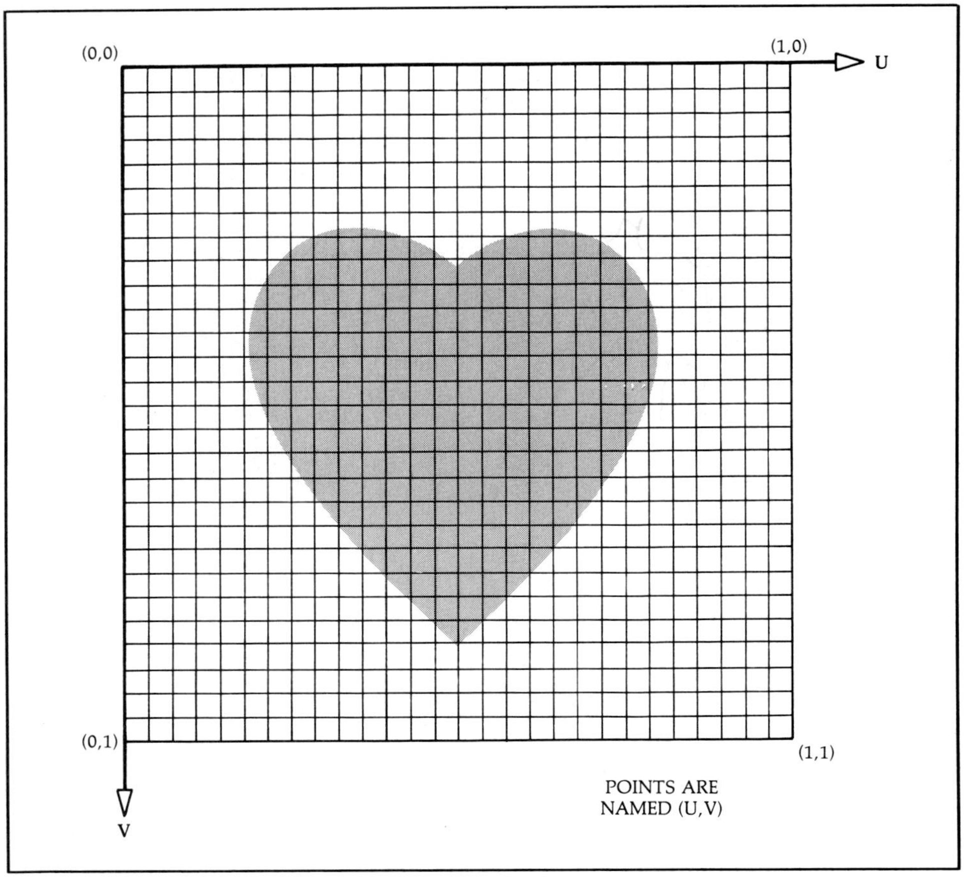

Fig. 6-3. Texture is referenced by (U,V) coordinates.

Another common surface we want to parameterize is our old friend the polygon. We usually parameterize polygons by assigning U and V values to each vertex, and then blending those values across the face of the polygon, much as we blend shade when we do Gouraud shading. Fig. 6-10 shows a four-cornered polygon and an interpolated point in the center.

SUMMARY

In this chapter we discussed how *mapping* can help us model small detail on the surfaces of objects. We said that the information that gets placed onto a surface is called the *map* or *source texture*, and the object that is affected is called the *mapped surface*.

Fig. 6-4. A mapped sphere.

Fig. 6-5. A mapped cylinder.

There are two major kinds of mapping: *picture mapping*, which paints a picture onto the mapped surface, and *bump mapping*, which causes the mapped surface to appear mottled or slightly reshaped.

Bump mapping is also known as *normal perturbation*. To "perturb"

Fig. 6-6. A mapped cone.

Fig. 6-7. We can change the scale of the map when we apply it.

something is to wiggle it, so we might also call bump mapping "normal-wiggle" mapping. The idea is that in the bump map, we have somehow stored a vector. When we apply a bump map to a particular point on a surface, we first find the surface normal of the surface at that point. We then "wiggle" that surface normal in some way, as directed by the vector

Fig. 6-8. A heart mapped onto a sphere.

Fig. 6-9. Again, we can change the mapping without modifying either the cone or the texture itself.

in the bump map. This wiggling of the normal causes it to point in a new direction, and thus, when it is compared to the light source, the shading at that point is not the shade that would be there if the bump map was not applied.

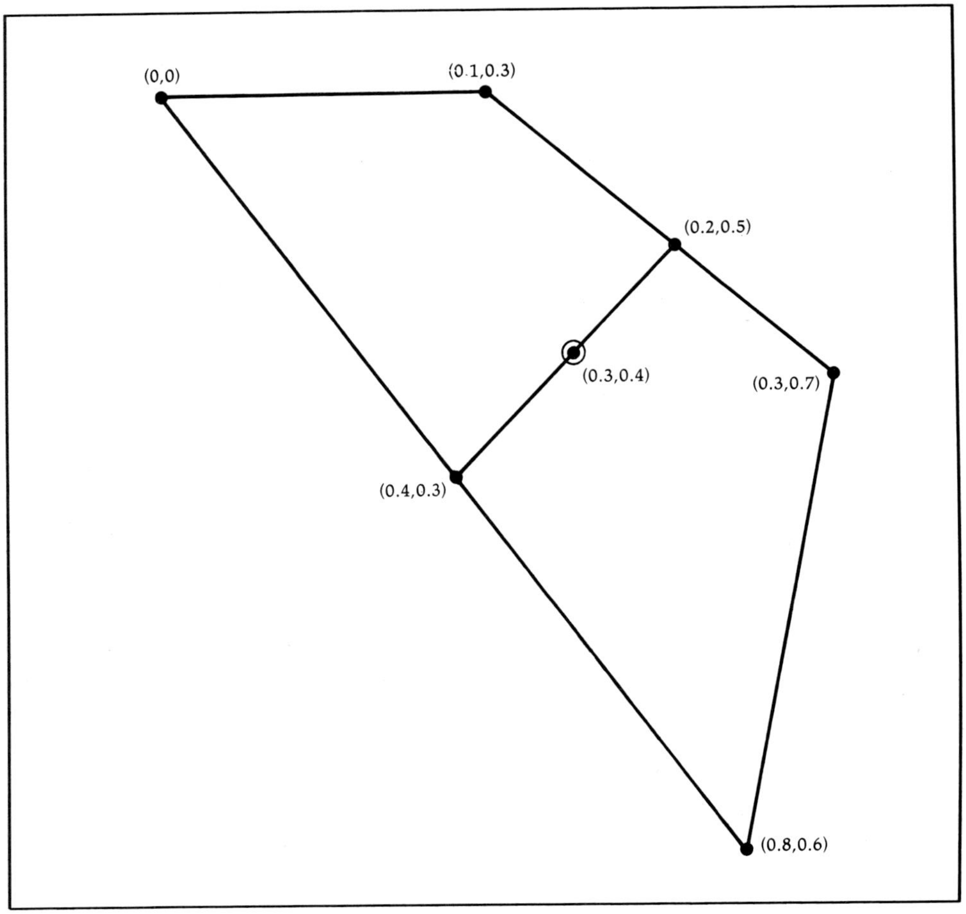

Fig. 6-10. Interpolating (U,V) coordinates across a polygon.

We then considered how texture was actually applied. We saw that various surfaces were *parameterized* by assigning a pair of numbers, or *parameters*, to each point on the surface. Each pair of numbers (referred to as U and V), referred to a particular point in the texture, and vice versa.

We saw typical parameterizations for spheres, cylinders, and cones. We then saw that we could change the application of the texture just by modifying the coordinates on the surface of the object being textured, without actually changing either the texture or the surface.

Next, we saw that to parameterize a polygon we assigned U and V values at each vertex, and blended them across the face of the polygon just as we blended shade in Gouraud shading.

Chapter SEVEN

Fractals

In this chapter we will look at a class of mathematical objects called *fractals*. Although they are relatively new to computer graphics, they have already helped create some of the most realistic-looking images ever generated.

We will consider an imaginary but realistic modeling situation where our old friend the polygon is completely inappropriate. We'll consider what properties we would want from a substitute modeling system, and then see that fractal objects fulfill those requirements perfectly. We'll then close the chapter with a gallery of computer-generated images, created with the help of fractals.

SOME BACKGROUND

The word *fractal* is new to the world. It describes a new system of mathematics so powerful, it can describe the structure of mountains, coastlines, galaxies, and much more. It was generally believed by mathematicians and scientists that such complex natural phenomena were almost beyond rigorous description. After all, a mountain looks so jagged and wild, it seemed impossible to capture the essence of its shape with the clean and elegant tools of mathematics.

Despite this general sentiment, Benoit Mandelbrot studied the structures of these objects, as well as many other shapes found in nature. He succeeded not only in describing them well for the first time, but he has shown they are all related to one another as well. His discovery was that one class of geometrical objects could describe the shapes of mountains, the distribution of stars in the galaxy, the patterns of moving fluids, and much more!

It is the traditional right of the discoverer of new territory to name his find. Mandelbrot coined the word *fractal* to encompass his new generalizations of complex shapes. The discovery of fractals was very exciting in many fields, including computer graphics. Let's now take a closer look at how fractals can help us make pictures.

AN AIRPLANE RIDE

A very good introduction to fractals can be found in the opening chapters of Mandelbrot's recent book on fractal geometry. We'll follow the same line of thought here. Our approach will be to learn about a particular fractal (a coastline), and then see some of the general properties of fractals from an examination of this particular one.

Imagine you're flying in an airplane high above the coast of France. If you look out the window at the coastline, you could sketch it on a small pad. If the plane then started coming in for a landing at a coastal airport, you would see the coastline grow larger and larger in your window, and you could keep resketching what you saw as the plane descended. Note that the large features you saw from a high altitude are still visible close up, but there is ever more detail visible in the coastline as you approach the airport. Figures 7-1 and 7-2 show a set of coastal sketches you might make.

If you wanted to simulate this sequence with a computer, you would run into trouble modeling the irregularity of the hills and the coastline. Most of the objects we have seen so far have been precisely defined. Polygons are flat and bounded by straight edges, and the curved surfaces we will see in Chapter 8 are all smooth by definition. Imagine how hard it would be to model such a coastline out of polygons!

Even if you were intrepid enough to start on a polygonal model of the coastline, there would still be a problem. To make an animation such as the sketches just described, you would need enough polygons to describe the coastline at each point in the film. The coast would have to look craggy from a great height, and there would have to be enough small detail so that when the plane is landing the coastline will still appear rugged. So even when we are far from the coast, the computer will have to draw all the little details even when they're really too far away for us to see them because the description of the coastline is a static model (as

A. From high up.

B. Slightly closer.

Fig. 7-1. Sketches of a coastline.

defined in Chapter 2), and if a polygon is in the model at the end of the film, it's there at the beginning as well.

The result is that a lot of computer time is wasted when we're very high up (drawing little details that usually won't make a difference on the

A. Closer still.

B. Finally, a close-up coastline.

Fig. 7-2. Closer sketches of the same coastline.

screen) as well as when we're close to the ground (because the computer processes all the polygons in the coastline, which means everything that was visible when we were high up!). Of course, you could have several coastlines defined, and you could draw different ones when the plane is at different altitudes, but that would also be a lot of hard work.

SOME CHARACTERISTICS OF FRACTALS

It would be very convenient if we could somehow get the computer to draw rough objects like the coastline for us automatically. There are certain things we would have to require of such a program, though. The first is that craggy objects (such as a coastline) have to be *self-similar*. We can think of this as meaning that if the coastline is very rough and jagged far away, it should be just as rough and jagged close up. In other words, the details should have the same general kind of shape as the overall structure. Another important requirement for our applications is that the computer should only generate as much detail as we need. For instance, we don't want fine details in our coastline from high up, but we do want them when we're close to the ground.

To consider another application, say you wanted to animate a scene in outer space, and you wanted to have asteroids pass by on the screen. Asteroids are very rough and craggy, and even if you modeled one out of polygons, every time you wanted to render it, you would have to wait a very long time. And then, every asteroid would be the same! What you really want is a computer program that can automatically generate asteroids for you, making each one different. From far away they should look like craggy rocks, and as the asteroid approaches the screen we should see increasing amounts of detail.

If you asked a programmer ignorant of fractals to write a program to "make asteroids," you would probably have a long time to wait. And then you might very well end up with some kind of "random" shape, roughly round, and certainly cragged, but as unlike an asteroid as a child's random scribble is unlike a coastline. Certainly natural objects have some kind of natural order to them. Although a coastline appears "random" to some extent, you can usually tell what might be a coastline and what might not.

HOW COMPUTER GRAPHICS FRACTALS ARE MADE

We should be careful here to distinguish between fractals in general and the particular objects we're going to study here and use normally in computer graphics. Fractals are a class of mathematical shapes, and it should be no surprise that they can get very complex and subtle. When we want to use the properties of fractals in our pictures, we're going to ignore many of the fine points of the theory and concentrate on making believable or visually pleasing pictures.

Let's look at how we can make a fractal. We'll pick a particular kind of fractal that has been around for a long time and is called a *Koch curve* even though it's made entirely out of straight lines!

We're going to take a polygon and change it in particular ways until it starts taking on the appearance we want. Fig. 7-3 shows our original polygon (a triangle), and an associated shape that Mandelbrot calls the

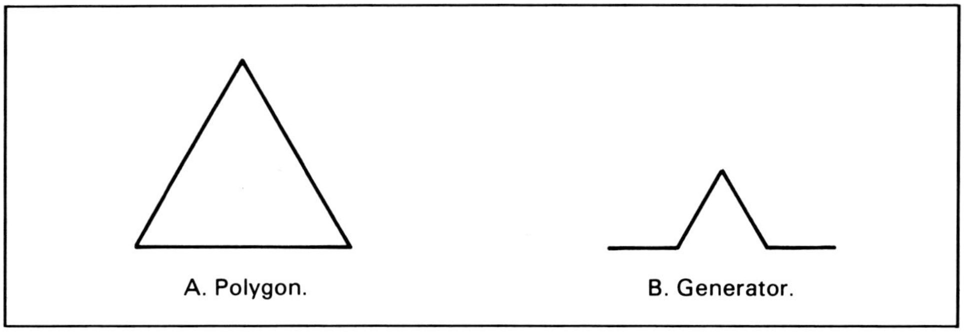

Fig. 7-3. A polygon and a generator.

generator. To make a Koch curve, we take each line in the polygon and replace it by the generator, as shown in Fig. 7-4. This new shape bears some resemblance to our original triangle, but now it looks a little more complicated. We now repeat the process of replacing every line in the polygon with the generator, yielding Fig. 7-5. Note that from a distance Fig. 7-4 and Fig. 7-5 may look very much alike, but Fig. 7-5 has more detail. We can repeat the application of the generator again and again (Fig. 7-6), as many times as we please.

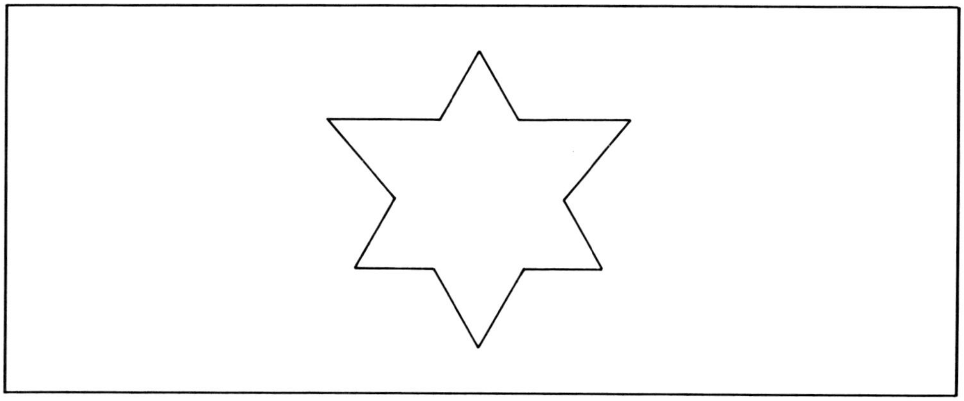

Fig. 7-4. Applying the generator once.

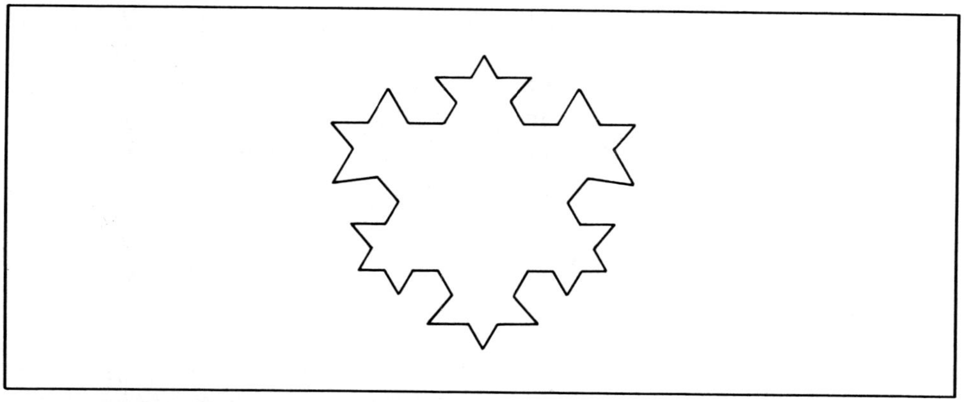

Fig. 7-5. Applying the generator twice.

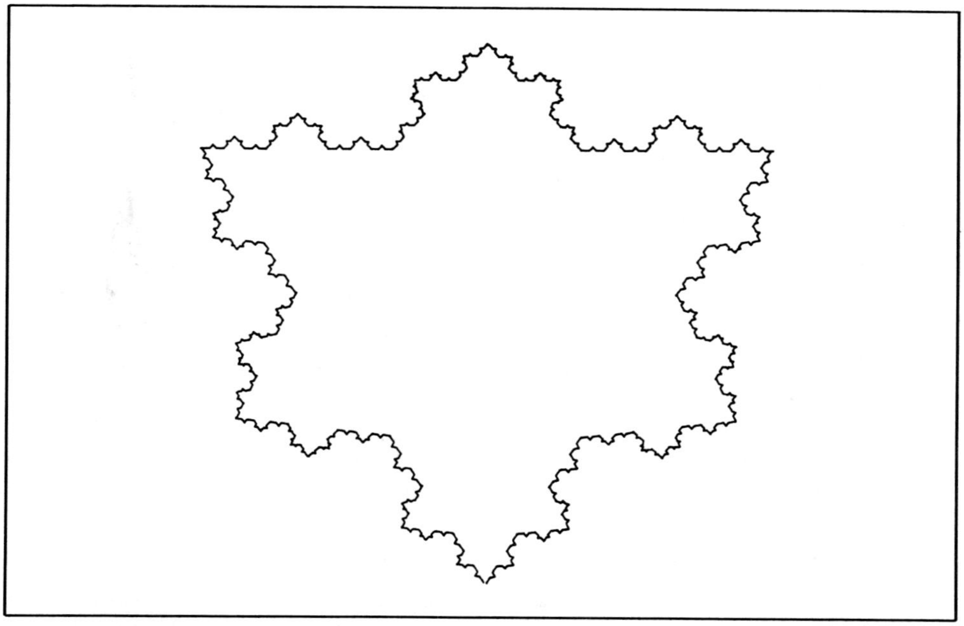

Fig. 7-6. This picture was made by applying the generator of Fig. 7-3 four times.

Let's make two important observations about the shape we have just made. The first is that they are all "self-similar." If we examine any section of a particular figure, it bears a strong resemblance to the whole. Thus, the details faithfully reflect the overall structure of the original form.

The other feature we should note is that we are able to control just how much detail we want in the evolution of the Koch curve. This control is helpful for the kind of situation as described in the imaginary airplane flight discussed earlier. When the shape is far away (and thus small on the screen), we only want the general shape to be rendered by the computer. Additional detail would not show up when the island is small and just makes the computer's job harder. On the other hand, when the island is close up (and thus large on the screen), we can generate as much detail as we want. Note that new detail is added to the old; it's not like we invented new, random shapes every time we wanted more detail. This may seem obvious, but until fractals were discovered and described, computers were not able to do this kind of thing very well at all!

Another line-type fractal can be seen in Fig. 7-7, where the original polygon is a line, and the generator is a pair of lines that form the other two legs of a right triangle with it. Fig. 7-8 shows this construction carried out eight times; it is often called a *C curve* for obvious reasons.

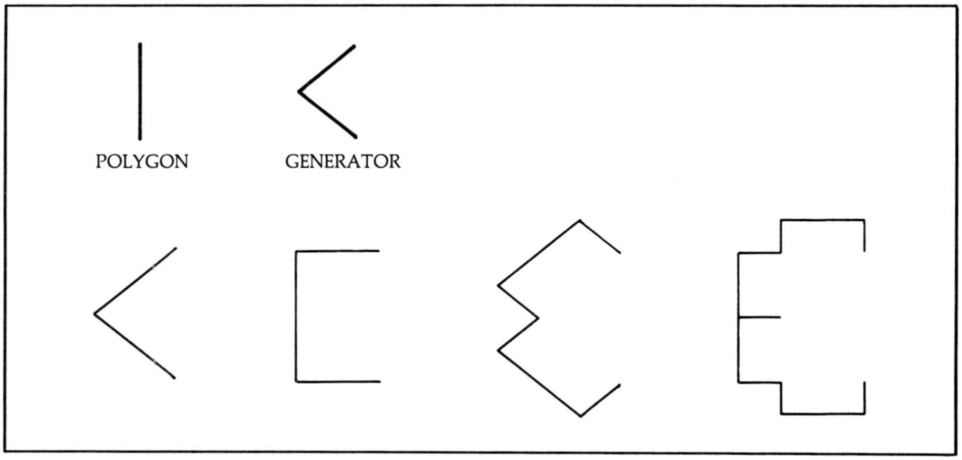

Fig. 7-7. The first few steps in constructing a C curve.

We can generalize this kind of technique from lines to surfaces, and although it gets more complicated, it is really just more of the same. For example, to create a coastline we use a single polygon and subdivide it repeatedly. If we want to create a three-dimensional object such as a mountain or asteroid, we create a three-dimensional polygonal object and do a more complicated kind of subdivision on it, as sketched in Fig. 7-9.

In the hands of talented programmers and artists, fractals can be used to create computer-generated pictures that were previously almost impossible. Figs. 7-10 through 7-19 show three-dimensional fractal objects. These weren't created to look like natural objects, but they seem to have very

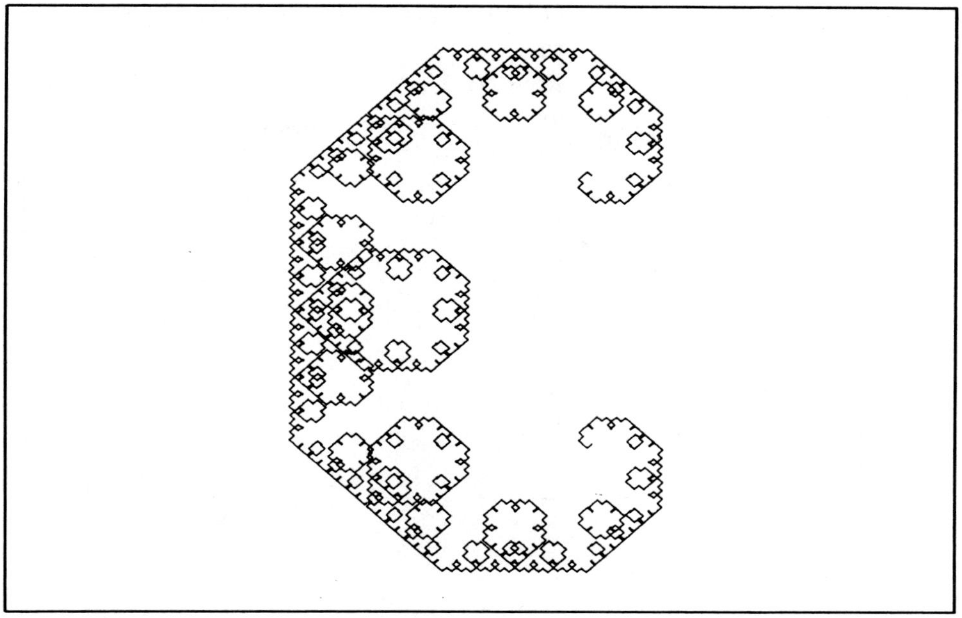

Fig. 7-8. C curve after eight repetitions.

pleasing shapes. On the other hand, Figs. 7-20 through 7-24 are some of the most realistic pictures every generated by computer. They are pictures of fractal shapes "grown" from a very small amount of starting information. Fig. 7-24 is a fractal planetrise. All objects were created by the computer with very little information from the modeler.

SUMMARY

In this chapter we started out by noting that until very recently, there existed no mathematical tools for describing some very important shapes found in nature. These tools were developed by Benoit Mandelbrot and were shown to have far-reaching applications in many fields of science and art, including computer graphics.

We took an imaginary airplane ride along the coast of France and noticed that as the plane descended we could see increasing amount of detail from the window. It was clear that a polygonal model of a coastline would be very difficult to construct and would not really even do the job very well.

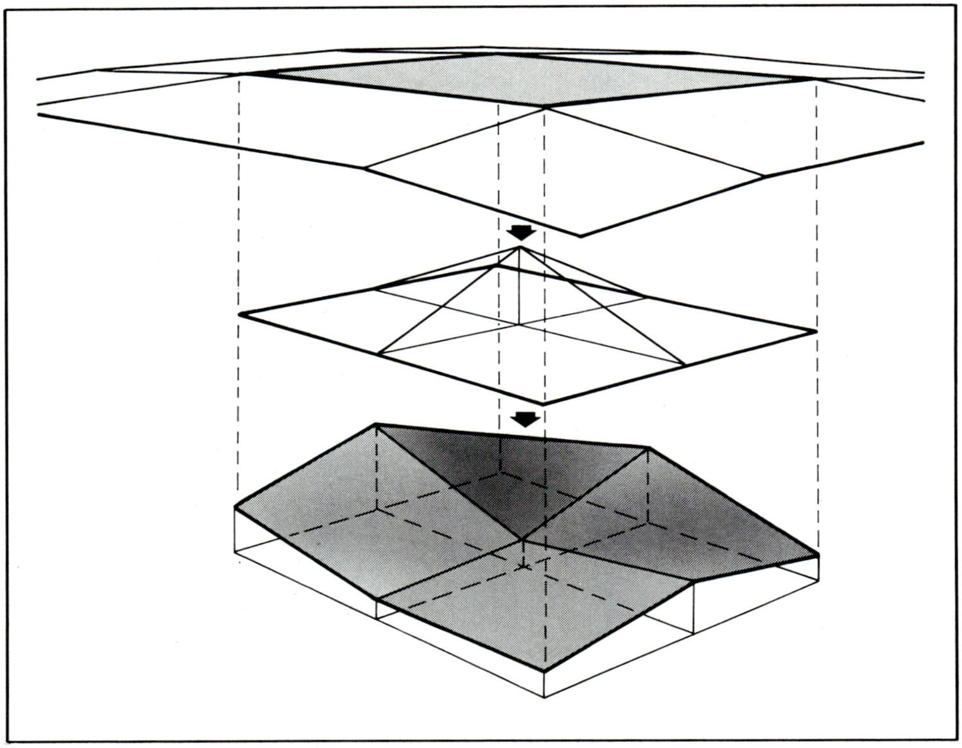

Fig. 7-9. Subdivision of a polygon into four polygons, making a crinkly surface out of a flat one.

Fig. 7-10. An abstract mathematical surface created with the tools of fractals. *(Image by Alan Norton. Used with permission of IBM Corp.)*

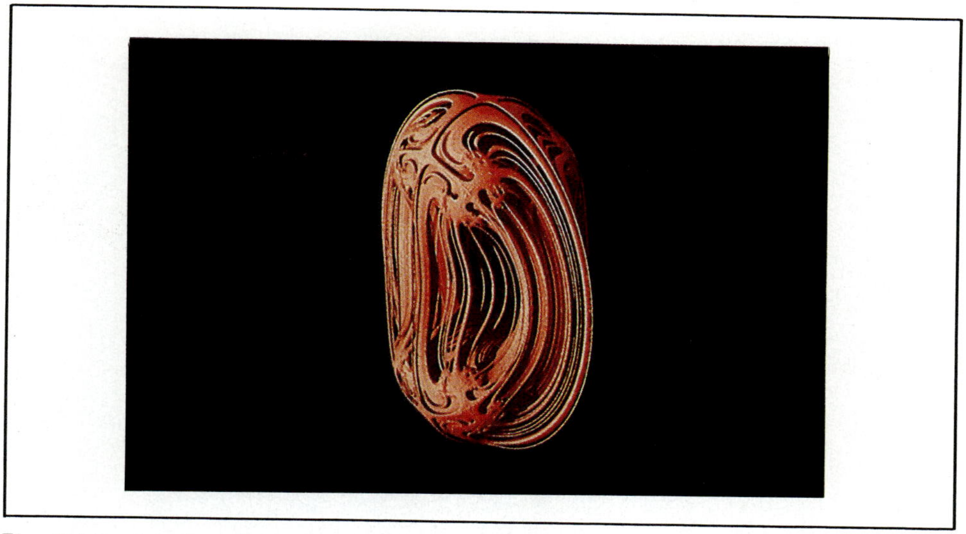

Fig. 7-11. Another fractal object. ***(Image by Alan Norton. Used with permission of IBM Corp.)***

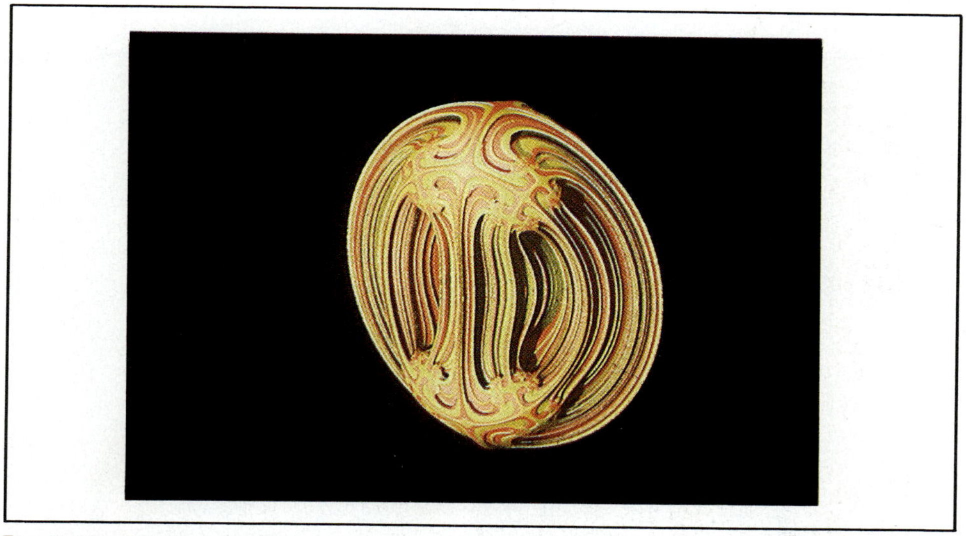

Fig. 7-12. An abstract fractal. ***(Image by Alan Norton. Used with permission of IBM Corp.)***

We stated that if we could find another kind of technique to model shapes such as coastlines, we would want it to generate models with certain properties. Two of the most important properties were those of *self-similarity* and arbitrary amounts of detail. Self-similarity tells us that small details bear a resemblance to the overall structure of the object, a

Fig. 7-13. Another abstract fractal. ***(Image by Alan Norton. Used with permission of IBM Corp.)***

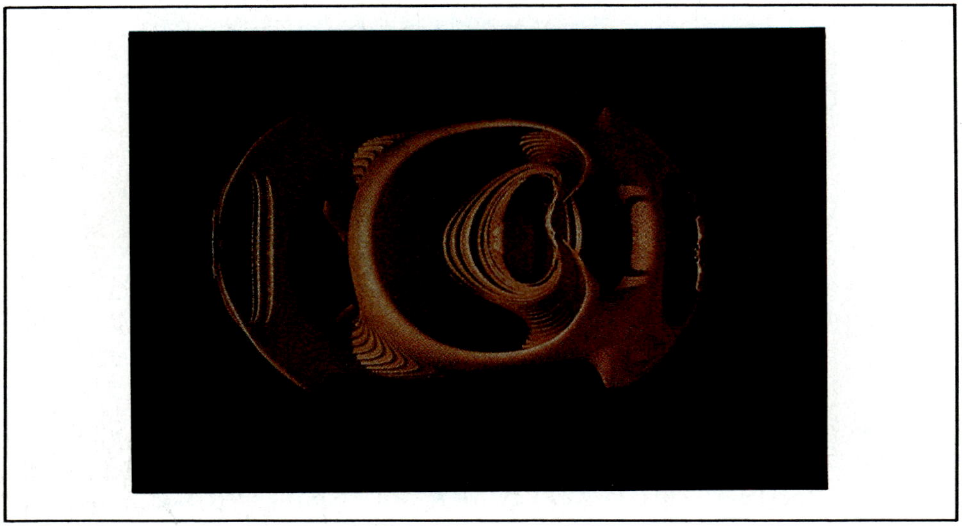

Fig. 7-14. Another abstract fractal. ***(Image by Alan Norton. Used with permission of IBM Corp.)***

property of many natural shapes. The arbitrary control over detail lets us make very rough shapes when they will be small on the screen, and increase the detail only when the object grows larger and the detail can be seen.

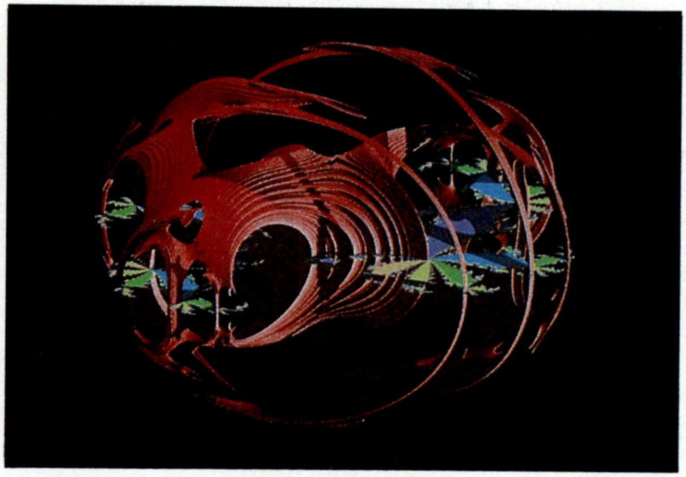

Fig. 7-15. Another abstract fractal. ***(Image by Alan Norton. Used with permission of IBM Corp.)***

Fig. 7-16. Another abstract fractal. ***(Image by Alan Norton. Used with permission of IBM Corp.)***

We saw two examples of fractals, the *Koch curve* and the *C curve*, both of which exhibited these properties. We saw that they could be constructed from an original polygon and a *generator*, that is applied repeatedly to the edges of the polygon. We then suggested that you could gener-

Fig. 7-17. **Another abstract fractal.** ***(Image by Alan Norton. Used with permission of IBM Corp.)***

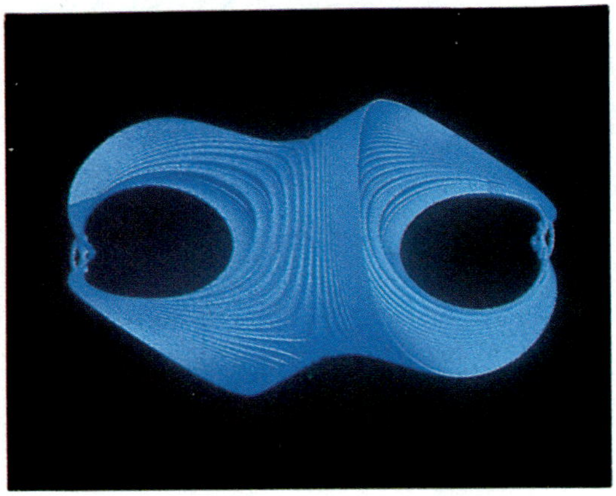

Fig. 7-18. **Another abstract fractal.** ***(Image by Alan Norton. Used with permission of IBM Corp.)***

Fig. 7-19. A fractal shape. *(Image copyright © 1982 by Benoit B. Mandelbrot. Programming by Mark Laff and Alan Norton. Used by permission.)*

Fig. 7-20. Fractal mountains. Note that these mountains were actually created by the computer using fractal geometry. *(Image copyright © 1982 by Benoit B. Mandelbrot. Programming by Richard Voss. Used by permission.)*

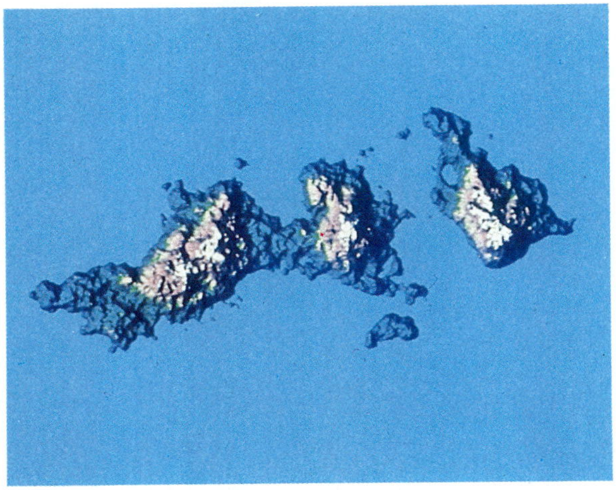

Fig. 7-21. Fractal islands. *(Image copyright © 1982 by Benoit B. Mandelbrot. Programming by Richard Voss. Used by permission.)*

Fig. 7-22. More fractal islands. *(Image copyright © 1982 by Benoit B. Mandelbrot. Programming by Richard Voss. Used by permission.)*

Fig. 7-23. A fractal gorge. *(Image copyright © 1982 by Benoit B. Mandelbrot. Programming by Richard Voss. Used by permission.)*

Fig. 7-24. A fractal planetrise. *(Image copyright © 1982 by Benoit B. Mandelbrot. Programming by Richard Voss. Used by permission.)*

ate a complex, three-dimensional fractal by making a three-dimensional object out of polygons like we usually do, and then subdividing it according to some rules of fractal construction. We closed with a brief gallery of pictures made with fractal techniques, ranging from abstract mathematical objects to convincingly real landscapes.

The power of fractals is being expanded every day, with new applications discovered in many diverse fields. For computer graphics, fractals can help us create complicated and previously formidable objects with relative ease.

Chapter EIGHT

Curved Surfaces

The only surfaces we have seen so far have been polygons. Polygons are very easy to work with and quite versatile, but by their very nature, they have limitations. For example, a sphere made up of polygons cannot get too large on the screen, or the silhouette (which is all straight edges) will show up, ruining the illusion of roundness. Also, it's a hassle to have to create a great many polygons every time you want to draw a complex, smooth, and curvy surface.

In this chapter we will look at a class of surfaces that are smooth and curved by definition. We will see how to cut them so that they are shaped just right for model making, and we will see how to get curved surfaces that touch each other and blend together so that the combination of several curved surfaces looks like one big surface.

SHADING AND DEFINITION

Recall from Chapter 5 that there are several methods for shading polygons, each with advantages and disadvantages. The reason for having more than one shading technique for polygons was that we wanted to make a polygonal surface look like a smooth surface, and the mechanism was the shading model.

For the curved surfaces we commonly use in computer graphics, the surface is defined by a mathematical expression in such a way as to guarantee us that the surface is already smooth. So to shade a curved surface, we first find the point on the surface that projects to the middle of the pixel under consideration (recall that a pixel is a single dot on the television screen). We then find the surface normal at that point, and compare it to the various light sources. We can also map a curved surface, causing the surface normal to be wiggled before being compared to the light sources, just like mapping polygons. So we can add small detail in coloration and shape in the same way as with polygons.

There are various kinds of curved surfaces that have proven themselves useful in computer graphics. Most of them we will only mention, because they require some mathematical sophistication to create.

A general class of curved surfaces are sometimes grouped under the category *patches*. We won't use patches in this book, but you may run across them in other people's models, so we'll just spend a little time discussing what they are.

The idea is that the user defines a small section (or patch) of a larger curved surface. An object may be created out of many patches placed next to one another, as Fig. 8-1 illustrates. For example, a barrel might be

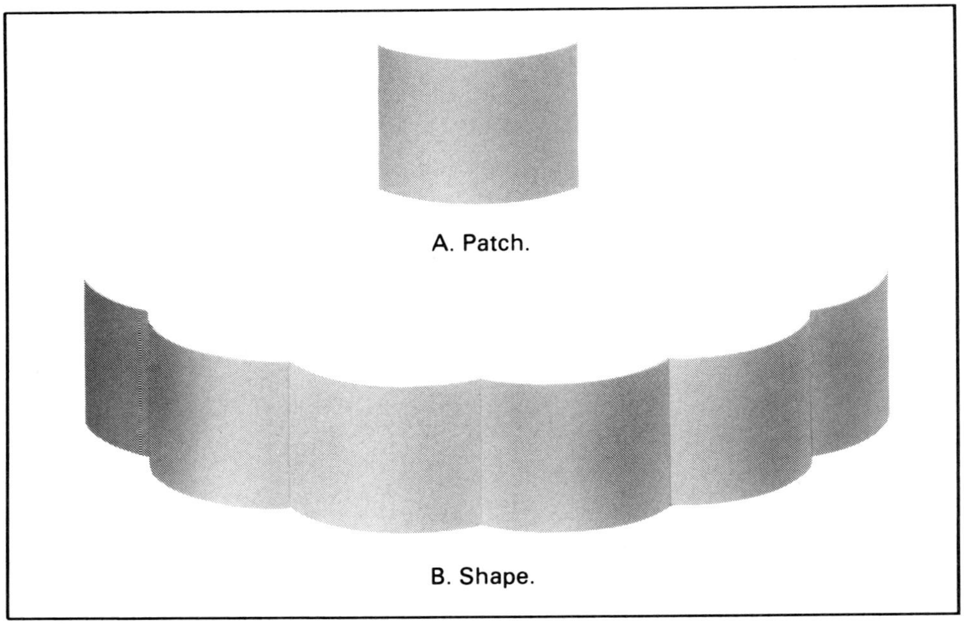

Fig. 8-1. A complicated shape built up of copies of one simple shape.

considered an object built up of many patches, where each patch is a stave. You might notice that we could say polygons are patches. In practice, we usually limit the meaning of "patch" to a section of curved, non-planar surface. Some types of patches are called bilinear patches, Bezier patches, and cubic patches. We will not look into how these small pieces of surface are created and entered; they are usually found more in mechanical engineering and design than in artistic modeling.

Another kind of curved surface is defined as the solution to a particular kind of mathematical equation, and we consider it in the next section.

QUADRIC SURFACES

A *quadric surface* is usually formally defined in computer graphics as the surface that is a solution to a quadric equation. What this usually boils down to is that quadric surfaces are a generic name for *spheres, cylinders,* and *cones,* as illustrated in Fig. 8-2. Other quadric surfaces are called *saddle* and *hyperboloid*, and are illustrated in Fig. 8-3, but these are usually more difficult to work with than spheres, cylinders, and cones. We will not consider saddles and hyperboloids further.

Fig. 8-2. Some modeling primitives.

Spheres are completely defined by a center and a radius as in Fig. 8-4. A cylinder is defined by a circular base and a height. Fig. 8-5 shows a collection of cylinders of different parameters, or values that control the shape.

The third class of quadrics, the cone, comes in basically two different varieties. Because of its mathematical definition, the cone can actually end up as two separated shapes! Fig. 8-6 shows several cones, each of which was entered as one surface.

Different computer systems have different methods for entering the variables that control surface parameters, just like for polygons, so we won't go into that now, except to note the diversity of shapes that the cone can lead to.

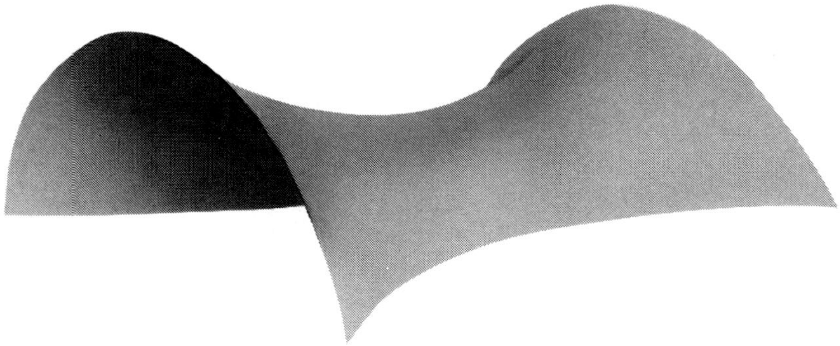

A. A saddle.

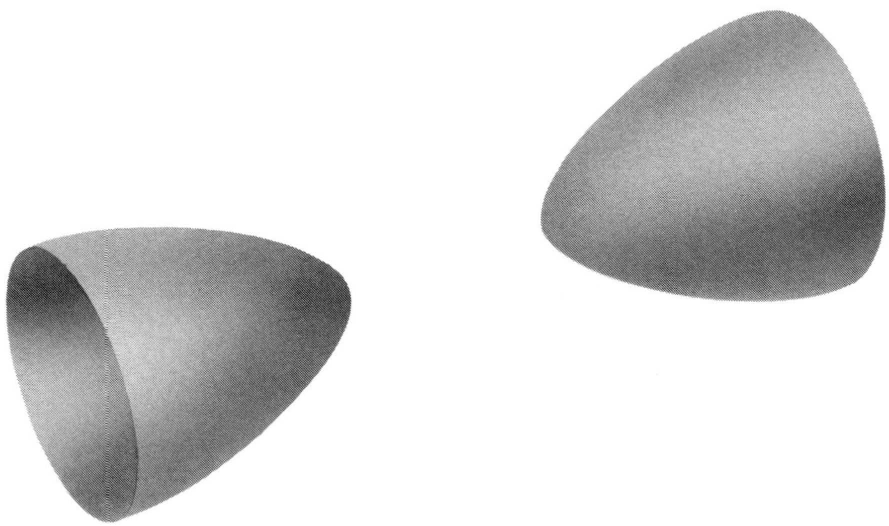

B. A hyperboloid of two sheets.

Fig. 8-3. Other quadric surfaces.

When we want to draw a cylinder on the screen, we have to be careful. The mathematical definition of a cylinder gives it infinite length, which is usually not what we want. Instead, we have to tell the computer to clip the cylinder off at certain points, or *bind* the surface. We also say we have to enter *bounds* for the surface, or that it must be *bounded.* Bounds are limits on the extent and size of the shape of a surface, beyond its initial mathematical definition. Fig. 8-7 shows several cylinders with the bounds that

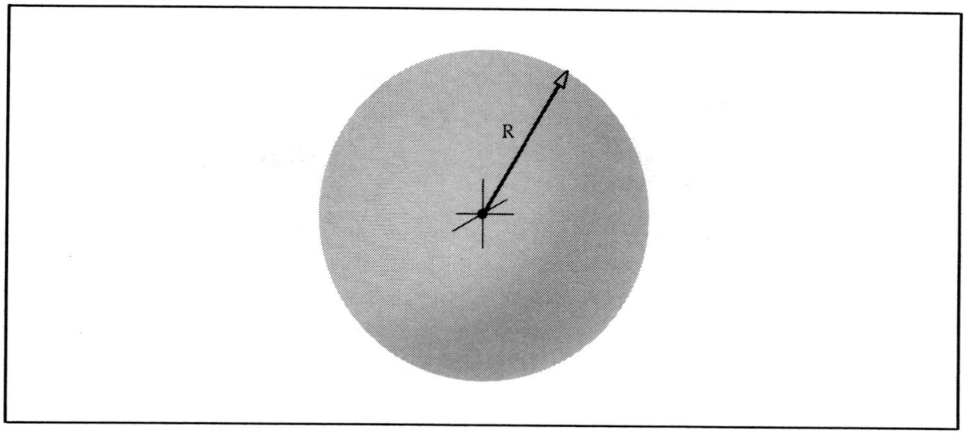

Fig. 8-4. A sphere is completely described by a center and radius.

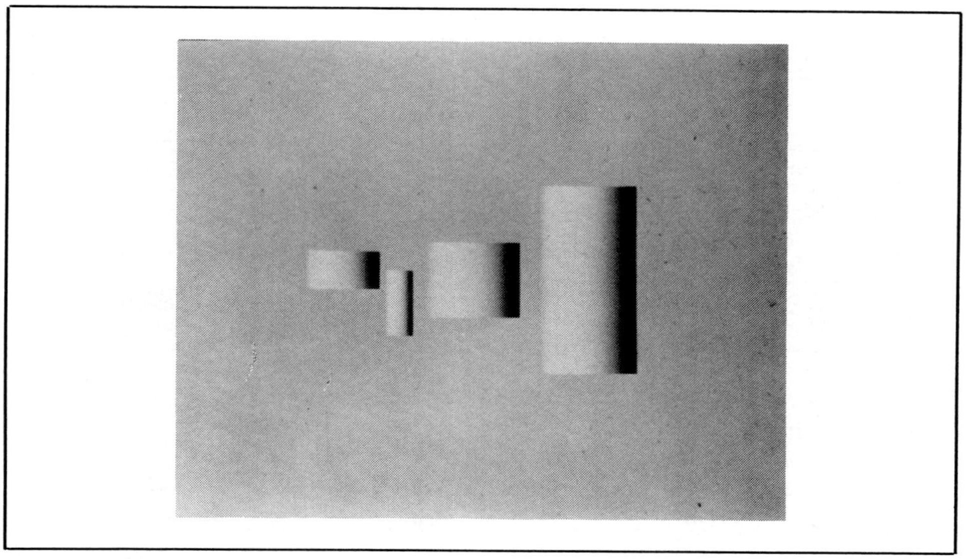

Fig. 8-5. Different cylinders.

must be included when we actually draw a picture: the lower and upper limits of the cylinder. Cones also need these limits, as shown in Fig. 8-8.

In addition to these bounds, the artist may enter additional bounds that actually cause additional pieces of the surface to be removed. Recall that we discussed subtractive modeling as removing pieces of volume from something, leaving behind just what you want. In this vein it is often possible to define some quadric surfaces (often just called "quadrics") as

Fig. 8-6. Different cones.

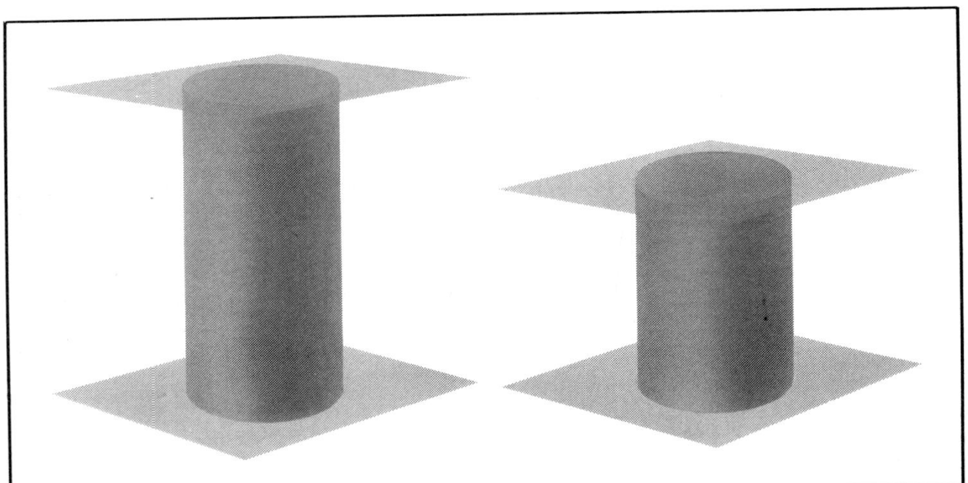

Fig. 8-7. How cylinders are bounded.

"negative volumes," or as pieces of the surface that should be removed. These new surfaces that don't get drawn instead act as bounds on the surfaces that are drawn. Fig. 8-9 illustrates how quadric surfaces may be used to bind (or limit) other quadric surfaces. In addition, some computer systems allow polygons to bind quadrics and vice versa.

Fig. 8-8. How cones are bounded.

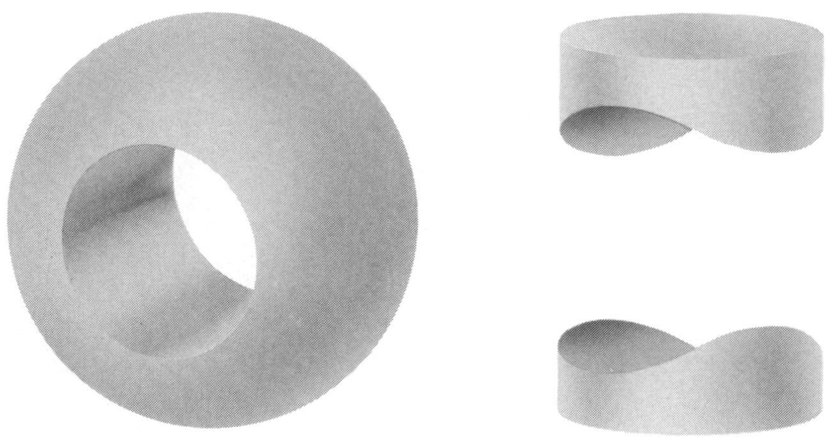

A. A cylinder putting a hole in a sphere. B. A sphere putting a hole in a cylinder.

Fig. 8-9. A sphere and a cylinder cutting holes in each other.

SUMMARY

In this chapter we looked at curved surfaces for computer graphics. We started by defining *patches*, which had a complex mathematically defined curved shape. We stated that any curved surface could be made up of enough correctly shaped and placed patches, and then moved on because of the difficulties inherent in modeling with patches.

We then defined a class of surfaces called *quadric surfaces*, because of their relation to quadric equations in mathematics. We said we would consider quadric surfaces to be the *sphere*, *cylinder*, and *cone*. We mentioned that there are at least two other surfaces that technically match the mathematical definition (the *hyperboloid* and *saddle*) but we did not discuss them because of the difficulty involved in using them. We then stated that although the sphere was naturally *bounded*, the cylinder and cone extended forever, and had to be cut at some point if we wanted to use them in models. We saw how both polygons and quadric surfaces can act as *bounds* on quadric surfaces for the purpose of defining their limits.

Chapter NINE

Model Making

So far we have been mostly concerned with the basic ideas and surfaces that we use in computer graphics. This chapter is to give you a flavor of how some of those ideas are combined to actually specify an object to the computer in such a way that not only can you get the computer to draw it, but you can animate it as well.

DESCRIBING A COMPLEX OBJECT

The first step in prepared model making is to prepare a drawing of the model. The drawing serves to identify the primitive surfaces used to make the model, and perhaps provides some information about the orientation and size of those surfaces. Once the modeler has some kind of idea of what surfaces are best to be used and how they are to be combined, then they can be entered into the computer.

When modeling, always remember that the model is built in the *global coordinate system*. This system is the overall set of axes (in the three-dimensional world of the object) that the entire object is defined in. You can think of this coordinate system as being permanently attached to the screen of your crt, with positive X to the right, positive Y going up, and positive Z going away from your nose. You may recall that this is the way a left-handed coordinate system looks.

Let's examine how the modeling procedure goes when the surfaces may be precisely defined in space from any point. Polygons fit this condition; a polygon is a list of coordinates (in the correct order) relative to a single set of coordinate axes.

Fig. 9-1 shows a cone and its relation to the coordinate system. Y is blue, X is green, and Z is cyan. Fig. 9-2 shows engineering-type renderings that help us locate all the vertices and their numerical positions in space. We

Fig. 9-1. A view of a cone.

then enter each polygon into the computer (the polygons may be named in any order), and the model definition is complete. We can then add lighting and special effects like mapping, transparency, and so on, apply perspective, choose a viewpoint, set up the viewing pyramid, and tell the computer to render the picture.

Fig. 9-3 shows a set of spheres and a cone in space. We will use these to describe the other kind of model making, which operates by keeping the relation between the object and a set of coordinates constant, but changing the coordinate system within some larger coordinate system.

For example, Fig. 9-4 shows the relation of the sphere and the cone to an arbitrary set of coordinates. The computer knows that every time we want to draw a sphere, it will draw a sphere with radius one about the origin of the current coordinate system. And the cone will always be drawn the same way relative to the current coordinate system: with the tip of the cone on the Y axis and the base on the X-Z axis, with a base radius of one and a height of one.

Recall from Chapter 3 that we are able to manipulate an entire coordinate system with transformations like translation, rotation, and scaling, which all take place within a larger coordinate system. For example, refer to Fig. 9-5. It shows a global coordinate system, and a new, temporary coordinate system created by the user. The mechanics of telling the com-

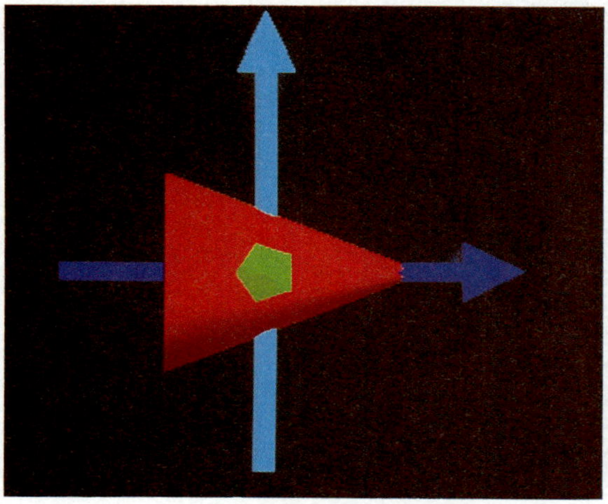

A. The Y-Z view.

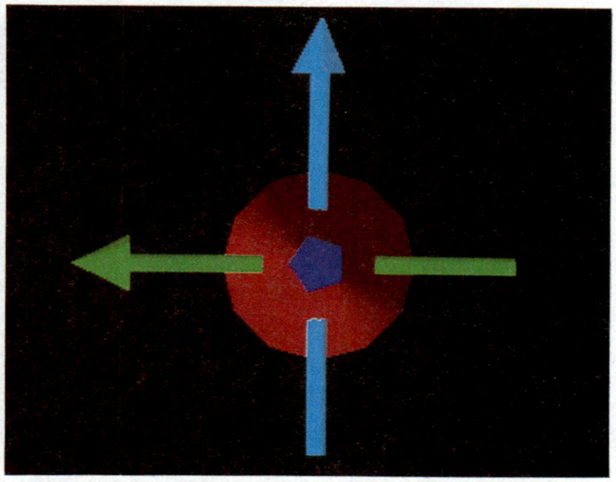

B. The X-Z view.

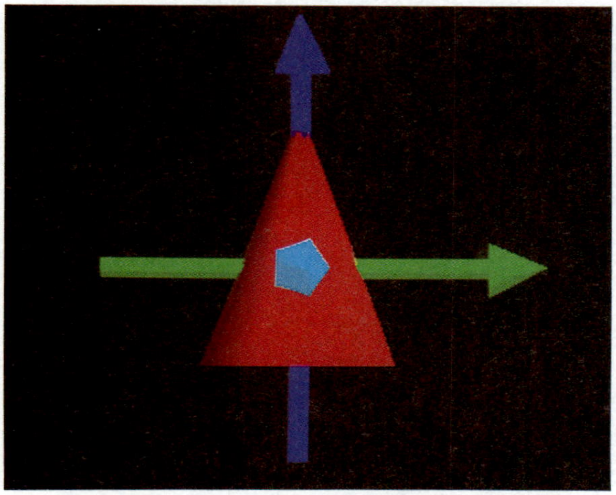

C. The X-Y view.

Fig. 9-2. Engineering-type renderings that help locate vertices and their numerical positions in space.

puter that you are defining a new coordinate system vary with each imlementation, so we will not go into this in detail. It will suffice to say that we instruct the computer that we are going to take the "current" coordinate system, create a new copy of it, and manipulate that new copy,

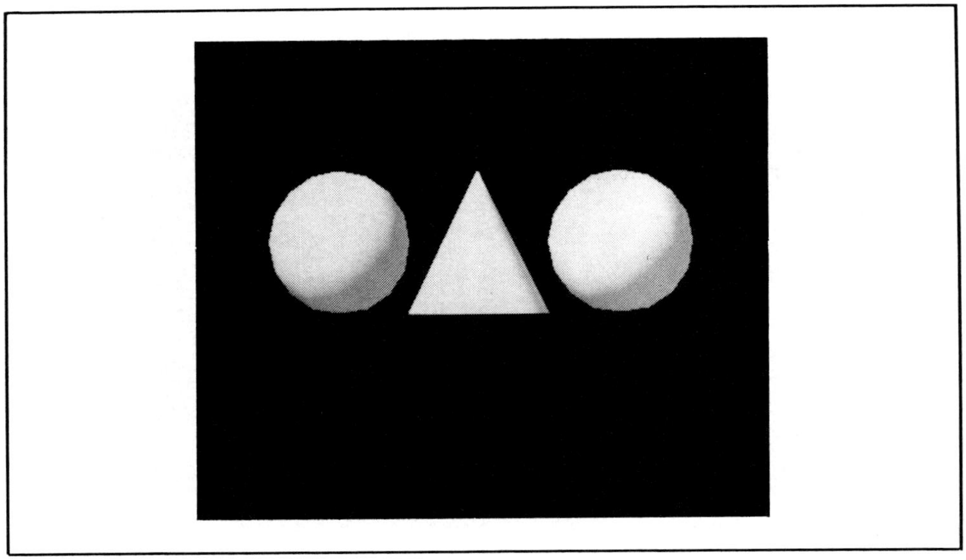

Fig. 9-3. A simple model.

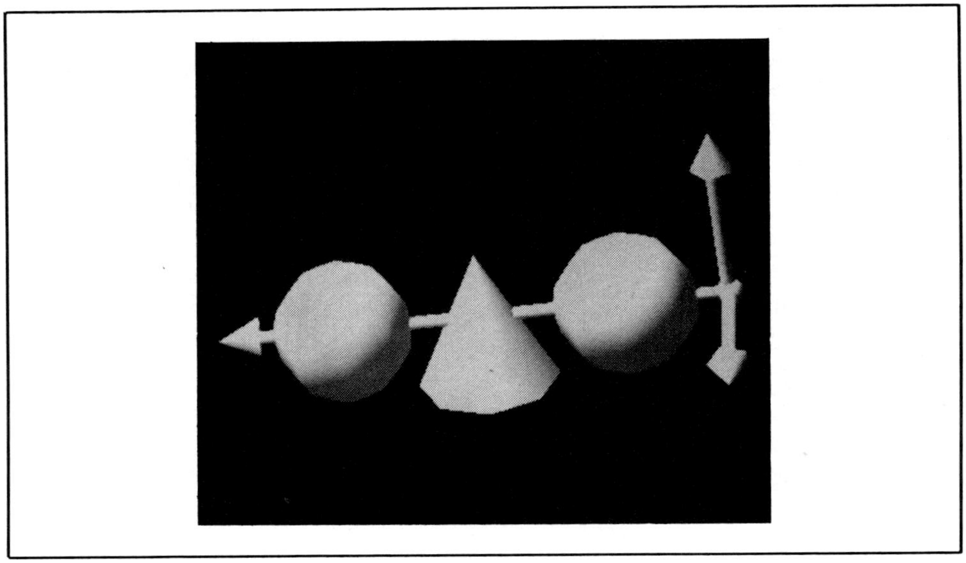

Fig. 9-4. The coordinate system for Fig. 9-3.

leaving everything that was done before unchanged. When we first begin defining our model, the global coordinate system is the current coordinate system.

Let's design the object in Fig. 9-6. It consists of two spheres of different

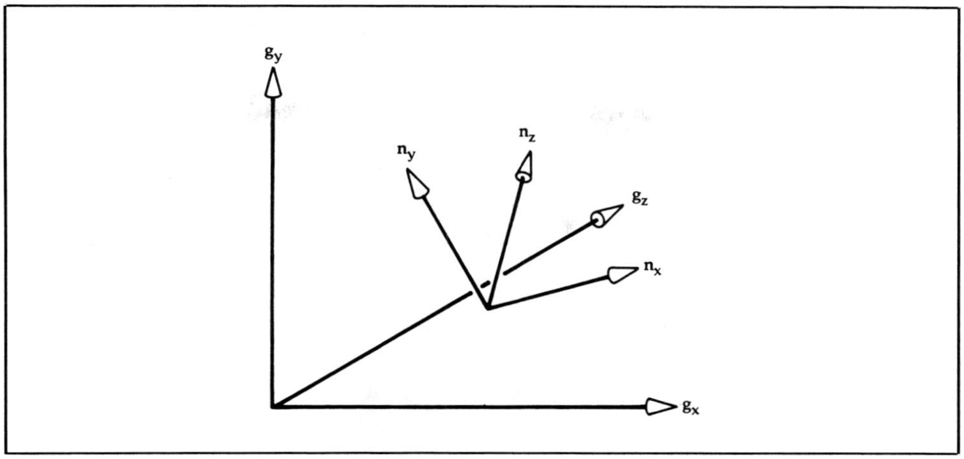

Fig. 9-5. Creating a new coordinate system.

sizes and two cones. To create this scene, we must create a new set of coordinate axes for each object, move the axes into position, rotate and scale them to make the object they contain properly oriented and scaled, and then tell the computer to "draw an object within the current axes."

Let's place the small sphere first. We create a new set of axes translated from the old one (Fig. 9-7), move them to the correct position in space, and scale them so that when we draw a sphere with a radius of one (relative to these axes), it will have a radius of three (relative to the global axes). We then tell the computer, "draw a sphere." Then, we do the second sphere in the same way, by creating a set of axes, moving and scaling them, and then drawing a sphere.

Now, we want to place one of the cones. The orientation of the cone is show in Fig. 9-8. Again, we create a new set of axes (Fig. 9-9) and move them so that the origin of the new set of axes (the center of the base of the cone) is in the correct place. We then rotate the axes to orient the cone in the correct direction (Fig. 9-10) and say "draw a cone."

We repeat the process for the fourth cone, and the description of the complete model is done. Later chapters will cover the placement of lights, selection of viewpoints, and other issues necessary to actually get the picture on the screen.

Usually, all this information is typed into the computer before you actually want the picture drawn. When it is all typed in and any typographical errors are corrected, the additional information mentioned earlier is added in and the picture is drawn.

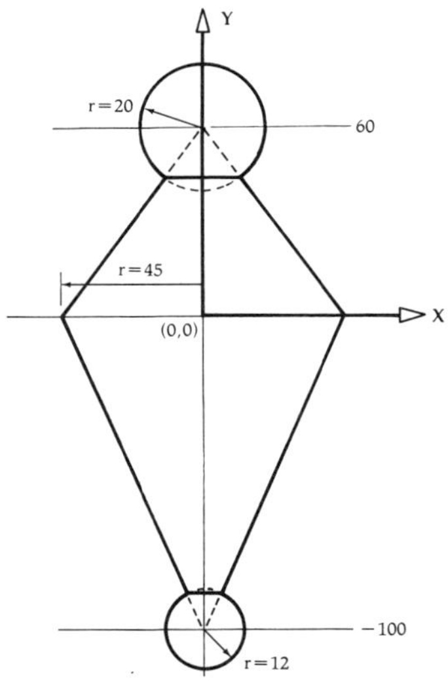

A. A model plan.

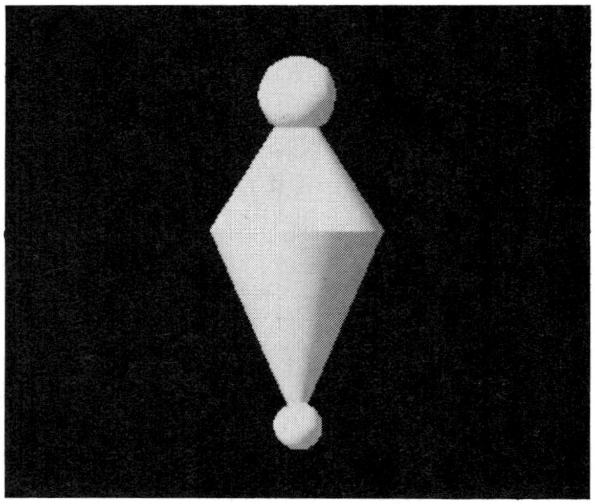

B. An image of the model.

Fig. 9-6. An image and its model plan.

INSTANCING

Let's say we want to create the model of Fig. 9-11. Note that this is really three copies of Fig. 9-6, placed in different positions and orientations. We

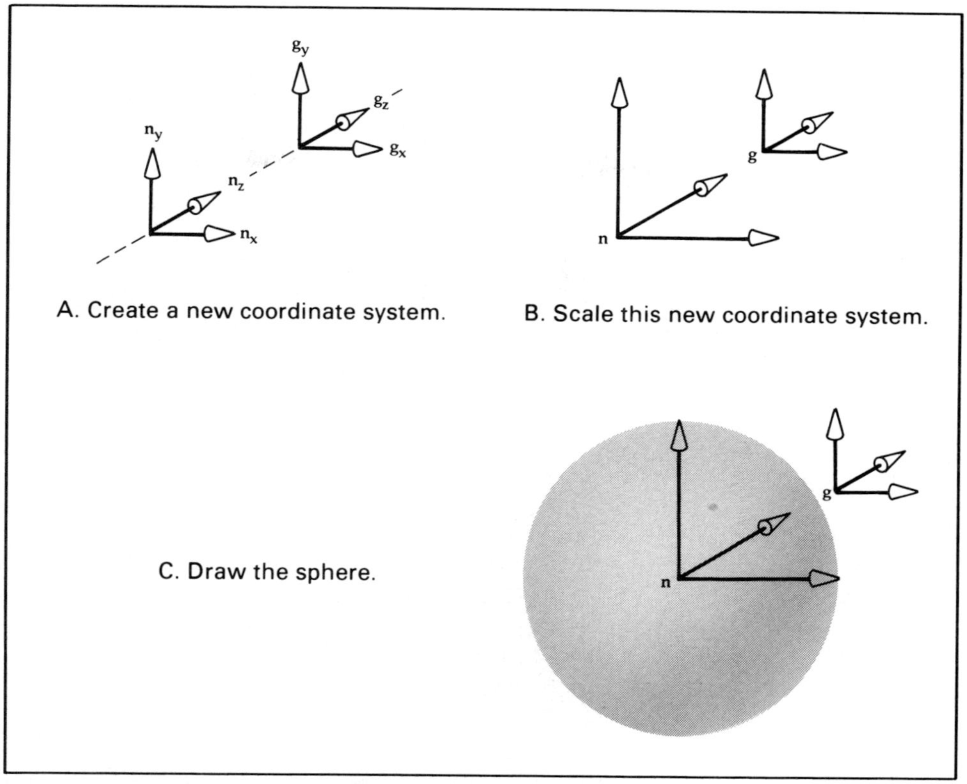

Fig. 9-7. Steps in modeling a sphere in space.

don't have to define the model three times. First, define one copy of the model the way we did earlier. This model is relative to the current coordinate system, which unless it has been previously modified (as we will do now), is the global coordinate system.

When this single unit of the model has been made, we give it a name; usually an English name is allowed. Again, the mechanics of naming will vary, but we will just ignore that and say that the name is "Rembrandt." As with other English names attached to user-defined objects, this name is completely arbitrary, equally good names might be "Saturday," "Highland_Park_NJ," or "Model3."

Then start a new model, beginning again with the global coordinate system. Create a new set of axes, and move them until they are oriented and positioned in the correct place for the origin of the global coordinate system relative to the model just defined (Fig. 9-12). Tell the computer "draw the model called 'Rembrandt' there."

Then, repeat this process two more times, moving a set of axes into

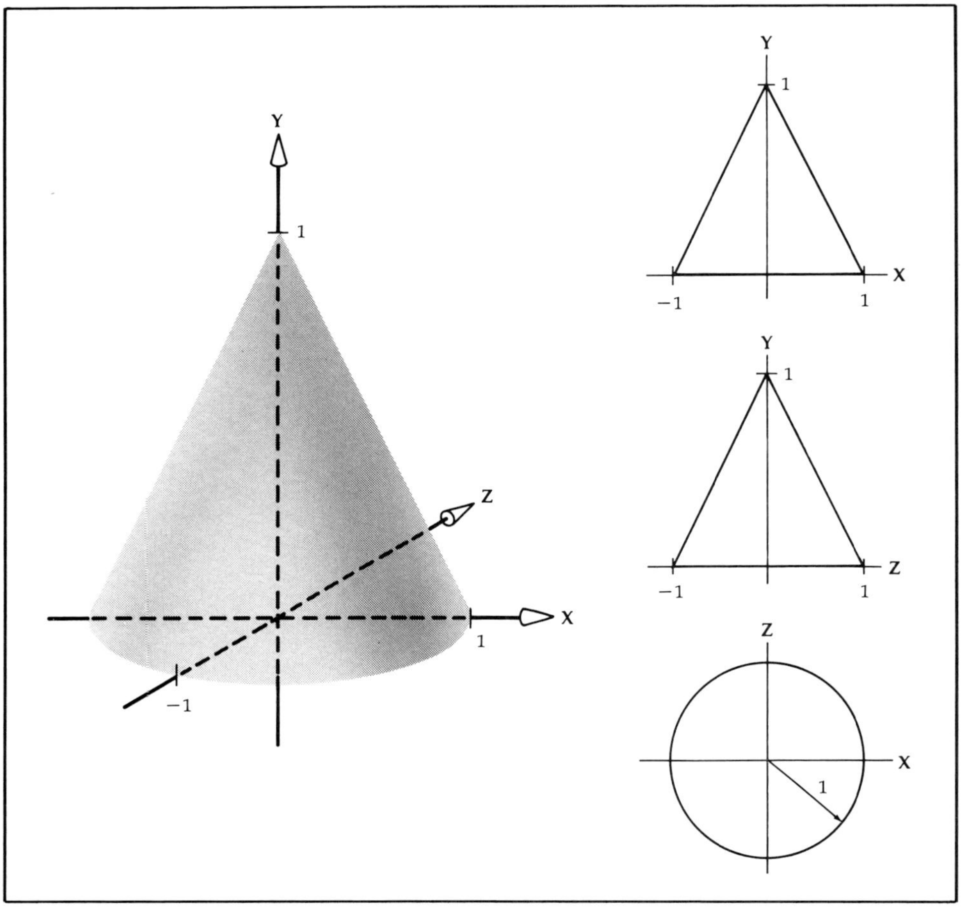

Fig. 9-8. Orientation of a cone.

position and drawing the model called "Rembrandt" instead of just simple surfaces.

The model definition of this larger model is now complete (see Fig. 9-13), and with the addition of the rendering information described later, may now be drawn.

This technique of using complex surfaces as simple surfaces is called *instancing*, and each complex surface that is just a copy of another complex surface is called an *instance* of that surface. Fig. 9-13 shows the actual model listing that created Fig. 9-11. The details are irrelevant; the numbers are set up for a particular modeling system. Compare to Fig. 9-6A.

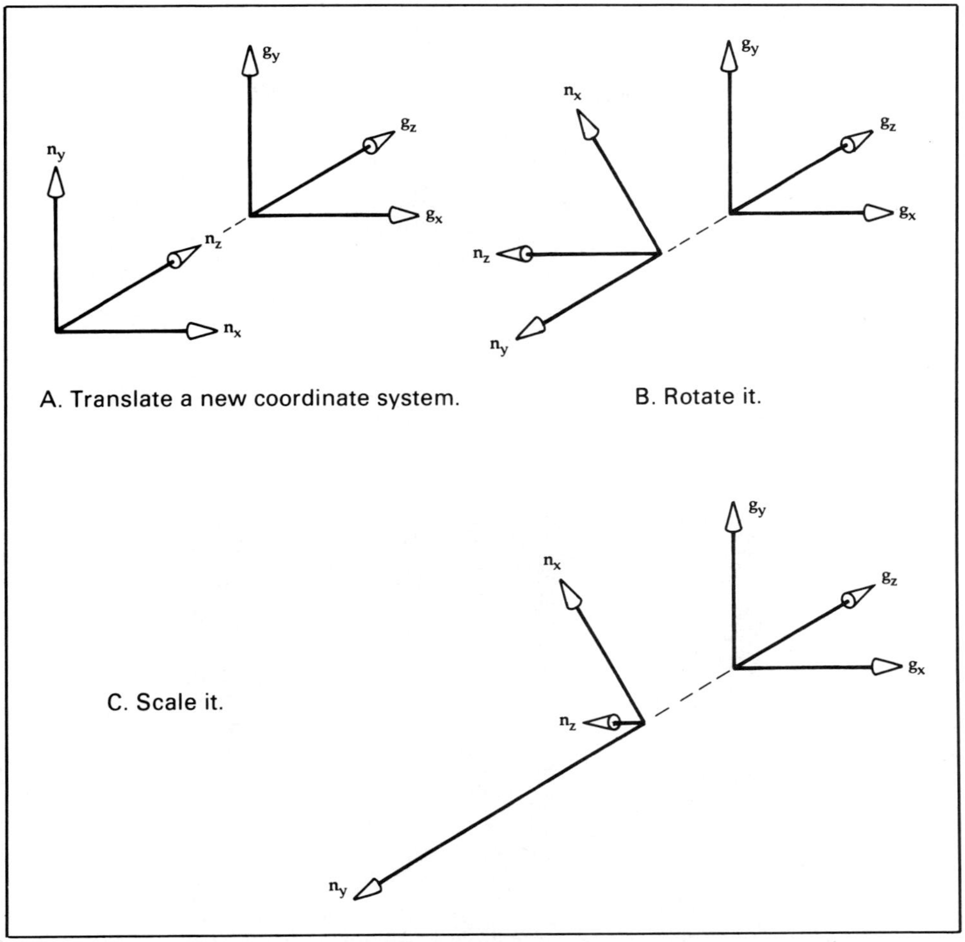

Fig. 9-9. To model a translated, rotated, scaled cone.

ARTICULATION TREES

Another way of describing the whole picture of Fig. 9-11 is through the use of a *tree*. The name "tree" comes from the similarity of Fig. 9-14 to an upside-down tree. Each branching point is called a *node*. The top node is called the *tree's root*, or just the *root*. The root is at the top, and the leaves are at the bottom. Branches and nodes are encountered along the way.

We start at the root with the current coordinate system set equal to the global coordinate system. Note that the root is always the global coordi-

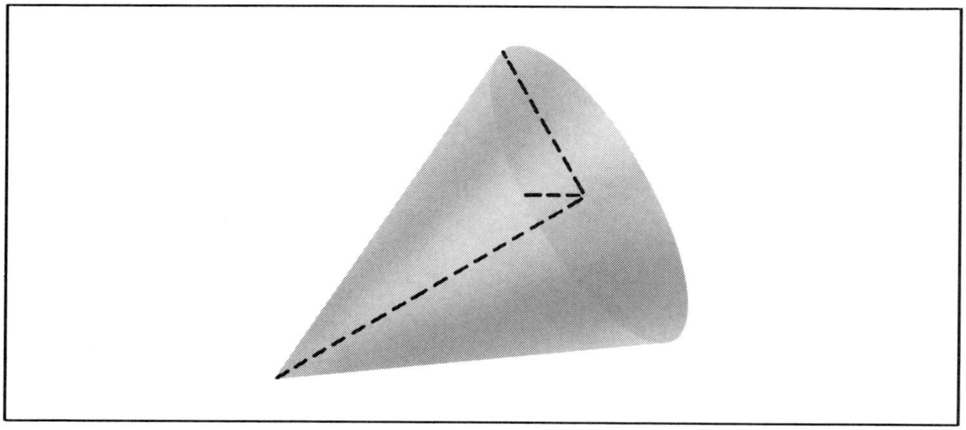

Fig. 9-10. A cone in the final coordinates of Fig. 9-9.

Fig. 9-11. A composite model, made of copies of Fig. 9-6.

nate system since there have been no transformations before it. As we progress down the tree away from the root we come to nodes, where new copies of the current coordinate system (meaning the coordinate system at the time we visit the node) are created. Following the tree down those new coordinate systems they get transformed, and then new copies of that system are made. The very bottom nodes, called *terminal nodes,* or *leaves,* actually command the computer to draw some kind of picture.

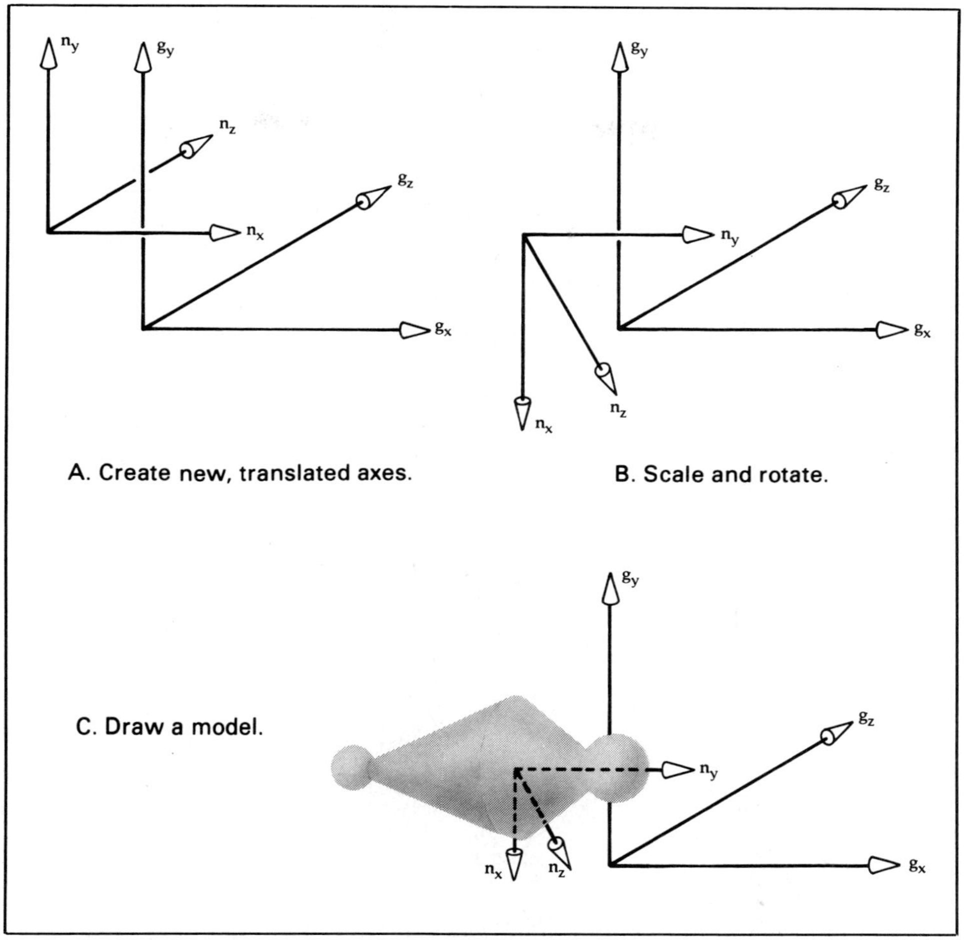

Fig. 9-12. Creating an instance of Fig. 9-6.

Terminal nodes may indicate a simple surface is to be drawn, or they may contain the name of a complex surface, which is a tree in itself. The act of following a tree in the way we have just described is called *traversing* the tree.

Surfaces may be as complex as you like. That is, a surface may contain (or use) a surface that contains a surface that contains a surface, and so on. The only requirement is that no surface contains a surface above it on the tree. Fig. 9-15 shows a tree that violates this rule. In Fig. 9-15 we have a tree called a "dollhouse," which includes several other trees as terminal nodes. When the computer reaches one of these trees, it starts following that new tree, until it has finally reached the terminal node of every tree in

```
comment Figure 9-11 / ASG
SCREEN=1,400,1,400
INIT
TX 200
TY 200
TZ 200
comment Draw the vertical-going shapes
PUSH
  TX -60
  comment The first one
  PUSH
    TY -100
    SPHERE 1 12 8 8
    POP
  CONE 1 -100 0 0 45 8
  CONE 1 0 70 45 0 8
  PUSH
    TY 70
    SPHERE 1 20 8 8
    POP
  TX 120
  comment The second one
  PUSH
    TY -100
    SPHERE 1 12 8 8
    POP
  CONE 1 -100 0 0 45 8
  CONE 1 0 70 45 0 8
  PUSH
    TY 70
    SPHERE 1 20 8 8
    POP
  POP
TZ -20
RZ 75
comment and the last one at an angle...
PUSH
  TY -100
  SPHERE 1 12 8 8
  POP
CONE 1 -100 0 0 45 8
CONE 1 0 70 45 0 8
PUSH
  TY 70
  SPHERE 1 20 8 8
  POP
RENDER
END
```

Fig. 9-13. The computer model for Fig. 9-11.

the picture. But notice that one of the leaves of "dollhouse" is "room," and one of the leaves of "room" is "dollhouse," implying that in a dollhouse you might have someone's bedroom with a dollhouse inside it, which contains a bedroom, which contains a dollhouse, and on and on.

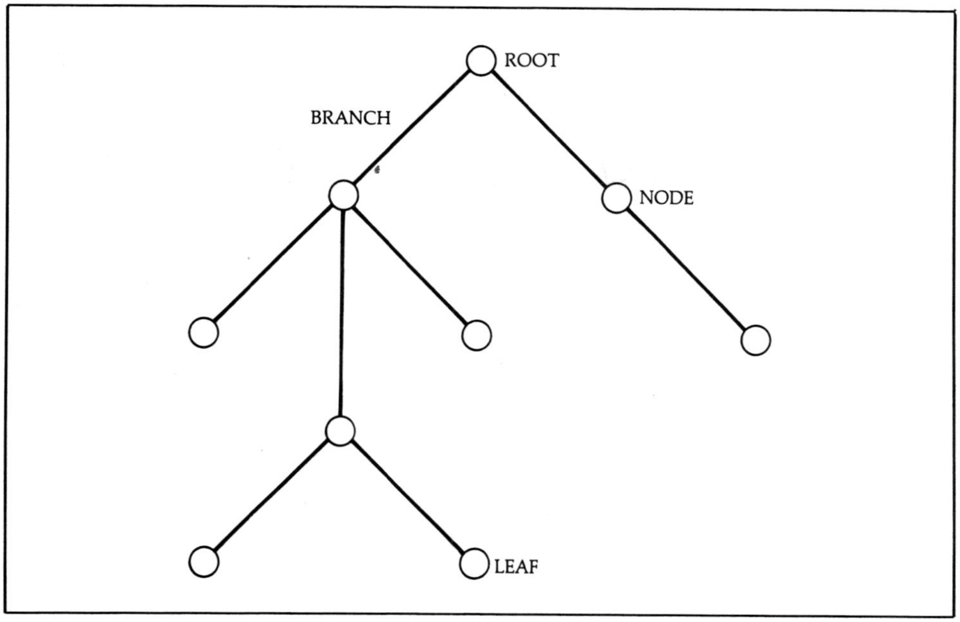

Fig. 9-14. A simple tree.

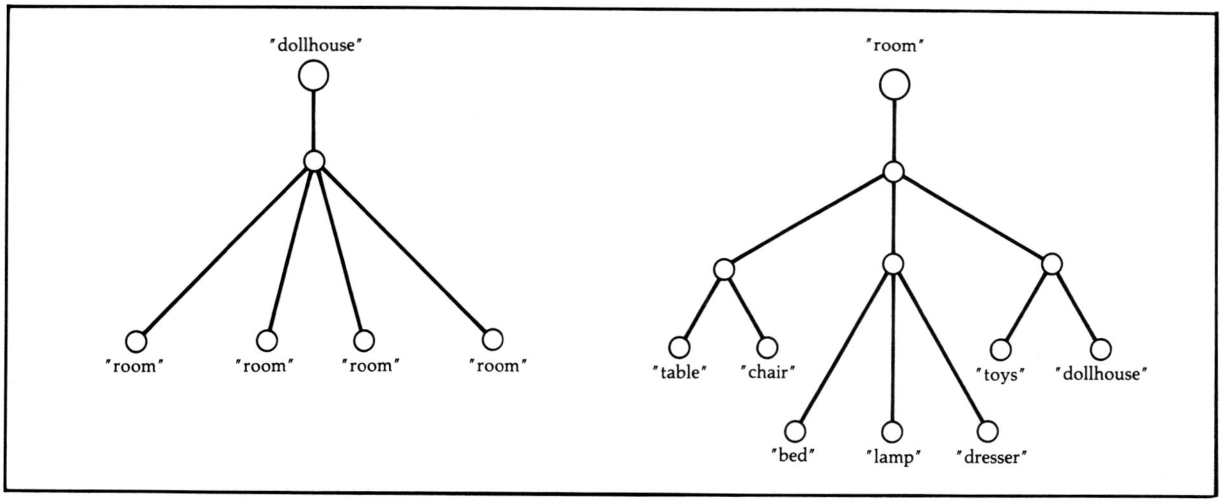

Fig. 9-15. Recursive modeling. Note the loop between the dollhouse and room.

This kind of tree is called a *self-referencing tree.* Some computer systems will not detect this error for you, and they may sit for a long while burning up computer time and resources going around and around the loop that has been accidentally created. Try to avoid creating such a situation.

Fig. 9-16 shows a tree for an arm that can be animated by changing the transformations at the different nodes. In other words, by replacing a "rotate" command at the elbow with a rotation by a different amount, the drawn model will appear as though it had rotated the lower arm at the elbow. Such a model is called an *articulated model,* and its tree description (which is a complete description of the model) is called an *articulated tree.*

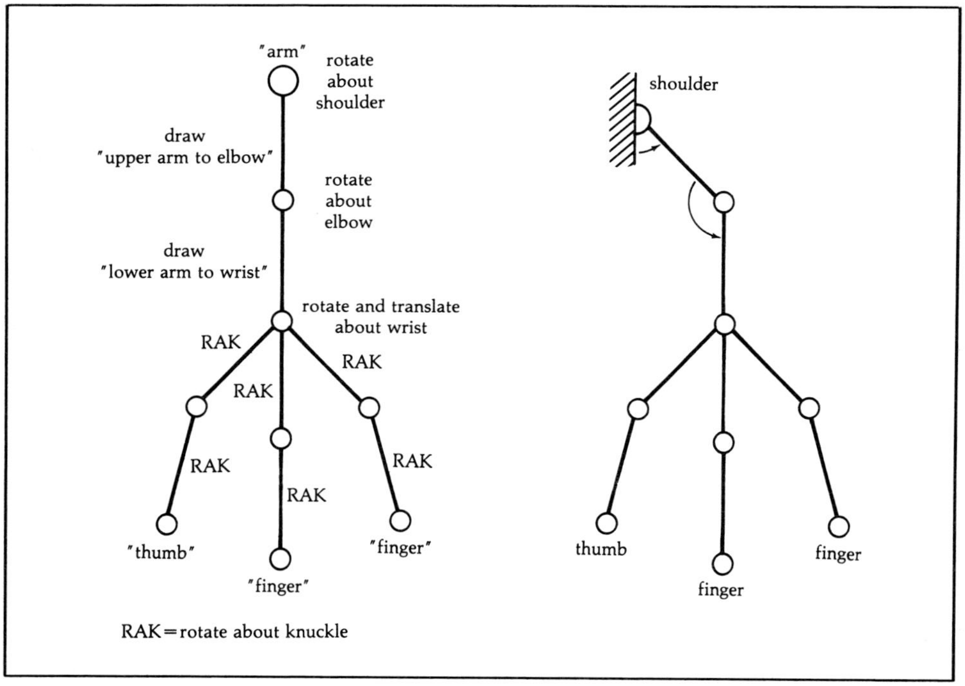

Fig. 9-16. A tree for a model of an arm.

SUMMARY

This chapter was a first view at a practical application of some of the techniques we have been discussing up to now. We started with the definition of a complex object within a *global coordinate system,* which can be thought of as the coordinate system fixed permanently to the screen of your shaded-graphics crt. We described how we instruct the computer to create new, movable coordinate systems within the global coordinate system. We then saw that we could manipulate these new coordinate systems to draw objects within them, which makes it easy to define an object: just create it in a convenient coordinate system and then move that coordinate system to a new place before telling the computer to place the object there.

We then saw how the technique of *instancing* can help us make a complicated model out of several smaller models.

Lastly, we saw that a model definition can be drawn in a special way called an *articulation tree.* We said that the top of the tree is called the *root,* and that the other ends of the tree are called *terminal nodes* or *leaves,* and that branching points are called *nodes.* Walking down the tree away from the root, applying transformations as we go, is called *traversing* the tree.

The idea is that at every node we create a new copy of the coordinate system exactly equal to the coordinate system we were working with when we hit that node. Then the next branch tells us how to transform that coordinate system. If we then hit another node, we create new copies of this new system and continue. If we hit a leaf, we draw the object indicated at that leaf. That object may either be a simple surface (like a polygon), or it may be the name of another articulation tree. In that case, we start traversing the new tree, where the root for this new tree is the coordinate system that we had at the leaf of the old tree.

We also saw that it is wise to avoid *self-referencing* trees, or trees that create loops. Such trees cause the computer to waste time going in circles until either you realize something is wrong and stop the computer, or it runs out of memory and quits. Either way a lot of time is wasted, so it is a good idea to check by hand for circular references if the computer is not set up to do it for you.

Articulation trees make models especially easy to animate, as we will see in Chapter 12.

Chapter TEN

Real-World Rendering

In this chapter we're going to discuss a few of the details involved in getting a picture described in three dimensions onto the two-dimensional screen of your crt. We'll discuss a couple of conventions that the computer adopts to draw the picture in a realistic way, and mention some of the devices available to keep a permanent copy of your images.

OBJECT SPACE AND SCREEN SPACE

When we describe an object geometrically, it is always in relation to some fixed origin and a set of axes radiating from it. The three-dimensional objects we have considered so far are all in relation to a three-dimensional coordinate system.

When an object gets drawn on the screen, it only has two dimensions. The third, depth, gets lost in the drawing because the screen has no depth. Since we often refer to both "objects in space defined mathematically" and "objects on the screen" as just "objects," it has become helpful to distinguish which category of objects we are referring to. We say "mathematical objects in space" are objects in *object space*, and "objects as drawn on the screen" are objects in *screen space*. This usage of the word "space" makes it synonymous with "category," a common technical practice. Fig. 10-1 shows an object and its representation in both spaces.

Not all objects in our scene description will make it onto the screen in the final image. Some will be blocked by others, but some objects will just not be visible from some points of view. To help us find out which objects will be visible in the final image, we can draw a picture that shows us what objects are representable on the screen and which are out of view. The picture is shown in Fig. 10-2 and describes the *viewing volume*, or that volume of space we can see. This particular viewing volume is very popular for computer graphics and is called the *viewing pyramid*. The pyramid

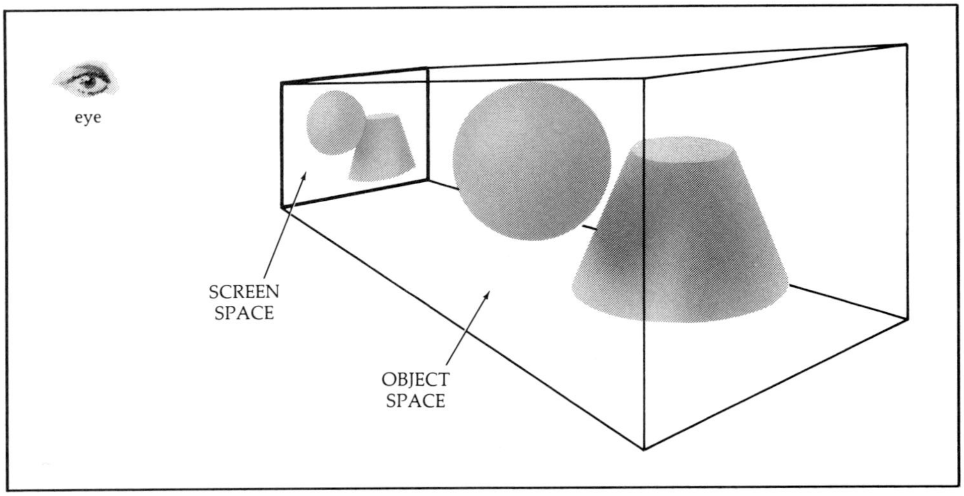

Fig. 10-1. An example of "screen space" (where we draw), and "object space" (where objects are modeled in three dimensions).

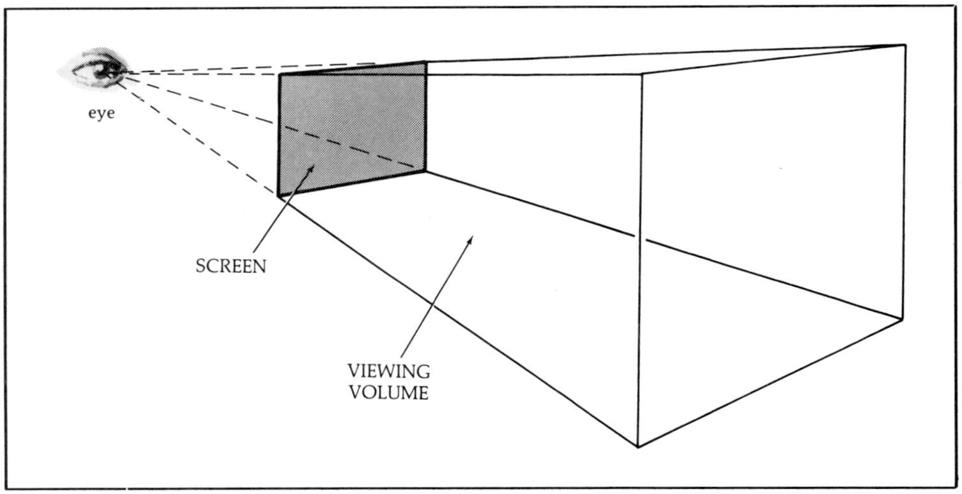

Fig. 10-2. The viewing volume pyramid.

is constructed with the viewer (normally drawn as an eye) at the top point (or *apex*) of the pyramid. The four walls of the screen make the four walls of the pyramid. The screen itself is sometimes called the *viewscreen*.

The figure shows us that objects outside the pyramid are not visible to us. But there are two walls to the pyramid we have not considered. These are the walls that make up the bottom and top of a cut-off section of the pyramid, as shown in Fig. 10-3. All six of these planes are called *clipping planes;* because if something touches them or goes through them, it gets "clipped" by the pyramid to only allow that part within the pyramid to be seen. The four walls are called *boundary walls.* The near wall to the eye is called the *hither* clipping plane, and the far wall is called the *yon* clipping plane. As indicated in Fig. 10-4, the viewscreen itself is often the near clipping plane.

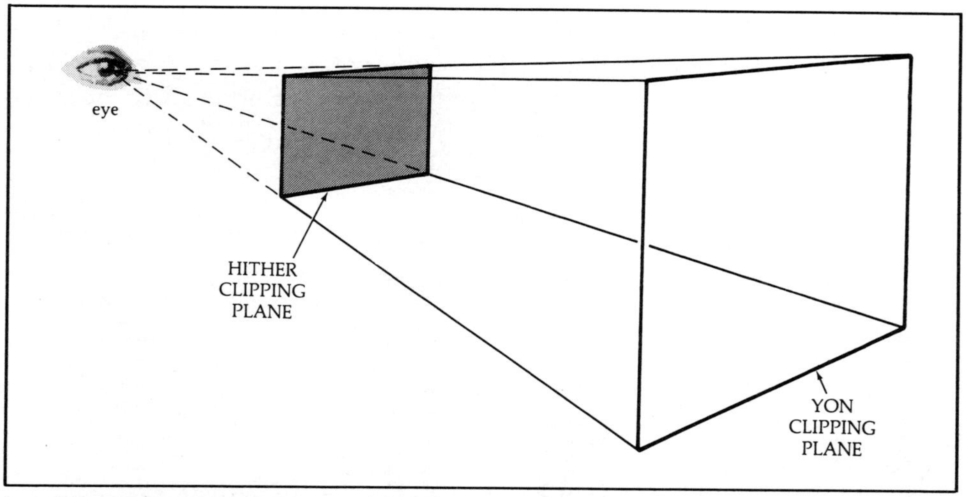

Fig. 10-3. The hither and yon clipping planes define limits on the height of the pyramid.

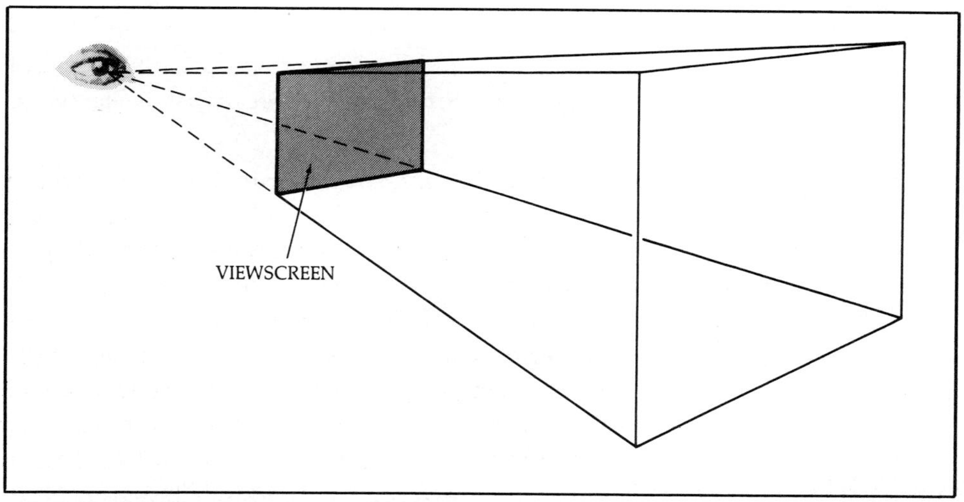

Fig. 10-4. A "standard" graphics setup.

PROJECTIONS AND PERSPECTIVE

Objects in the viewing volume are three dimensional, and those on the viewscreen are only two dimensional. We need a consistent way of getting those three-dimensional objects onto the screen that simulates the way a real camera would do it. This kind of operation is called a *projection*, and there are many ways of doing it, so there are many projections. We'll look at two.

The first is called *orthographic projection* and is illustrated in Fig. 10-5. Lines are drawn from the object to the viewscreen, intersecting the viewscreen at right angles. This kind of projection is often used to produce engineering and drafting illustrations, but it doesn't usually produce pictures that look like they were photographed.

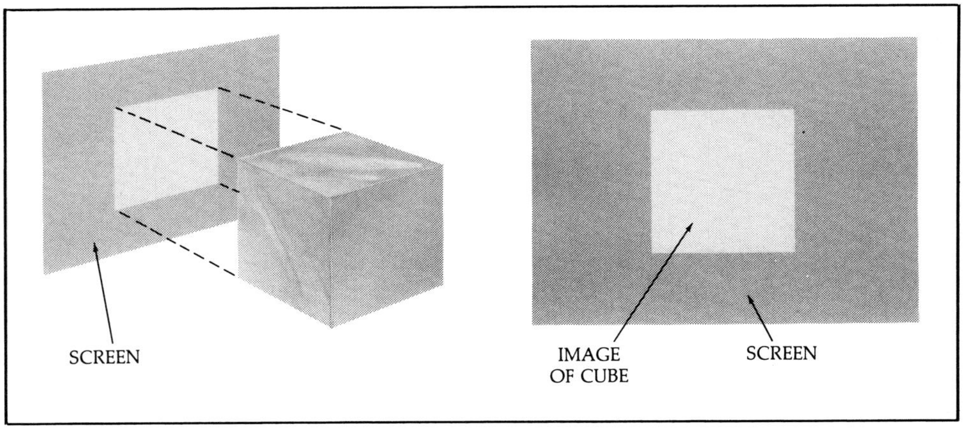

Fig. 10-5. An example of orthographic projection. All lines are perpendicular to the screen.

Another kind of projection, called *perspective projection*, does create that photographed effect. Note that the viewing volume is larger as it recedes from the eye. The objects farther away from the eye must appear to shrink if the entire yon clipping plane is to fit on the viewscreen. This accounts for the phenomenon of *perspective*, a component of photographs taken with a real camera. Note that as the yon clipping plane increases in size, the objects near it decrease in size on the screen. We say that a viewing volume with a large yon clipping plane has a sharper perspective than one with a smaller-sized clipping plane, as in Fig. 10-6.

We usually don't specify the size of the clipping planes. The parameters that we specify for the viewing pyramid are usually: the distance of the

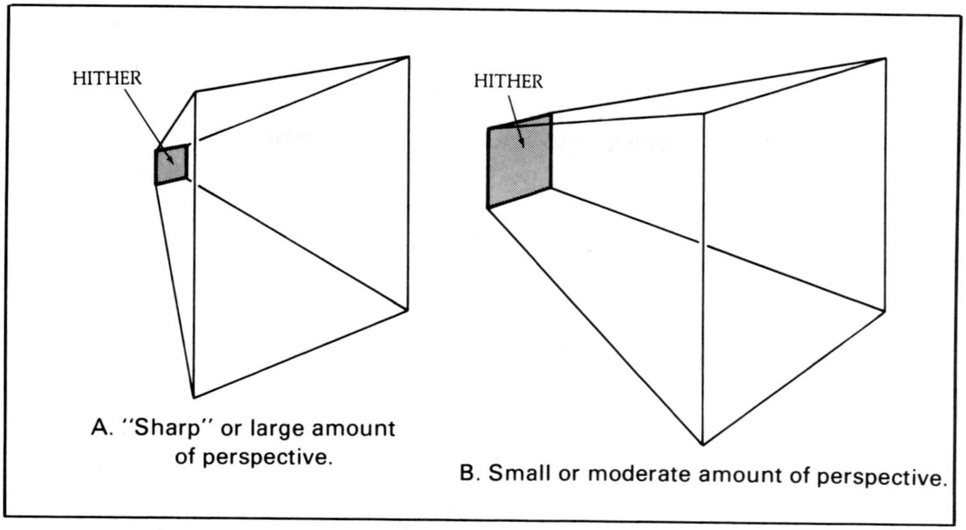

Fig. 10-6. Large and small amounts of perspective projection.

hither clipping plane along the Z axis; the distance of the yon clipping plane along the Z axis; and the half-angle of the apex of the pyramid, as indicated in Fig. 10-7. This last is called a *pyramid half-angle* because of its definition as the angle between one wall of the pyramid and the line going through the center of the viewscreen from the eye. If it's more convenient, sometimes you may specify the *full-angle* instead, which is two times the half angle.

OUTPUT TECHNIQUES

Once you've generated an image with the computer, you possess a *soft copy* of that image. You're looking at a computer's picture tube, and the soft copy of the image is what you see. When the power goes off, the image goes away. If you decide to take a photograph of the picture, or print it out in some way to make a permanent record of it, you've made a *hard copy*.

There are different ways to get hard copy of a computer graphics image. The most primitive is to print it out with a line printer, like the "computer portraits" found in shopping malls, illustrated in Fig. 10-8. Or, if you have access to a camera, you may just point it at the screen and shoot a picture. You may also find a videotape recorder and record the frame onto videotape.

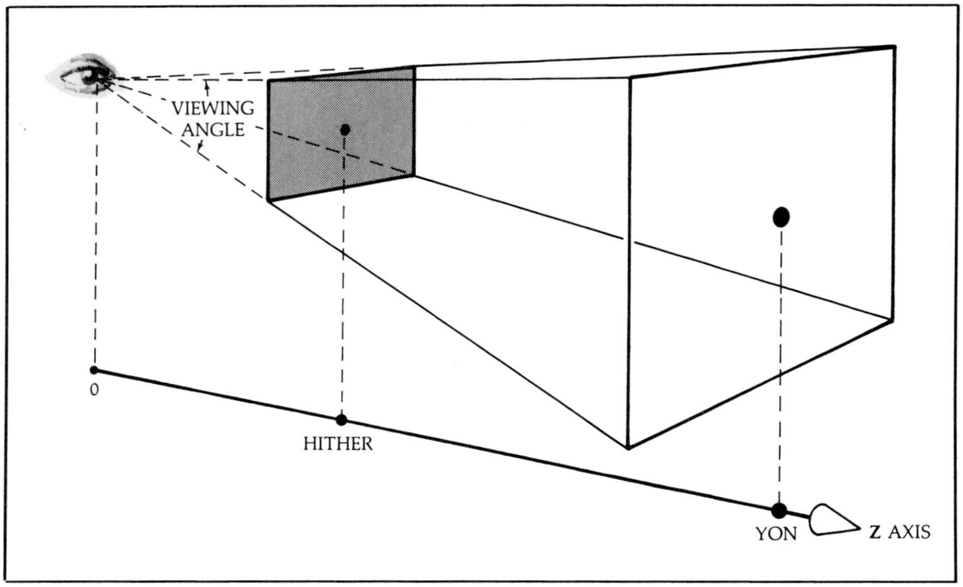

Fig. 10-7. We define the viewing pyramid with the location of the hither and yon clipping planes along the Z axis, as well as the viewing angle.

Or, you can use a professional film recorder that will take very high-precision photographs from its own internal monitor. The best of these machines are often very expensive but produce beautiful photos. Additionally, these machines can take three-color separations, slides, and movies.

SUMMARY

In this chapter we discussed some of the details involved in getting a three-dimensional scene onto the two-dimensional screen of your crt. We defined the object as a three-dimensional structure in *object space,* which creates an image on the crt, which is an image in *screen space.*

We mentioned the fact that the only objects we can see on the screen in the final picture are those that are capable of fitting onto the screen. We said that such objects are within the *viewing volume,* or that volume of space that is visible from our particular eye position. We defined the most common viewing volume used today—the *viewing pyramid.* We placed the eye of the observer at the *apex,* or tip of the pyramid, and said the four walls were defined by the four edges of the *viewscreen.* We said that each

Fig. 10-8. A supermarket computer's eye view of the author with a beard.

wall of the pyramid could be called a *clipping plane*, or *boundary wall*. We placed additional limits on the viewing pyramid by saying that only objects between the *hither* and *yon* clipping planes would be visible, in addition to the restrictions of the four walls of the pyramid. Usually, the hither clipping plane is the viewscreen itself.

We then looked at how the three-dimensional points get *projected* onto the two-dimensional viewscreen. The first kind of projection we looked at is called an *orthographic projection,* and it causes the points to project directly onto the screen at right angles to the screen. We said that such a projection is good for engineering applications but doesn't usually look very realistic.

The problem is that it lacks *perspective,* the familiar phenomenon that makes railroad tracks in the distance get closer together and makes buildings far away look smaller than equally tall buildings close up. The *perspective projection* includes the effects of projection. We control the amount of perspective in a computer-generated scene by adjusting the angle at the tip of the viewing pyramid. This angle is often called the *pyramid half-angle* or *full-angle.*

We then said that an image on a television screen is called a *soft copy* of that image; it disappears when the power goes off. In contrast, we can make a photographic record of the picture, and thus, have a *hard copy* that we can keep and reproduce.

Chapter ELEVEN

Raster Rendering

In this chapter we will discuss a very important piece of computer graphics hardware, and the various special techniques of computer graphics that have grown up because of and around it. Recall that the television screen on which we draw shaded images is called a *raster crt*. The word "raster" will appear in this chapter always referring to shaded images in some way.

The hardware we will concentrate on here is called a *frame buffer*, and it is probably the only piece of hardware (besides a computer terminal) that you will find at every computer graphics site. We will discuss frame buffers in some detail because they are really the key to understanding a whole range of computer graphics techniques.

FRAME BUFFERS

In this section we will examine the characteristics of a piece of hardware known as a *frame buffer*. To really understand it, we're going to take a slight digression into the mechanics of how a television picture is produced.

An electrical signal is received from the antenna, amplified, and used to control three different-colored "guns" inside the tv picture tube. They are called "guns" because they shoot a tight beam of electrons towards the face of the picture tube. The beams themselves really aren't colored.

Actually, the face of the picture tube is coated with triplets of different colored *phosphors*, one set of red, green, and blue for each "dot" on the screen (Fig. 11-1). Phosphors are chemicals that glow for a short period of time when hit by an electron beam. Just as any pigment can be made from the three primary colors of pigment, so can any color be made from these three primary colors of light. To make a given color appear at a given spot on the screen, the three guns point to the triplet at that spot and make the phosphors glow with the correct brightnesses.

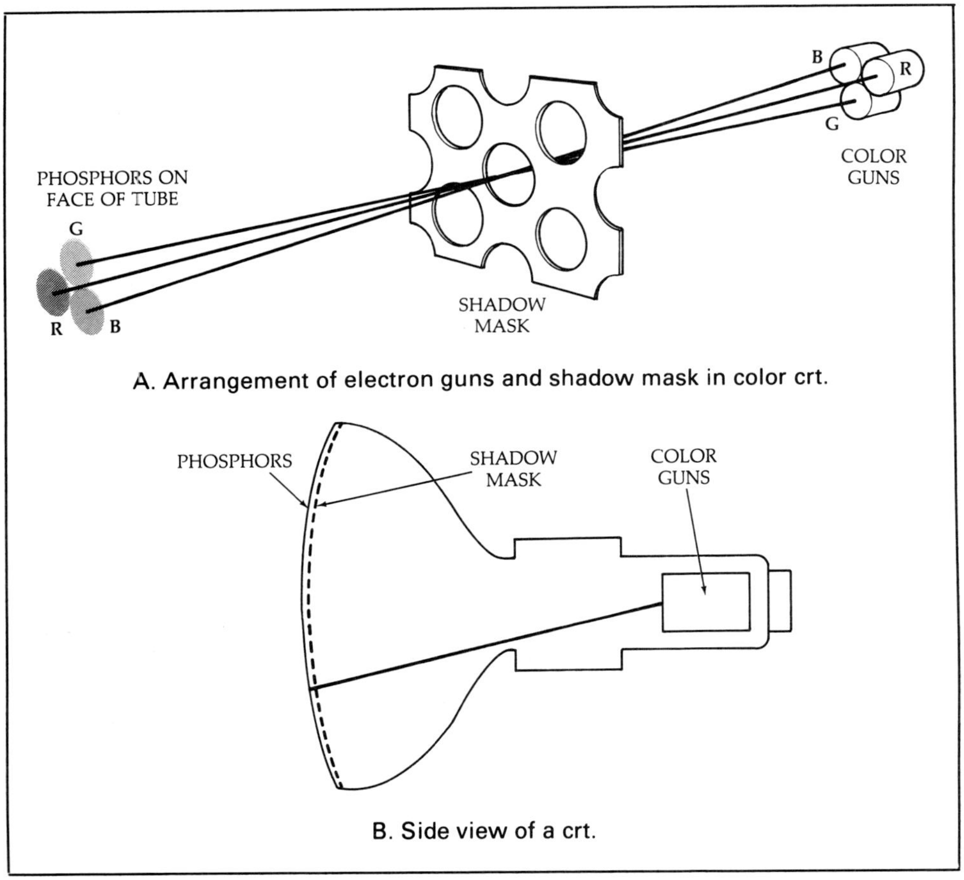

Fig. 11-1. The face of a picture tube has many triplets.

The internal circuits of the tv set cause the electron beams to sweep the surface of the tube once every 1/30 of a second. Two sweeps are made from the upper-left corner to the lower-right corner, much in the way an English book is read. The picture is created by building up many scan lines, which are the individual horizontal traces of the electron beams. See Fig. 11-2 for a picture of this process.

There are two *fields*, or sets of lines, which are *interlaced*, or alternated

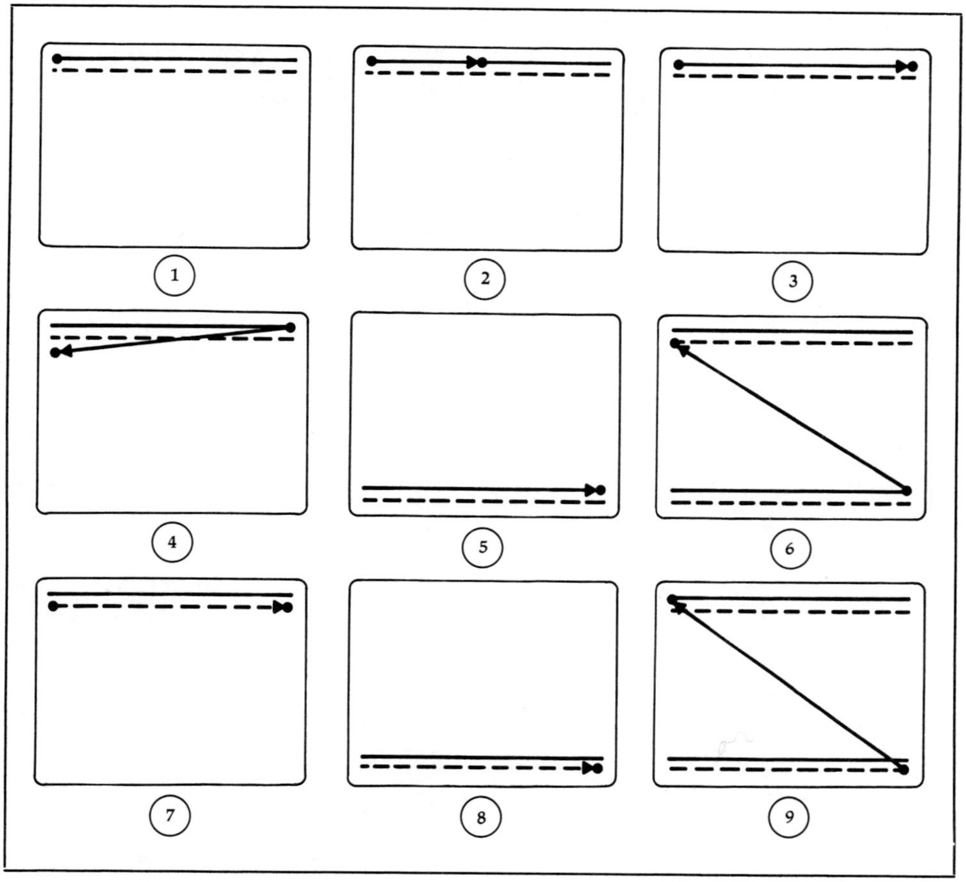

Fig. 11-2. The travel of an electron beam.

in drawing. The beam starts at the upper-left corner and sweeps out all the even-numbered scan lines, or the *even field*, as in Fig. 11-3, and then the odd-numbered scan lines, or the *odd field*. Each field takes 1/60 of a second to complete, so it takes 1/30 of a second to complete the entire picture. A complete picture is called a *frame*.

Then, the beam goes back to the upper-left corner and starts drawing the next frame.

Whatever colors (if any) the beams draw as they travel are controlled by the signal arriving from the antenna. For each dot on the screen, the signal describes the color and the brightness of the color at that point. The internal circuits of the tv then control the beams to make the correct

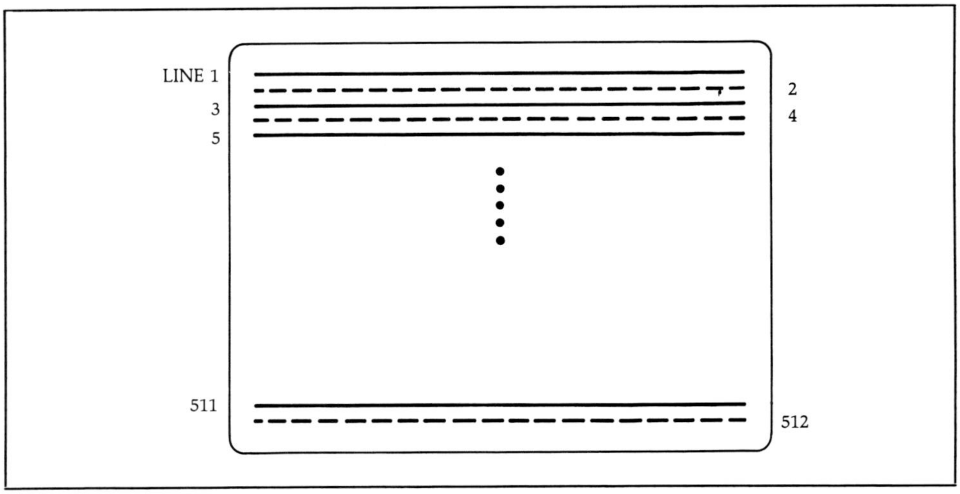

Fig. 11-3. Even lines are dashed, odd lines are solid. Each set is a field and is drawn in 1/60 of a second.

phosphors glow the correct amount to get that color to appear. The signal arrives in the correct order for the tv to scan the picture tube as we just described: upper left to lower right, alternating fields referred to as *interlaced* scanning.

If you could make a videotape recording of that signal and replay it 30 times a second into the tv set, you would get the same picture over and over. But instead of receiving it from the air, you would have your own copy of the instructions to the tv, and you could modify it at will. For example, you could change the colors at certain points by changing the videotape in a careful way.

Although computers actually often have a kind of tape recorder attached to them, they use a faster type of memory for most tasks. This kind of memory is called *solid-state*, or *semiconductor* memory. It is also sometimes called *core* memory, for historical reasons. A large piece of this memory can be thought of as the tape and tape recorder in one and contains the information for every dot on the screen.

Such a piece of "video memory" is called a *frame buffer*. "Frame" comes from the single complete frame that is stored, and "buffer" is computer slang for memory. So with a large piece of memory set up and controlled by the computer and connected to a tv, a television can be made to draw a picture under control of the computer.

Another way to think about frame buffers is to consider the tv tube as a giant grid of small squares, as illustrated in Fig. 11-4. Each square (or dot)

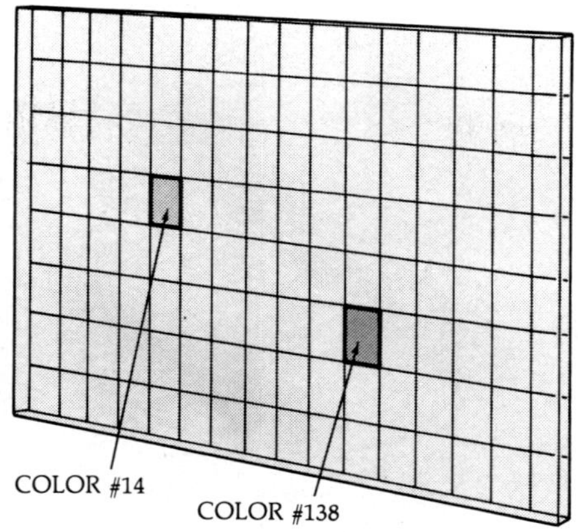

Fig. 11-4. The face of a tv screen. Each square holds a number describing which color should be used to paint it in.

corresponds to a place in the computer's memory. When the tv is ready to fill in that dot with the correct color, the computer supplies the correct intensities of red, green, and blue at that dot, which causes that color to appear at that point on the screen.

A particular dot on the screen is sometimes called a *pixel*, a contraction of *picture-element*, which is sometimes also called a *pel*.

COLOR MAPS

In the previous section we closed our discussion by comparing a tv set to a large grid of dots, each of which was to be filled in by a color from the frame buffer. The question now arises: how is the color stored in the frame buffer? The answer to this question opens the doors for an explanation of many special effects and tricks.

The frame buffer can be thought of as having a number stored for every dot on the screen. The number is like the numbers used in a paint-by-numbers set (Fig. 11-5): it doesn't describe the color itself, it just identifies which color it is from a given set of numbered colors.

For the following discussions we will consider frame buffers to be eight bits *deep*; that is, every dot on the tv screen has an associated set of eight bits in the frame buffer, which means for each point on the screen the

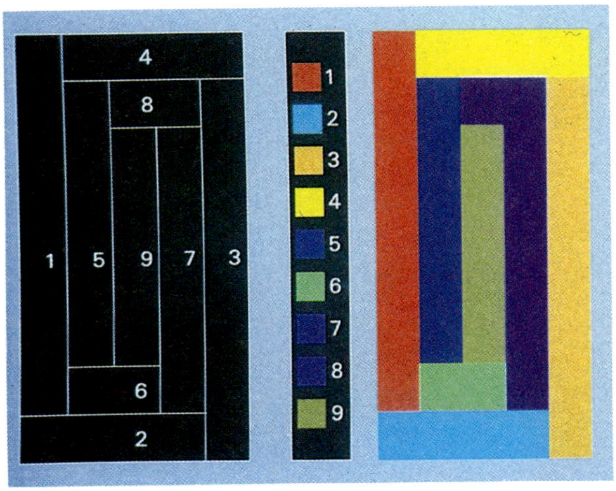

Fig. 11-5. Paint by numbers. The frame buffer doesn't hold colors, just the numbers of colors in a table.

frame buffer can hold 8 bits of information to tell which color is to be used at that point.

With 8 bits we can represent 256 different numbers from 0 to 255. So if we number a certain shade of red as color number zero, a shade of yellow as color number one, a shade of orange as color number two, and so on, we can have a total of 256 different colors on the screen mixed in any way from a single 8-bit frame buffer.

A small piece of memory is usually set aside within the frame buffer to hold the information about the actual color content of the 256 different colors. Each color is represented by three numbers: the amount of red, green, and blue light that make it up. Since the frame buffer is 8 bits deep, each location can hold a number from 0 to 255. So the color black would be no color at all, and would be represented as (0,0,0) (R,G,B). Pure red would be (255,0,0); a mixture of red and blue would be (124,0,44), and so on.

The table of color intensities has one entry for each color on the screen, so there are 256 entries for an 8-bit frame buffer. The computer is generating the signals for the tv set, so it knows which dot is next to be filled in by the tv. It finds the correct number in the frame buffer, and then looks in the table at the correct place for the intensities of the primary colors needed to make that color. This table we have been discussing is variously called a *color map*, *color table*, or *video lookup table*. Fig. 11-6 shows this process graphically.

Different color maps can give rise to significantly different images even with the same data in the frame buffer. An example of the same image with different color maps is shown in Fig. 11-7.

Incidentally, whenever the computer itself looks at the contents of the frame buffer, it gets the actual color number in the buffer at that point, not the RGB intensities that it represents. Therefore, remember that you're always looking at a picture that is very dependent on the particular color map in effect at the moment; a different color map can make the picture look very different, without any alteration to the frame buffer contents.

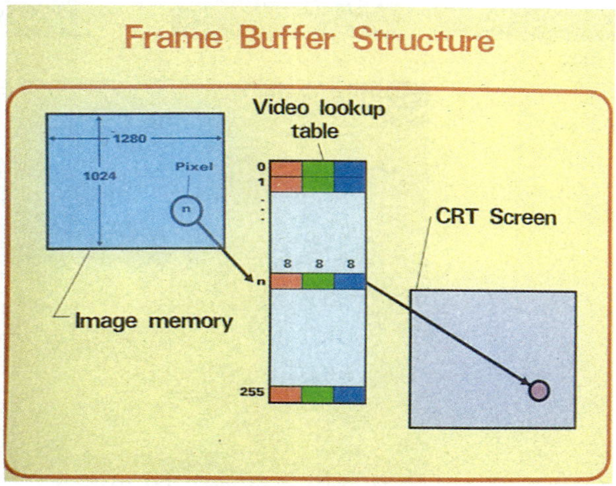

Fig. 11-6. The value of each pixel is looked up in a table of RGB values. *(Image by Paul Sholtz. Used by permission of IBM Corp.)*

FRAME BUFFERS WITH MORE THAN EIGHT BITS

With one 8-bit frame buffer, there are 256 different colors available. These colors can be any color the user desires by manipulating the color map, but only 256 different colors can be on the screen at once.

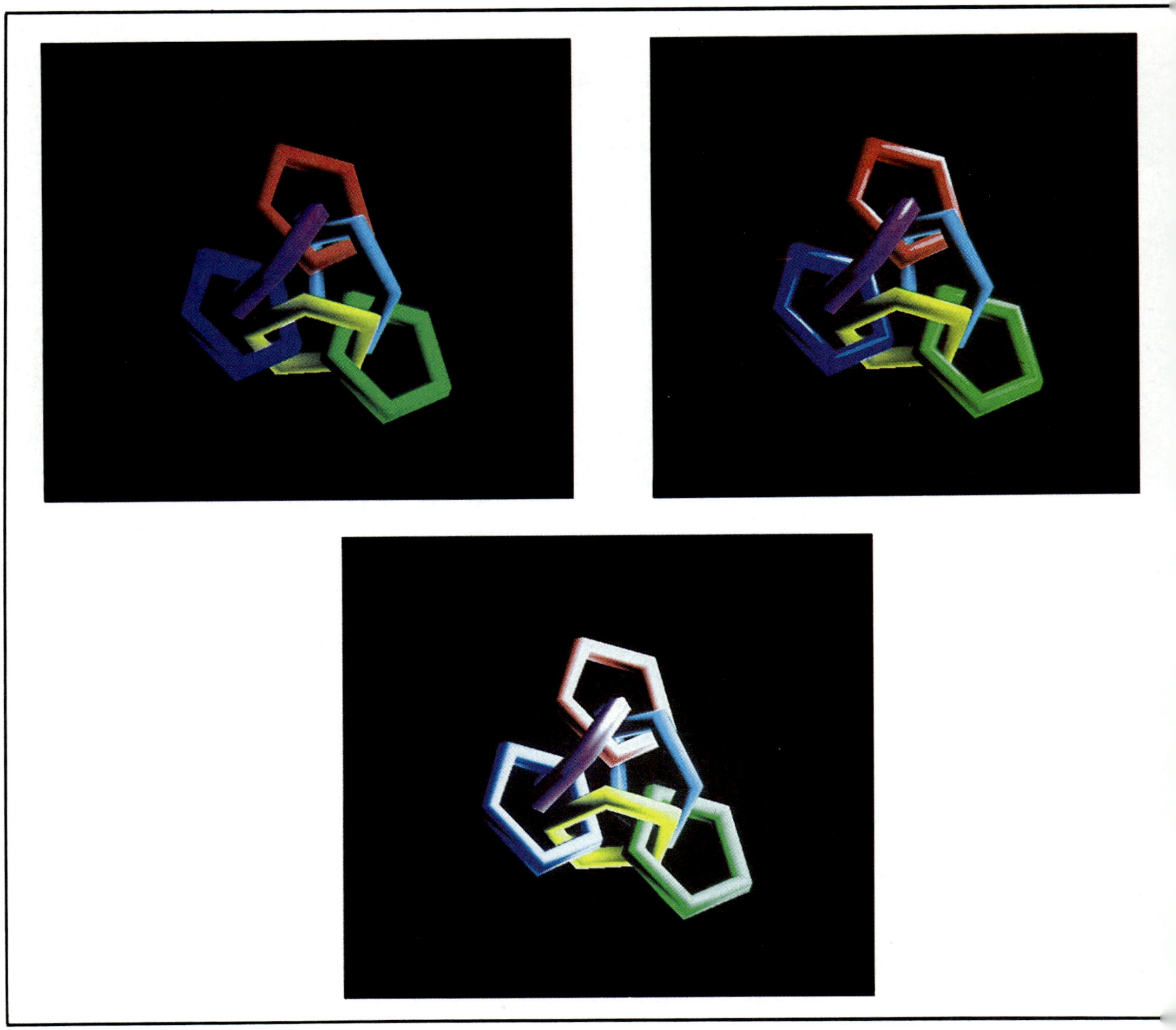

Fig. 11-7. The same picture with different color maps.

However, the situation changes if we have more bits available at every pixel. Let's take for example three 8-bit frame buffers used at the same time to provide 24 bits per pixel. Fig. 11-8 shows how this looks. With this kind of storage available we don't need a color map anymore. Each pixel has three sets of eight bits or 24 bits associated with it. It's easy to tell the hardware to treat the first eight bits of every pixel as the red intensity for that pixel, the next eight bits as the blue intensity for that pixel, and the last eight bits as the green intensity. So every square in the frame buffer, instead of representing which color is to be selected from a table, now holds the red, green, and blue components of that color itself.

The result is that every dot on the screen may be a different color since each dot defines its color directly. If we consider a "standard" frame buffer to be 512 pixels wide and 512 pixels tall, there are 512 times 512 or over a quarter million different colors possible on the screen at once!

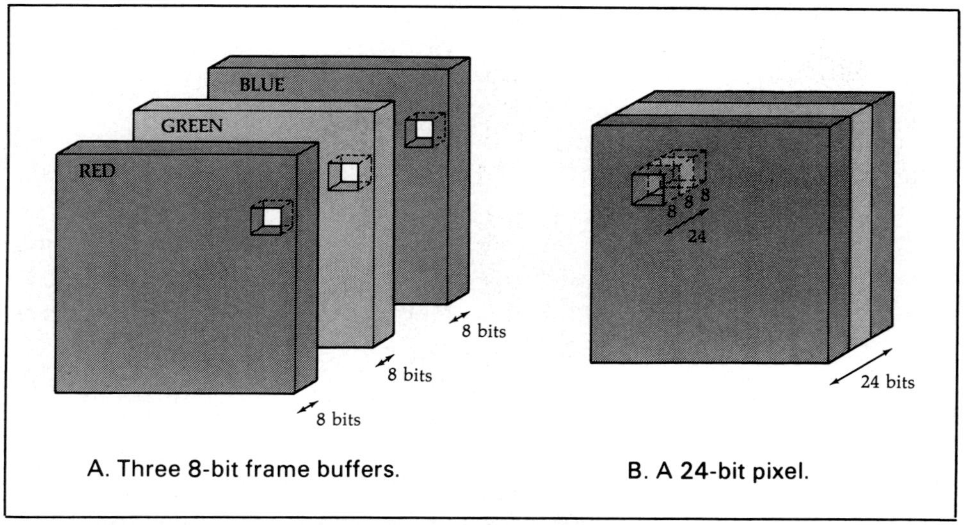

Fig. 11-8. We can look up RGB directly in the frame buffer if it's big enough.

Z-BUFFERS

Frame buffers are not limited to storing pictures. They are large pieces of computer memory that can hold numbers: one number for each point on the screen. The number may be a color number from a color map, it may represent the RGB components of the color at that point, or it may be something else. This "something else" turns out to be extremely useful when we want to actually generate shaded pictures, and special techniques have been developed to take advantage of this. The basic idea is that if you want to store information about a picture on a pixel-by-pixel basis, a frame buffer is a natural place to put it. Let's look at a popular technique that uses this idea.

A complex scene is usually made up of a collection of objects. The objects, in turn, are usually complex surfaces made up of simpler surfaces.

The process of actually rendering objects on the screen consists of two main steps, which we can pose as two questions. The computer has chosen a point on the screen and wants to know if anything should be drawn there. It chooses an object and poses the first question: "Is this object visible from this point? If so, is it the closest object to the eye, or is it blocked by some other object?" If the object is both visible and the closest to the eye, we ask, "What is the correct shading (color) for this object at this point?" Once we know the shading, we then fill in the point on the screen with that color. Then, we move on to the next point and ask the whole sequence again. Once we have gone over the entire screen for this object, we get the next object in the scene, go back to the upper-left corner, and start again. We repeat this process for every object in the scene.

The process of shading, once we know a point is visible, we have considered in Chapter 5. It now turns out that the frame buffer can help us determine whether a visible object is the closest one to us (from a given point of view). Let's examine how this happens.

Imagine several objects arrayed in front of you in random ways. To make an accurate picture, those objects that lie closest to the eye should be visible; those objects behind them should not be in the final picture. We have seen this situation before in Chapter 4 and called it the *hidden surface problem*. So if two opaque objects both project (projections were covered in Chapter 10) to the same point on the screen, the closer one to the eye is the visible one. Also note that we said that the nearer object should be the visible one in the final picture. If other objects are drawn on the screen while we build up the picture, there's no problem because the final picture is all we care about and the computer's picture (that's in the frame buffer) is completely erasable. As long as the picture is correct when we're all finished, then it's fine.

This set of ideas is the heart of the technique we are about to describe, known as the *Z-buffer algorithm*. The Z-buffer algorithm allows us to build up objects and then scenes by drawing them simple surface by simple surface. The name comes from using a frame buffer to store some information instead of a picture. The information stored in this extra frame buffer is the "Z-depth" of the visible object at that point, hence the name Z-buffer.

Let's see how the algorithm works. Suppose we have defined a dumbbell made up of a cylinder with the two spheres of different sizes at opposite ends, as shown in Fig. 11-9. We would like to draw this on the screen from the point of view indicated in the figure.

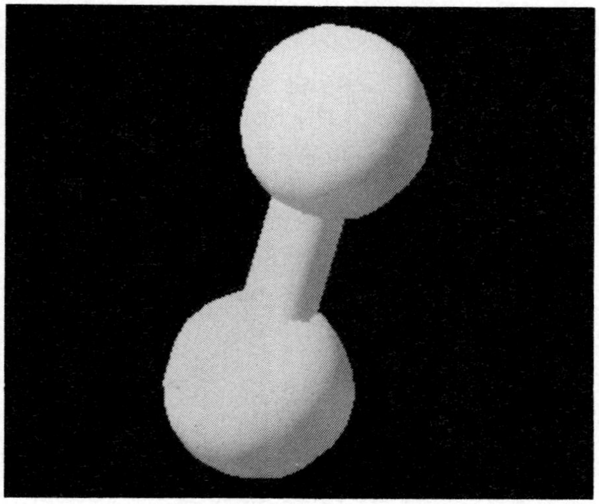

Fig. 11-9. An object we'd like to draw. Note the near sphere covers some of the cylinder, with covers for the sphere.

The Z-buffer algorithm says to select a simple surface and find any points on the screen where it is visible. It doesn't matter what order we take the surfaces in the total scene; the picture will look different as it's built up, but the final image will always be the same no matter what order we take the surface in.

So let's take the small sphere, the cylinder, and the large sphere in that order, completely arbitrarily.

The first step is to clear the image buffer to some background color. We will draw the picture in the image buffer, and we'd like to erase anything that might be accidentally in it at the time we start the new picture. For simplicity, we'll assume that the image buffer has only 8 bits to it, so it uses a color map. Clearing the buffer then just means selecting a color from the color map that makes a nice background color and setting every point in the frame buffer to the number that represents that color.

Now we'll set up another frame buffer. This buffer will not hold a picture. We don't care about the color map, and whatever the frame buffer looks like is only of curiosity value: it will hold numerical information, not picture information. This second buffer is called the *Z-buffer*, and will hold numbers that represent not colors, but the distance from the eye of points represented in the image buffer. The term Z-buffer comes from the common orientation of the image buffer (or screen) as an X-Y plane, so the Z-buffer represents the distance of each point in it along the Z-axis (Fig. 11-10). Initially the Z-buffer is cleared to represent the value of the Z-axis on the yon clipping plane.

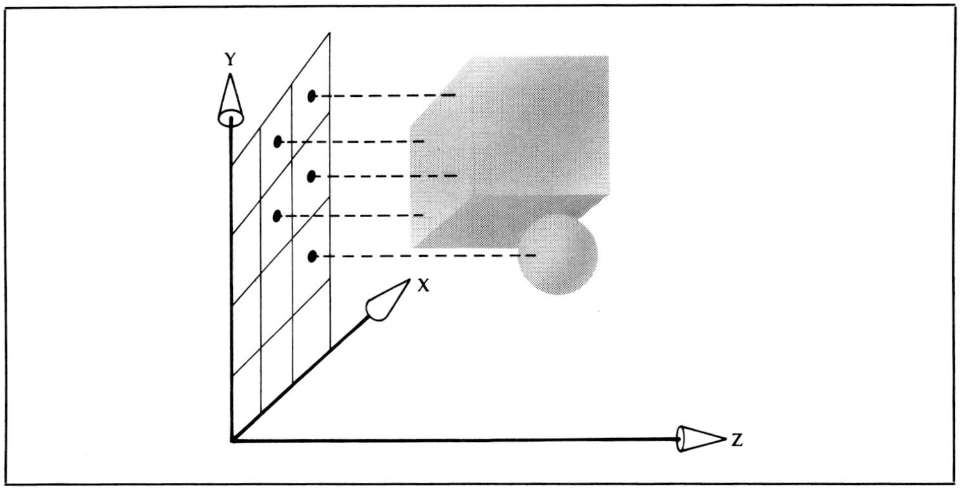

Fig. 11-10. The Z-buffer holds the depth of the object at each pixel.

The first point on the screen is examined and the computer checks (mathematically) to see if the sphere is visible there, which is the first part of the first question illustrated in Fig. 11-11. If it is not there, then none of the following work is done, instead the computer just selects the next point on the screen and checks to see if the object is visible there. Finally, the computer will find a point on the screen where the sphere is visible. Let's say that this point is identified on the screen by the (X,Y) coordinate of (230,210) in the image buffer, as in Fig. 11-12. Let's also say that the sphere is 85 units down the Z-axis from the eye at this point. (We always concern ourselves with the closest point of the surface if more than one point of the surface is in the line of sight, as in Fig. 11-13.)

Now we know that the sphere projects to this point, and we ask the second part of the first question, which is to determine if this object is the

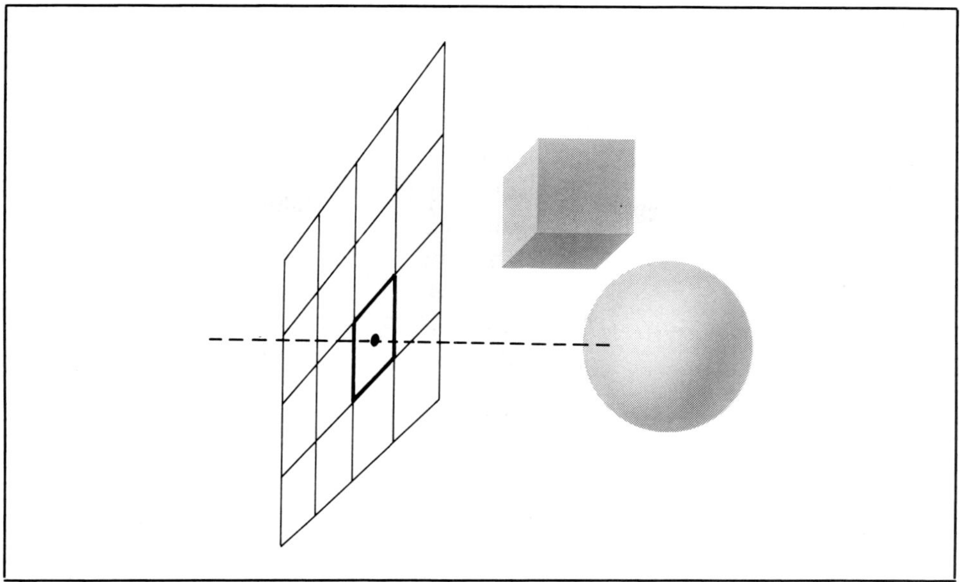

Fig. 11-11. The sphere can be "seen" by the current pixel, and the cube cannot be "seen" by it.

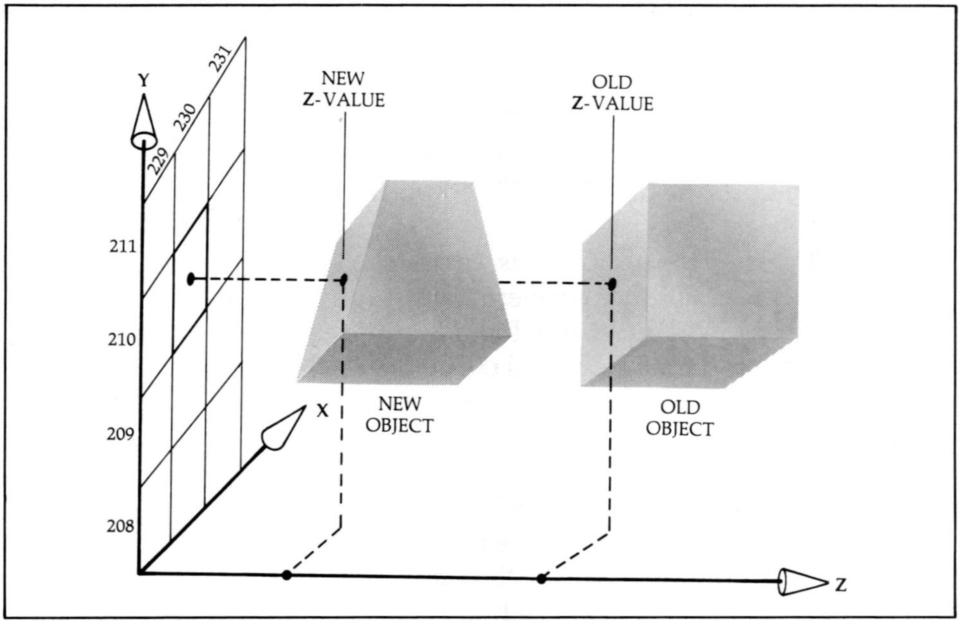

Fig. 11-12. The new object will be drawn at the given pixel because its Z-value is less than that previously stored.

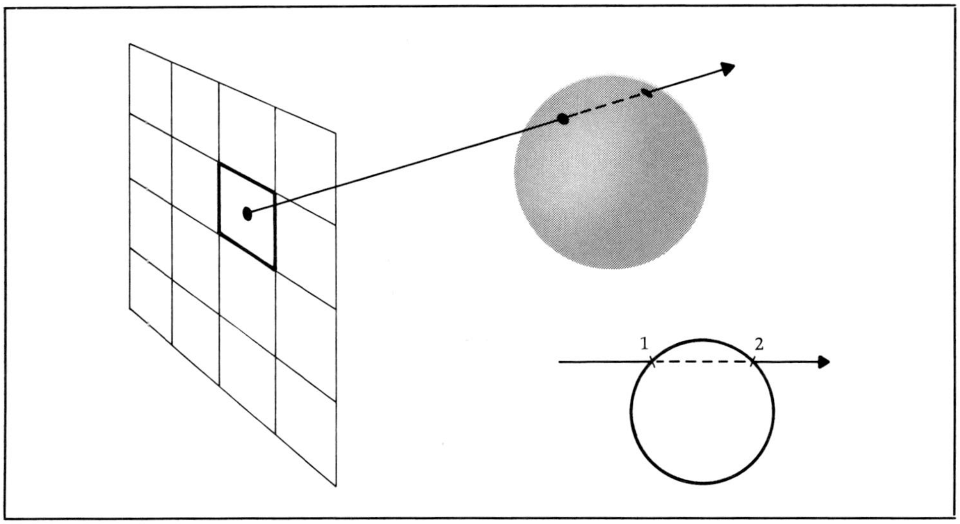

Fig. 11-13. A line may intersect a sphere twice. We see only the closer surface so that is the depth (Z-value) we store.

closest at that point. In the Z-buffer algorithm we ask, "Is this object closer to the eye than whatever object is currently represented in this pixel?" We know the distance of this object from the eye at this pixel; the computer determined it for us when it calculated the projection of the object on the screen (in this case we said it was 85). Now we have to know the depth of the object currently represented on the screen at this pixel.

We know that this is the first pixel to be filled in so the visible object here is the yon clipping plane. We want to generalize the algorithm, so we'll check for the Z-depth anyway by looking at the value in the Z-buffer for this pixel. It contains the number 500 (the yon clipping plane, to which it was initialized). Our pixel of interest on the sphere has a depth of 85 units, which means it is closer than the object currently in the image buffer at that point so it obscures (or covers up) the image there. So coordinate (230,210) in the image buffer is replaced with the color represented by the answer to our second question. The contents of the Z-buffer at (230,210) are replaced with the value 85. Now any other objects that project to (230, 210) will have their Z value compared to the new value of 85. Only if their Z value is less, will the new shade be placed in the image buffer, and the Z-buffer changed. Otherwise, we know the object lies behind some other object at that point, and we just move on to the next pixel on the screen. An illustration is in Fig. 11-12.

We can then finish the object (Fig. 11-14). If there are more surfaces to be drawn, we handle them in the same way. Note that it doesn't matter what order we take the objects in. The closest object at each pixel will always be the one remaining there in the end.

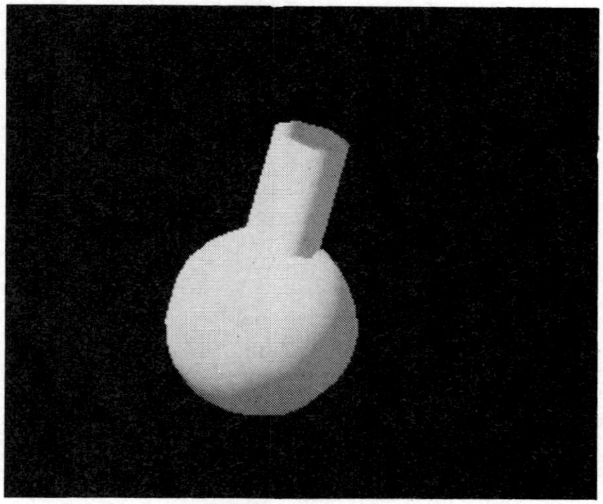

A. A sphere and a cylinder. Note the exposed part of the cylinder.

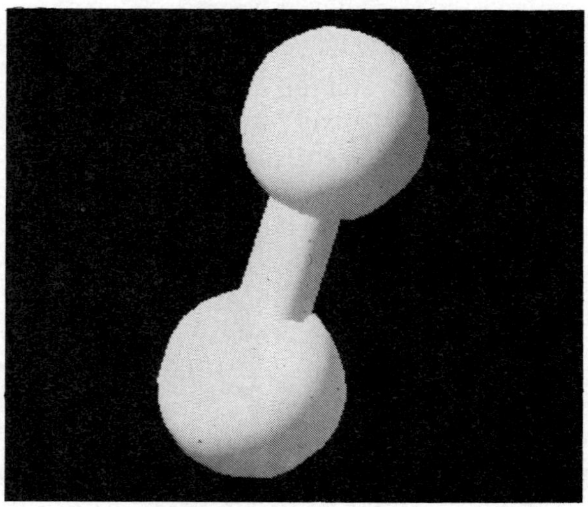

B. The second sphere covers some of the cylinder.

Fig. 11-14. Two steps in finishing the object.

In practice, we usually use more than eight bits for the Z-buffer, either by using a larger frame buffer or by using several buffers at once. Image buffers may also be deeper than eight bits for additional colors.

Although the Z-buffer is not intended to be a picture, it does hold an image of some kind. Often it holds a pretty moire pattern that bears a resemblance to the picture in the image buffer. A picture of a Z-buffer is in Fig. 11-15.

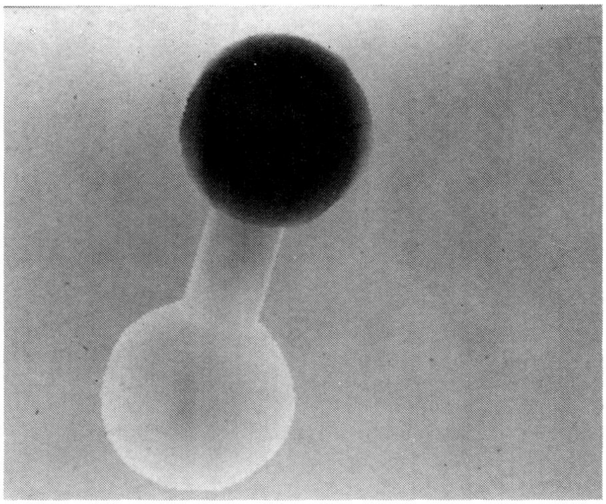

Fig. 11-15. A Z-buffer drawn with a black-and-white color map.

Z-BUFFER ALGORITHM PROBLEMS

The Z-buffer algorithm is valuable for its speed and generality in rendering. However, it suffers from its own set of problems like everything else.

Transparency is not handled in the algorithm as described. It can be "faked" if objects are first sorted in their Z coordinate, and are rendered farthest object first, back-surface first. The extra programming necessary to sort the objects before drawing becomes an expensive addition to the algorithm.

Reflections aren't modeled in the Z-buffer algorithm at all. Mirrored surfaces require programs to be written to create textures to apply to surfaces to make them look at all reasonable, and if a good number of surfaces are reflective, then this algorithm becomes very unattractive. It also particularly suffers from the problems of aliasing and sampling, to be discussed later in this chapter.

Z-BUFFER ALGORITHM ADVANTAGES

Now that we understand some of the principles of the Z-buffer algorithm, let's look at the advantages and disadvantages of the technique. In this section we'll look at some of the more significant advantages.

Perhaps the strongest point in favor of the Z-buffer technique is that it allows us to make pictures with as many objects as we wish. Many other rendering techniques require the computer to hold in memory all the objects that will eventually make it to the screen. Since computer memory is limited, so is the number of objects that we may render with such a technique.

But the Z-buffer algorithm draws each object one at a time, and needs no information about previous or following objects. Thus, pictures may contain an arbitrary number of objects.

Another advantage of the Z-buffer technique is that we may have many different kinds of objects in a single picture. Each object is rendered independently, so there may be different programs for each kind of object. To correctly render an object, a program needs only to get to the picture buffer and the Z-buffer. Thus, a modeler may draw five thousand polygons, followed by a hundred curved surfaces, followed by a fractal mountain range, and then add some more polygons. Each of these sections of the picture may be created by totally independent programs, which is good; when you want to add a new kind of object to your computer's primitive object repertoire, you need only write a new program; you don't have to make additions and changes to existing programs, which is much harder.

Although it is time consuming, the Z-buffer algorithm can be used to create a final picture with shadows. Shadows are normally a very desirable effect in all images. Many types of rendering techniques make shadows almost impossible to achieve. There is a technique using Z-buffers for drawing shadows but it requires a lot of storage and rendering the picture several times.

Here's the heart of the algorithm for including shadows with the use of Z-buffers. The key observation is to notice that all objects that are illuminated by a light source can be "seen" by an observer placed at that light source. Any objects or parts of surfaces that such an observer cannot see are thus not illuminated by that light source, which places them in shadow.

Let's say you're about to render an image. First you render the entire image from the point of view of the first light source. You can ignore the image, but you'll want to keep the Z-buffer. Again note that those objects that are visible in the image buffer are illuminated by the light source, and those that are not are thus in shadow from that light source. In terms of the Z-buffer, any point that is farther away from the light source than the nearest point (as found in the Z-buffer) is, therefore, blocked by that first point and thus in shadow.

Render the picture once for every light source, saving all the Z-buffers. Now we're ready to draw the final picture. For each point we're going to render, we consult the Z-buffers we have saved. We have to do some mathematical transformations, but we can eventually see where the current point lies with respect to each light source. If the Z-buffer for that point for that light source tells us that an object is closer to the light than the current point we just don't illuminate the point with that light source, effectively leaving it in shadow. We check each light source and then render the point.

The fact that the Z-buffer algorithm can be used to create shadows is important, but remember that you must save all the Z-buffers, which can take a great deal of storage, and that you must render the entire image once for each light source for each frame. Thus, if you have five light sources illuminating a scene, it will take at least five times longer to draw the final picture than without shadows.

Additionally, the technique just described will not let light fall through transparent or translucent objects so that some objects are only partly obstructed from the light source. It essentially forces all your objects to be fully opaque.

Another advantage of the Z-buffer algorithm is that since each object is drawn independently of the rest of the scene, very little internal computer memory is needed. The image buffer and Z-buffer hold almost all the information needed; the computer needs only to hold the program and a single object in its memory at a time, which is important for small computer systems.

TYPES OF RENDERING ALGORITHMS

The various rendering techniques we have considered so far suffer from some problems because of the way they fill in the image buffer. The first thing they all do is select a pixel, and then see about perhaps shading or reshading it. Usually the pixels are chosen in order across a scan line, and are therefore called *scan-line algorithms*.

Despite the problems mentioned in this chapter, scan-line algorithms are very popular because if a particular problem is really bad, it can be solved at the expense of more computer time and modeling effort. All the algorithms discussed so far have been scan-line algorithms.

There are some rendering techniques that do not work well in this way because the mathematics of trying to find where a ray from the eye (through a pixel) hits a surface is either very slow, very expensive, or unknown for a particular surface. A different rendering process is used for these surfaces, and we can lump them all together without too much generalization under the heading *subdivision algorithms*. This name refers to the mathematical technique used to draw the picture. We won't discuss them any more here, except to note that although they are the only way of drawing some surfaces, the edges of these surfaces usually look ragged, and animation with them suffers from jaggies and movement jump.

ALIASING AND MOTION BLUR

In this chapter we have so far concentrated on studying the Z-buffer technique for rendering. The Z-buffer is perhaps the most straightforward technique commonly used, and it's also quite popular, but the Z-buffer technique has problems in addition to those we have seen although these problems are not restricted just to Z-buffers.

The general class of problems we will look at in this section fall under the category of *aliasing*. To alias is to masquerade, or appear as something else. Mathematicians have studied aliasing in a variety of places, and recently it has become an important issue in computer graphics.

We won't go into the mathematics of aliasing but we can generalize its effects as the result of not doing something often enough, which will cause us problems.

For example, a current research problem in computer graphics is to solve the problem of motion blur, which we referred to before. Motion blur is the result of how conventional film is shot. Each frame of film passes in front of the lens, gets exposed, and is then moved away from the lens and eventually back into the can. But when the film is being exposed, objects in front of it might be moving. Since the film records what it sees for a very brief but noninstantaneous moment, moving objects will show up as a blur on the film. The faster the movement of an object, the bigger its blur.

It is very difficult to simulate motion blur in computer-generated images. When the computer draws a picture (either a two-dimensional picture or a three-dimensional rendering), it is effectively "freezing" the action at the moment of rendering. For example, in a three-dimensional scene, the positions of the various objects are determined and then they are drawn. No information is kept about where the objects are going or how fast they are moving.

Recall that the motion blur is the result of an object moving, so it is necessary to know that information to really simulate motion blur.

Now that we've seen that current computer graphics systems are not equipped to handle motion blur, we might be willing to just forget about it and proceed. But, motion blur is really very important in animation.

We have seen that a great deal of work has gone into methods for making computer-generated images look realistic. What's the point, though, if the final animation is lacking important visual cues? Most stop-motion animation in horror films (*King Kong*, *Godzilla*, and so on) has a particular "look" or style to it; somehow the monsters don't seem very real. Why not?

The monsters are usually very good models, so they look all right. And the animators often know how to animate well; some are excellent. But still, the motion is jerky. As you may have guessed, this jerky motion is because there is no motion blur in this kind of animation. The monster is posed and then photographed. It is then repositioned and photographed again. Each time the frame of film is shot, the monster is frozen still. Thus, there is no "streaking" on the film as a result of its motion.

But most people have seen so many films that they just "know" that moving figures leave a small blur; their eyes are used to it. Thus, when that motion blur is missing we automatically pick it up and notice something is "wrong."

The general problem of motion blur is one of the most significant research issues in computer graphics today. Until really good methods for simulating motion blur are found, there are a couple of choices open for producers of animation.

The first is to forget about motion blur completely. Despite the previous warnings, motion blur has almost never been incorporated into conventional two-dimensional animation; for example, the Disney classic *Snow White* has none of the effects of motion blur anywhere in the film. Of course, *Snow White* was not designed to appear "real," like current three-dimensional computer-generated animation.

If you want to simulate motion blur in three-dimensional animation, there is a rather crude trick that is sometimes helpful. When you finish rendering a frame of animation, copy into the frame buffer previous frames with a much lower intensity. It's as though you drew the current picture in the frame buffer without the previous frame having completely faded. Often people will add the previous two or three frames, though with greatly diminishing intensity for each.

Fig. 11-16 shows motion blur simulated with this technique. It does not always work well, and does not alleviate all the problems of motion blur, but it's often better than nothing.

Let's now return to our original topic of aliasing. We can now see that indeed motion blur fits our definition of "not doing something often enough." In this case, we're not showing new pieces of film often enough. (Of course, this statement isn't a good analysis of the problem, but if we were able to show, say, 100 frames per second, then the movement on the screen would be so continuous we wouldn't need motion blur.)

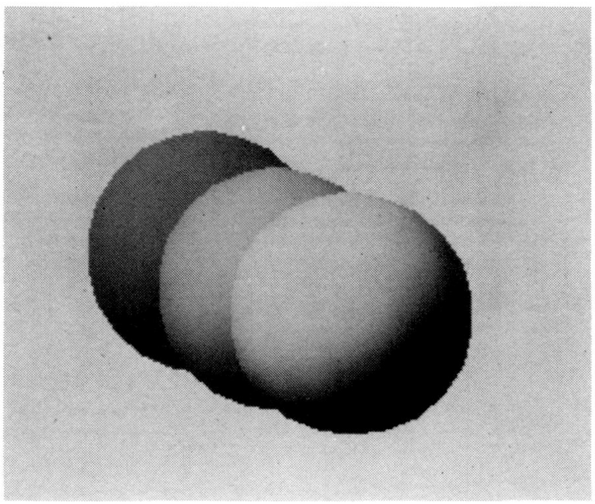

Fig. 11-16. Faking motion blur with previous frames added at lower intensity.

Viewed in this slightly off-center way, we could say motion blur is a result of not taking a large enough number of exposures of film in time, so it's aliasing due to time, which is also called *temporal aliasing*. Sometimes people will say *temporal aliasing* to emphasize the mathematical way of looking at this problem.

Another form of aliasing is due to not looking at the picture we're drawing enough when creating a three-dimensional, synthesized image. For example, we usually draw our pictures in a frame buffer. The frame buffer only has a limited number of squares. Usually that number is big, but when we draw images, we often draw the image that is seen by the center of each pixel. Thus, sometimes small objects will slip between pixel centers, as in Fig. 11-17. If this object is moving, or we're moving the camera around a still scene, this object might flicker on and off as it variously hits and then doesn't hit pixel centers.

Fig. 11-18 shows a narrow cylinder that we would like to draw on the frame buffer. Note that only some of the pixels see the cylinder completely, and those are the ones filled in, which gives rise to the "jaggies," or "staircasing" of edges. For film and animation it's quite important to get

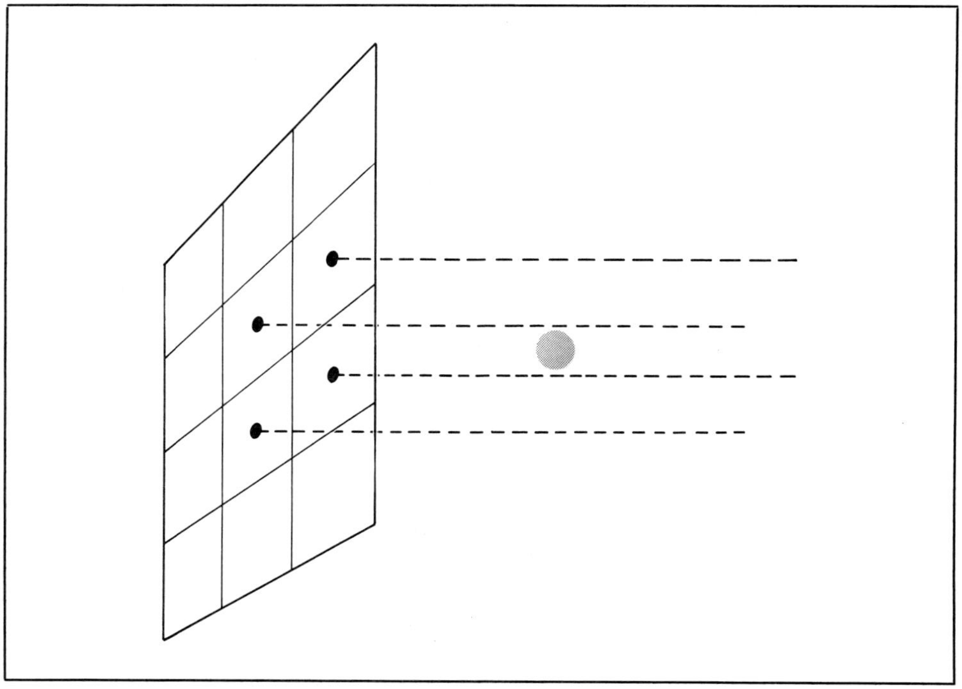

Fig. 11-17. We can miss small objects if the pixel's center doesn't see them.

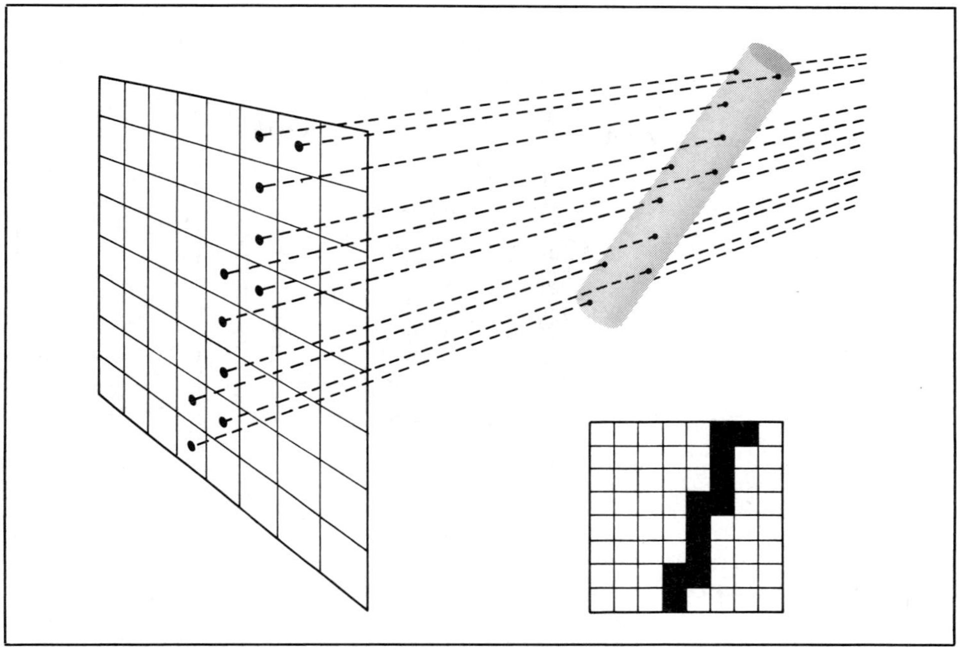

Fig. 11-18. A chunky cylinder, created by those pixels who see it.

rid of these annoying effects. For very high-quality still images, we would like to get rid of them as well.

The cure is called *anti-aliasing*, and there are plenty of ways to correct for aliasing with computer programs. Fig. 11-19 shows a pair of objects, with and without anti-aliasing.

Although there are many mathematical techniques for doing anti-aliasing, they all end up doing the same thing—slightly blurring the image. Blurring isn't always bad; to convince yourself just look at Fig. 11-19 again. The blurring is very slight and carefully controlled.

Fig. 11-20 shows how sharp edges are gently blurred to smooth them out. Note that we're now using several shades of gray, no longer just black and white. Fig. 11-21 shows this technique applied to colored edges.

Anti-aliasing is also very important when we want to display text on a frame buffer. If we want to draw very small characters, we might find that there aren't enough pixels to allow us to draw a good-looking character. The result is a choppy letter or number, which is displeasing to look at.

Fig. 11-22 shows how anti-aliasing is applied to a large character to shrink it down to a smaller size. The original letter B is 190 by 122 pixels, the final result is only 30 by 21. If we didn't anti-alias the character when

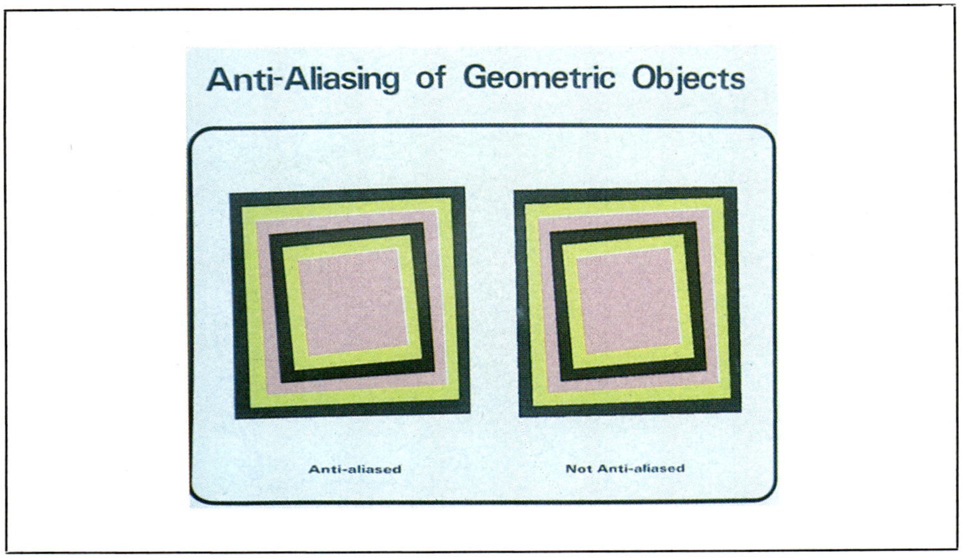

Fig. 11-19. **A comparison between aliasing and anti-aliasing.** ***(Image by Paul Sholtz. Used with permission of IBM Corp.)***

Fig. 11-20. **How anti-aliasing works.** ***(Image by Paul Sholtz. Used with permission of IBM Corp.)***

Fig. 11-21. Anti-aliasing in color. *(Image by Paul Sholtz. Used with permission of IBM Corp.)*

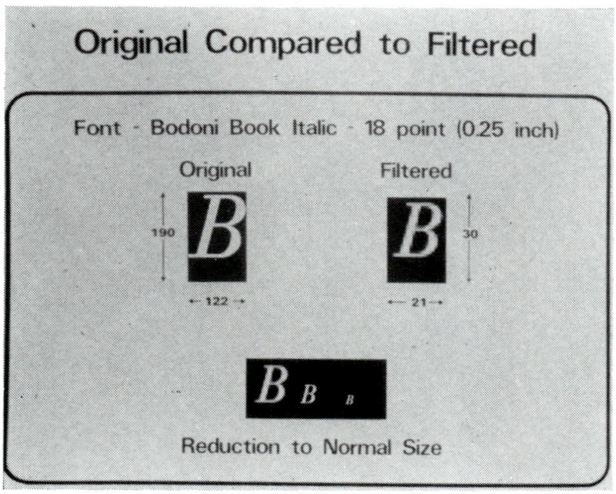

Fig. 11-22. Shrinking a letter so it still looks good. *(Image by Paul Sholtz. Used with permission of IBM Corp.)*

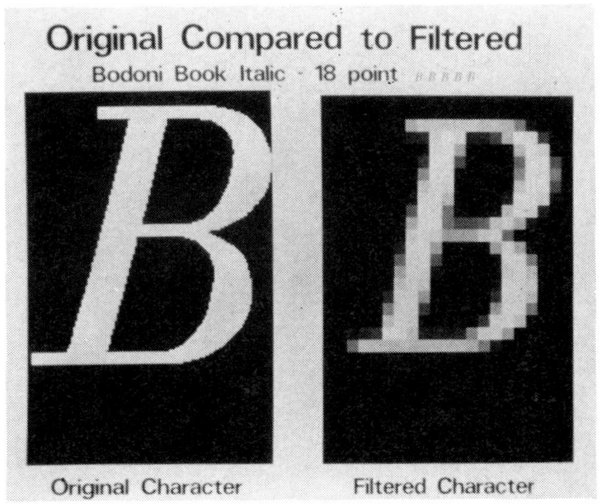

Fig. 11-23. Anti-aliasing a character for reduction. ***(Image by Paul Sholtz. Used with permission of IBM Corp.)***

Fig. 11-24. Anti-aliasing a character for reduction. ***(Image by Paul Sholtz. Used with permission of IBM Corp.)***

we shrank it, the little letter B would be very chunky and ugly. Figs. 11-23 and 11-24 show the technique applied to a script E and an italic B. All the computer-generated text in the pictures in this book is anti-aliased.

Unfortunately, anti-aliasing is often a slow procedure. Thus, only a small fraction of the pictures in this book have been correctly anti-aliased. But the surprising thing about anti-aliasing is the quality improvement you get when you apply it.

Anti-aliasing has become so popular that there is now an "international anti-aliasing symbol" (Fig. 11-25).

Fig. 11-25. The international anti-aliasing symbol—no jaggies! ***(Image by Paul Sholtz. Symbol© by Craig Reynolds. Used by permission of Craig Reynolds and IBM Corp.)***

RAY TRACING

Another type of rendering algorithm is called *ray tracing*. Ray tracing is perhaps the oldest of techniques discussed in this book although it has just recently become very widespread and popular.

The goal of ray tracing is to draw a picture that is based on the laws of light and optics that have been used for years to describe how prisms, lenses, and other objects affect light.

Imagine a light source as sending out an almost infinite number of *light rays*. Each ray starts at the light source and goes in a straight path until it hits an object. The object may then absorb the light, reflect some of it, or perhaps also allow some light to pass through if the object is somewhat transparent or translucent.

If you followed every light ray from the light source, as it bounced and reflected and otherwise moved around a three-dimensional scene until it hit the screen of your crt (if it ever did!), you would be able to build up a complete picture on your screen. Unfortunately, this technique is not quite right for practical purposes. In the first place, there are far too many rays coming out of any light source for us to be able to follow them all with a computer in any reasonable amount of time. Secondly, most of these light rays will not reach the screen. You can spend a great deal of time following light rays that just disappear into nowhere and don't help you make a picture at all.

You can modify the scheme simply by tracing the rays the other way. Instead of following rays from the light source to the screen (and thus the eye), we can trace them from the eye back to the objects in the scene. This way we know that every ray we trace will somehow contribute to at least one pixel on the screen since that's where it started.

Ray tracing is perhaps the slowest rendering algorithm used in computer graphics today. So why does anyone use it? The reason is that ray-traced pictures are among the most realistic images ever created by computer.

The reasons for this realism are straightforward. First, ray tracing can handle almost any kind of object you would like to use for modeling, and new techniques for ray-tracing new kinds of objects are being developed constantly. Additionally, ray tracing correctly handles three very important effects that most other rendering algorithms are unable to model—reflection, transparency, and shadows.

Fig. 11-26 shows our old friend the viewing pyramid, with the eye looking right down the center, and the screen located at the hither clipping plane. We can see a ray drawn from the eye, through a pixel on the screen, and traveling into the viewing pyramid, where our three-dimensional model is located.

We are interested in what happens to the ray when it hits different objects, because it is these interactions that will create our picture. Fig. 11-27 shows an example of a ray hitting an opaque, matte-finished sphere. The sphere has a dull surface, so it doesn't really reflect much light back to the eye (so we don't get a highlight), and because it's opaque, no light passes through the surface of the sphere into the inside (and then perhaps out the back of the sphere). When a ray hits an object like this, it just stops; it doesn't bounce off because of the matte finish, and it doesn't travel through because the surface is opaque.

Fig. 11-28 shows a ray hitting a sphere that is both glossy and transparent, like a shiny Christmas tree ornament. Some of the light bounces off

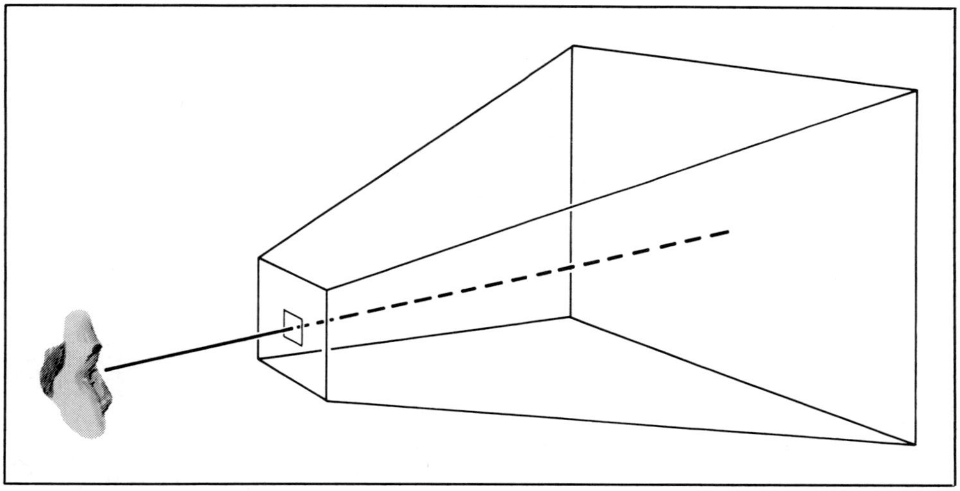

Fig. 11-26. A ray entering the viewing pyramid.

the surface of the sphere as a *reflected ray*, and some passes through the surface of the sphere as a *transmitted ray*. Note that the transmitted ray has bent as it passed through the surface of the sphere. Why?

You can answer this question with a ruler and a fishtank. Fig. 11-29 shows a stick dipped into a water-filled fishtank. The stick doesn't look straight at all! The reason is that light travels at different speeds in air and water causing the stick to appear bent and transmitted rays to bend as they pass through transparent objects. More detailed explanations are possible with the aid of some physics, but we need only notice the effect and think about how to model it into our pictures.

It turns out that the amount of bend depends on both surfaces at the place where the light actually bends. In our example with the fishtank, the light passed from water to air (or vice versa, the order doesn't matter in this discussion). For our Christmas-tree ornament the light passed from air to glass. All such glass-air boundaries will cause the light to bend at a certain constant angle.

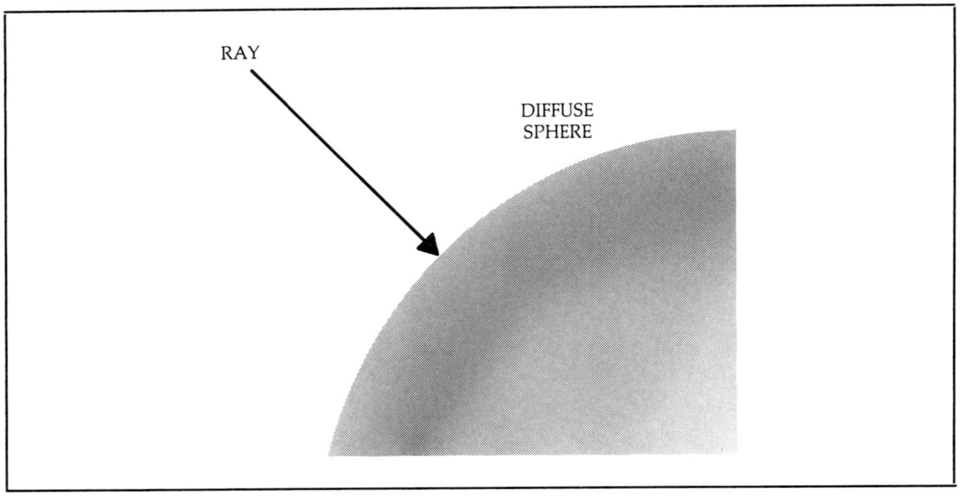

Fig. 11-27. A ray striking a diffuse sphere.

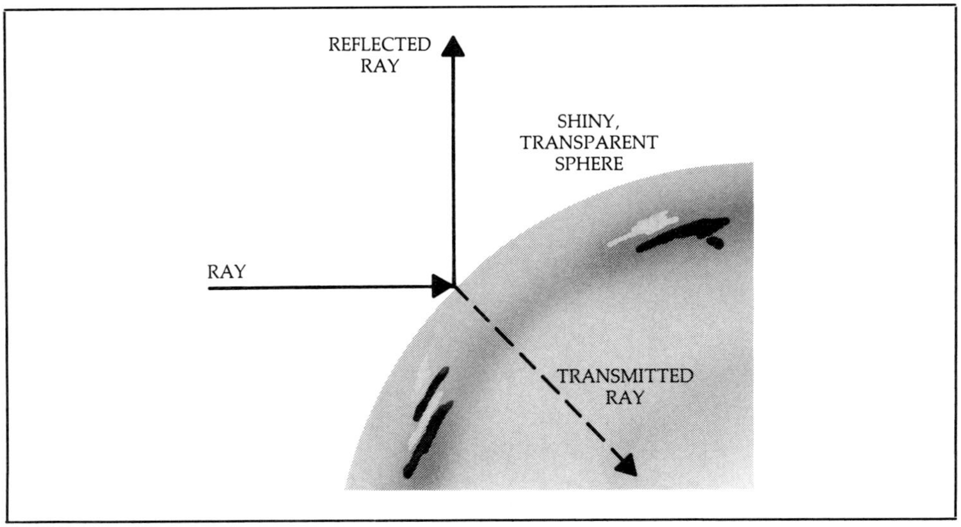

Fig. 11-28. A ray striking a transparent, shiny sphere.

Physicists have measured this angle for a wide variety of surfaces, and have written up their results as a table of indices of refraction. Basically, an *index of refraction* is a number, describing how much bend there is to the light ray passing through a boundary between two media. When modeling, we usually associate an index of refraction with each object. Good values are usually in the range between 1.3 and 1.7.

Fig. 11-29. A ray of light bends like this ruler appears to bend when passing from one medium to another.

Fig. 11-30 shows a ray entering a more complicated scene. Note that each time a ray hits an object, that ray stops and two new rays (a transmitted ray and a reflected ray) begin. It is the effect of these rays that gives us transparency (the transmitted ray) and reflection (the reflected ray).

We generally tell the rendering program that we only want to follow the original ray from the eye to a certain depth. We use the word "depth" because we can associate an abstract picture of a tree with a ray from the eye, as illustrated in Fig. 11-31. Each row of the tree has more rays than the previous row; the exact number of new rays is dependent on how many light sources are illuminating the scene. We will discuss the "light source" rays illustrated in this figure in a little while, but for now notice that each time we proceed to a new row of the tree, we suddenly encounter many more rays.

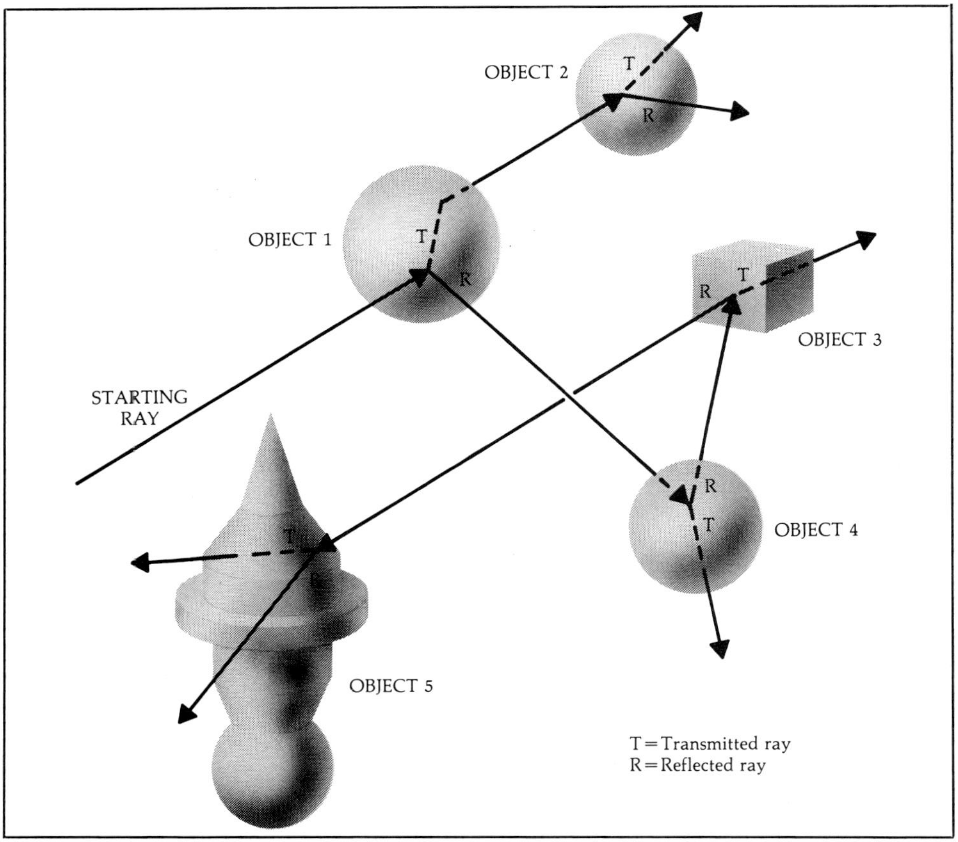

Fig. 11-30. A ray entering a complex scene.

You can see that we can quickly have a lot of rays going at once causing the computer to go really slowly when rendering a picture; each ray takes a long time to follow. So we limit the depth of the tree before we begin.

We can't limit the tree too much, though. It's hard to say where a good point is for stopping the tree, but we can establish a least value pretty easily. Fig. 11-32 shows a ray going through a wine glass, hitting a mirror, and returning, along with the tree for this picture. To get the ray back to the eye from the mirror we need at least six levels to the tree, so six is certainly a minimum depth for the tree. More complicated pictures may need much deeper trees, causing them to take much longer to render.

The ray-tracing scheme is very good at handling hidden surfaces. The mathematics of ray-tracing tells us very easily which is the first object hit by a ray; this is the object that we use for reflections and transmissions of

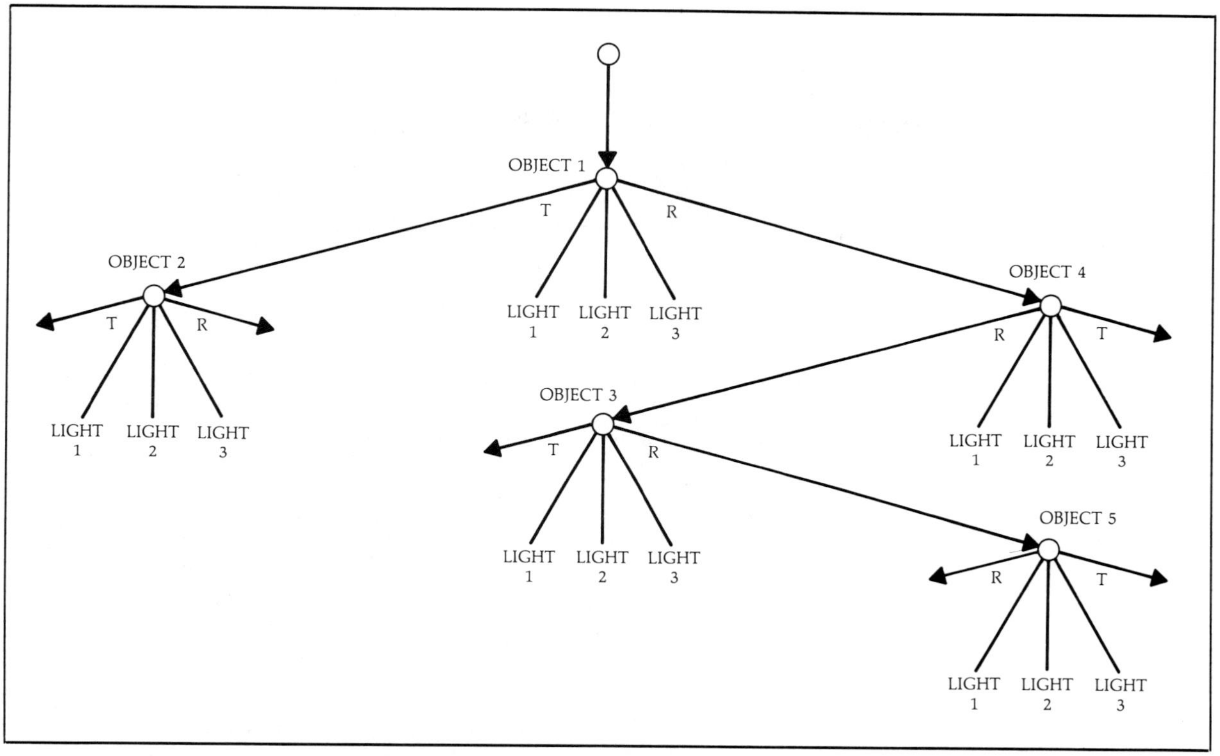

Fig. 11-31. A tree for a ray entering a complex scene.

new rays. We don't need a Z-buffer, but we do need to keep all the different objects around the entire time we are drawing a picture.

We should also note that although the viewing pyramid is important in ray tracing for determining perspective and hither/yon clipping planes, we might end up seeing objects outside of the pyramid itself. Fig. 11-33 shows a sphere reflecting the image of a sphere outside the viewing pyramid. Although rays from the eye can't hit this "outside" sphere directly, we can certainly see it in the picture. Thus, our model can exist in a large volume of space, much more than just the viewing pyramid.

Since our models can occupy an unlimited region of space, the computer has no way of "knowing" when a ray has passed outside of our model. It's easy to imagine a ray missing all the objects in a scene and traveling off to infinity. We certainly don't want to trace this ray forever!

To stop rays from shooting off into space forever, most modelers place

Fig. 11-32. A ray passing through a wine glass, reflecting off a mirror, and returning.

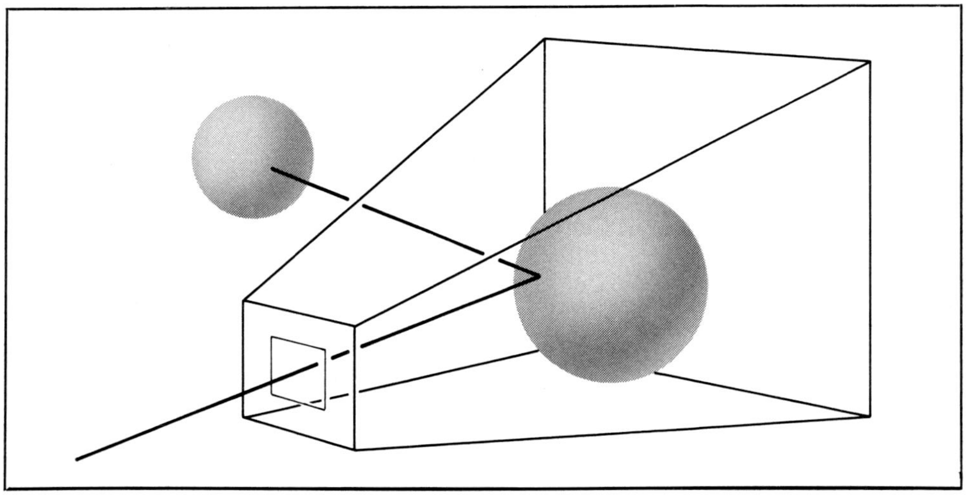

Fig. 11-33. A ray may strike an object outside the viewing pyramid.

a *world sphere* around the universe of the eye and the model, as in Fig. 11-34. This sphere is colored with some background color for the picture. If a ray hits this background sphere, it stops and assumes the color of the sphere where it hit.

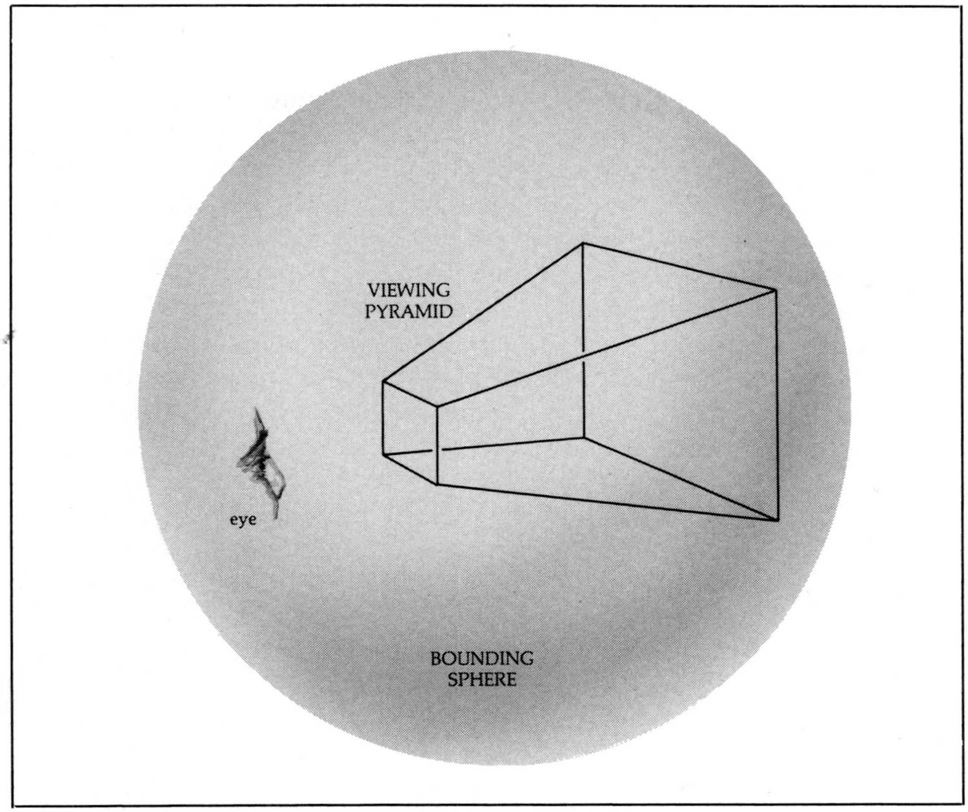

Fig. 11-34. Most modelers enclose the whole universe in some surface, usually a "bounding sphere."

So we have seen how ray tracing creates a ray starting at the eye, passing through a pixel, and continuing into the world of the model. We've seen how that ray can be absorbed, reflected, and transmitted off of objects, and maybe hit the bounding sphere. Let's now see how all this information is used to actually create a picture.

The game actually consists of two steps: first we build up the tree of rays, and then we process the tree. We have seen something of how transmitted and reflected rays come about, but in the illustrations of trees we have also seen rays going off to light sources. What are they for?

These rays are sometimes called *illumination rays*, just to distinguish them from the other rays; but they are still just straight lines in space. When we are at a particular point on a surface, we always need to know what the color is at that point, what the index of refraction is, and so on.

We also need to know how to shade it; that is, how many lights are hitting that point, and what is then the intensity of each light that does strike that point of that object?

So first we need to know which lights actually manage to strike that point. Not all the lights will get to every point on the model; some will be on the wrong side of some objects, and some lights will be blocked from some points by other objects. It's easy to tell if a given light source strikes a given point on a surface. Just start a ray at that point on the surface, and direct it to the light source in question. If that ray strikes any object on its way to the light, then there is not a direct path from that light to that point, and that light source does not contribute to the shading for that point. If the light ray makes it all the way to the light source, or to the bounding sphere on its way to the light source for an infinite light source, then we add in the illumination of that light source to the given point.

Note that this scheme automatically creates shadows for us! If a light source does not illuminate a given point, then that point is in shadow relative to that light source. We automatically get shadows as complex and curvy as they ought to be; and just for the price of a single ray towards each light source for each object on the tree.

Now that we can shade objects, we're ready to start the actual business of rendering the picture, which is the second step of the create-the-tree/process-the-tree procedure given before.

The color that we will place in the pixel pierced by the original eye's ray is the result of the color of the object first struck by that ray, the transmitted ray at that point, and the reflected ray at that point. The color of that point's transmitted ray is the result of the shade of the object it first hits, and the transmitted and reflected rays at that point, and so on down the tree. Each step in the tree requires the colors of the rays below it to create the final color at that point.

So the second step in the rendering process, after creating the tree, is to color it from the bottom up. First, we find the shades of all the final objects where either the ray was absorbed by an object or the bounding sphere, or where it was stopped because the tree got too deep. Fig. 11-35 shows an example of coloring all the final points in the tree.

Then, we start working our way back up, using the results of the lower rays to create new composite colors. We combine the rays according to the characteristics of the surface at each point. For example, if a surface is very reflective and only slightly transparent, then the color there will be dependent on the light source rays, the reflected ray, and only a little bit on the transmitted ray as it "comes back" to the point with a color.

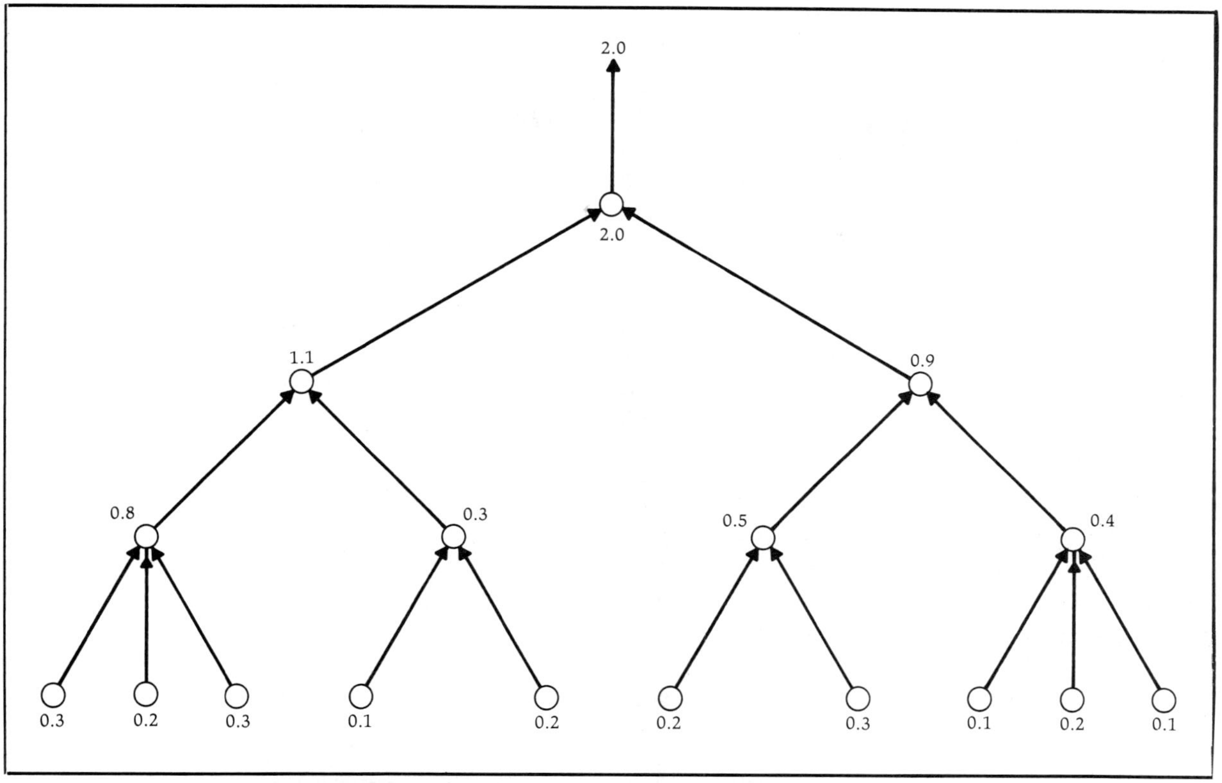

Fig. 11-35. Ray tracing actually shades the tree from the bottom up.

When we finally reach the top of the tree, we have the color for the first object we struck with the original ray that started at the eye. This is the color of the pixel and the same ray passed through. At this point we color in that pixel on the screen, and then move on to the next pixel where we start all over again with a new eye ray and a new tree.

Ray tracing is very slow because of the mathematics involved, but it is very versatile because of the special effects it can handle and the wide range of objects that may be used in the models being rendered.

SUMMARY

This chapter was fundamentally concerned with a piece of hardware called a *frame buffer*, and the computer graphics techniques that make special use of it.

We motivated our discussion of the frame buffer by discussing how a television signal is generated. We saw that it is "drawn" on the screen by beams of electrons that go from top down, left to right. These beams only draw every other line each time they go down the face of the tube so that it takes two passes to complete one picture. We say that each of these two sets of lines, the even and odd ones, are called the *even field* and the *odd field*, respectively.

We saw that if we could videotape the signal that controls these electron beams and carefully modify it, we could control the image on the screen. We said that the computer does something like this, only instead of videotaping onto magnetic tape, it stores the picture in *solid-state memory*, also sometimes called *semiconductor memory* or *core memory*.

We said that a *frame buffer* is a chunk of computer memory large enough to hold one image of the raster crt. Each dot on the crt is called a *picture element*, sometimes also called a *pixel* or *pel*.

We started our discussion of frame buffers with the assumption that the "standard" frame buffer is eight bits deep. This means that there are eight bits available for each pixel on the screen. Eight bits is enough room to hold a number from 0 to 255, so there can be up to 256 different colors on the screen at any one time.

These colors are put up on the screen through a process involving a list of 256 colors called a *color map* or *color table*. For each pixel on the screen, there is a number from 0 to 255 associated with it inside the frame buffer. When the computer wants to draw that pixel on the screen, it gets the number from the frame buffer for that pixel. That number is then used to select a color from the color table. For example, if the frame buffer holds the value 219 for a certain pixel, the computer draws color number 219 on the screen at that point.

The color table is a list of 256 triplets of red, green, and blue intensity values for the pixel at that point. There are 256 intensity values available because the color table itself is only eight bits deep although there are three sets of these eight bits for each color (one set each for red, green, and blue).

We then looked at frame buffers that are more than eight bits deep. For example, a 24-bit deep frame buffer can be considered three eight-bit deep frame buffers put together, so the computer can directly get the red, green, and blue components of the color at a given pixel by looking at the first eight, second eight, and third eight bits in the frame buffer respectively.

We then saw one way the computer renders complicated, complete scenes, using another frame buffer as a kind of depth memory for every pixel in the frame buffer where we're actually drawing the picture. This *depth-buffer algorithm* is also called a *Z-buffer algorithm*.

We render a complete picture by setting the Z-buffer initially to the Z-depth of the yon clipping plane (recall that's the farthest point that we will be able to see on the screen). Then, every time we draw a new object, we compare the Z-depth of every pixel to the Z-depth currently in the Z-buffer. If the new pixel is closer to the eye than the one that's currently in the Z-buffer (that is, its Z value is smaller than the one in the Z-buffer), then the value in the Z-buffer is replaced with the new Z value, and the corresponding pixel in the image buffer is replaced with the image of the object at that pixel.

Although the Z-buffer technique is conceptually straightforward and easy to implement, it suffers from some drawbacks. Most visible drawbacks are that it does not have any provisions for handling transparent objects, nor for accurately displaying reflections of one object off another.

We then looked at some of the advantages offered by use of the Z-buffer technique. We can have as many objects in our scene as we please since the computer need only think about one object at a time.

We can also mix types of objects with relative ease so that curved surfaces, patches, and polygons can all share a single set of image buffer and Z-buffer to make a complete image.

We then saw that by rendering the picture once for each light source and saving the Z-buffers, we can create shadows in a final image. Unfortunately, there are no provisions for transparent or reflective surfaces in this shadow-generating scheme.

We then closed with a discussion of various kinds of rendering algorithms. All the techniques we have looked at so far fall under the heading of *scan-line algorithms* because they generally fill in pixels along a scan line, then move to the next scan line, and so on.

Alternatively, there are *subdivision algorithms* that can be found in many computer graphics sites. They are all much more bound up with programming than the Z-buffer algorithm, so we didn't discuss them. When all the problems have been corrected for, all the different kinds of rendering algorithms should theoretically give you the same picture.

We then looked at the general problem of *aliasing* and started with a discussion of *motion blur*.

We saw that in conventional film, each frame of film is exposed long enough so that quickly moving objects on the screen will leave a definite "blur" on the film itself. This blur is an important psychological cue for viewers of film, and when it isn't there, we notice that something is wrong.

Although techniques for handling motion blur are still being invented, and almost all are very expensive (thus time consuming) to apply, we looked at a "fake" for simulating motion blur. The idea was to add in previous frames to each frame, with a diminishing intensity as we go back in time. This sometimes works well and is often better than doing nothing at all.

We then saw that we might miss small objects with a frame buffer/Z-buffer system. Since each pixel in a Z-buffer can hold only one depth value, it holds the value for what is seen by the line drawn through the center of the pixel. Small objects might slip through between pixels, and sometimes catch a center line and sometimes miss it, causing the object to flicker on and off as time goes on, which is clearly undesirable.

We saw that *anti-aliasing* is the solution to these problems, and that it generally works by applying a very carefully controlled kind of blur to the image. Anti-aliasing comes in many flavors and forms, but some kind of anti-aliasing is necessary to eliminate the "jaggies," or staircased edges caused by the limited resolution of a frame buffer.

Another important class of rendering technique is called *ray tracing*. The essence of ray tracing is to trace a line from your eye into the screen, and see what you hit. If you hit a reflective object, you bounce the ray off the surface and continue following it to see what might be reflected in the first object. If that object was also transparent, then we send another ray through into the inside of the object.

These reflected and transmitted rays are each followed until they hit another object where the process is repeated. Although a reflected ray is just bounced off the surface of the object, a transmitted ray is bent from the line of the ray that originally hit the object by an amount controlled by the *index of refraction* between the media on both sides of the object boundary.

When we have built up a complete *tree* of rays, we are ready to trace them back and shade each ray as we go. We first trace *illumination rays* from each object to all the light sources, to determine the shading at that point on that object. If a particular light is not blocked by an object between the point we are examining and the location of the light itself, then we shade the surface with one of the shading techniques we looked at before. If the light source is blocked on its way to the object, then that object is in shadow, and that light does not contribute to the shading of that point.

We combine rays as we work our way back up the tree, until we hit the original eye ray. That ray has the value of the first object seen by the eye, and it is that shading that is stored in the frame buffer for the pixel that started the whole thing off.

Chapter TWELVE

Animation

In this chapter we will examine the process of conventional animation as it has been done for years. We'll first look at the principles that tell us why animation works at all, and then we'll look at what goes on in an animation studio and see how an animated film is designed and produced.

We'll then see how the computer can help us do conventional animation and not only save us time and effort on the boring and uncreative tasks that must be done, but how it can actually help us make animation that would otherwise be virtually impossible.

Then, we'll see how the computer can help us do a whole new kind of animation: three-dimensional animation. Actually, three-dimensional animation has been done for years—*King Kong* was an early three-dimensional animation, but with the computer the process has become much faster and easier, and now we can animate objects that could be prohibitively expensive to build and animate. We can also animate impossible objects—optical illusions that exist only in the computer's memory but look real on the screen! We begin with the human eye.

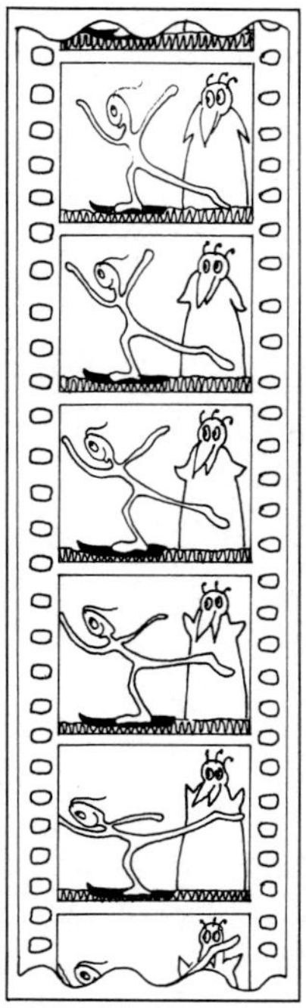

Fig. 12-1. A piece of film. Note that each frame is unmoving.

PERSISTENCE OF VISION

When we see a film on television or in the theater, the motion appears smooth and continuous. But if we look at a piece of film (Fig. 12-1), we can see that it is not really this way at all. Instead, film consists of a strip of still pictures, flashed in rapid succession on the screen so as to give the illusion of movement. Because each picture is slightly different from the one preceding it, we perceive motion when these frames are shown to us quickly enough.

This illusion exists because of a peculiarity in the human visual system. When shown a picture, we tend to retain it for a very brief period of time, which is called *persistence of vision*. If the pictures arrive fast enough, one after the other, then we automatically sense motion, and we perceive a smooth movement. If the difference between successive frames is too large or the time between them is too large, then the illusion is shattered, and the motion no longer appears smooth.

The persistence of vision is what makes conventional film, video, and animation possible. As we will mention later, 24 frames per second has become a standard rate for the showing of still pictures in the film industry. Actually, the projection rate is 48 frames a second, but each frame is shown twice so only 24 pictures per second are needed. This rate turns out to be the best compromise between economy in the amount of film that must be projected and the necessity of simulating movement for the human eye. For comparison, video (television) images are broadcast at 30 frames per second.

CONVENTIONAL TWO-DIMENSIONAL ANIMATION

The production of an animated film is a very time-consuming process normally involving many people. Thirty minutes of film at 24 frames per second requires 43,200 different frames, each of which must be drawn, inked, checked, rechecked, and photographed!

When an animated film project is begun, a story is first written in script form. This script is then turned into a series of pictures that show important moments in the story or animation. Fig. 12-2 shows such a set of panels for a very short film. This set of panels is called a *storyboard* and can easily consist of dozens or hundreds of pictures. These storyboards help the animators envision how they will tell the story, plan nuances of the character's features, and perhaps plan special effects and other important points of the film.

When the storyboard has been completed and refined, the actual work of animation can begin. To understand the different steps, it is useful to understand how a complete frame of animation, or *cel*, is created and photographed. Cel is short for cellulose, the clear plastic material that frames of animation are drawn upon.

A single frame is actually a photograph of many cels laid over one another. Each cel in the stack is a piece of clear plastic with one character, or one piece of a character, drawn upon it. Fig. 12-3 shows several cels, and Fig. 12-4 shows how they may be stacked to create a complete image. The advantage of this technique over drawing each frame individually is a savings in human labor and time. If a character is standing still and speak-

1. The artist works on a new film.

2. Wonders what to draw.

3. Gets idea.

4. And goes to work.

5. Zoom into drawing board.

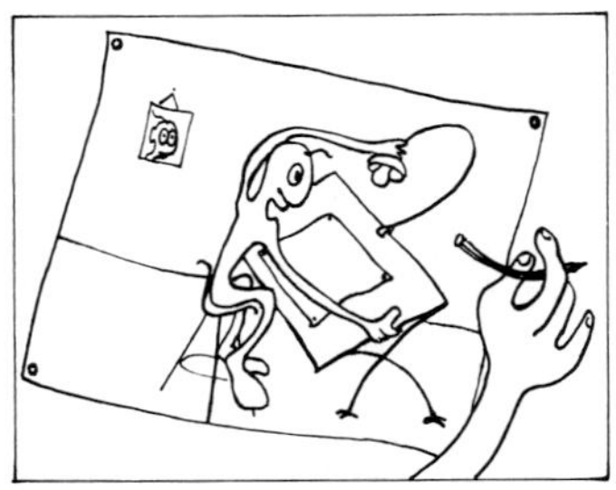

6. to show the new film.

7. The last board.

Fig. 12-2. A simple storyboard showing action and camera moves.

Fig. 12-3. Many individual cells may be drawn.

ing, then it might be reasonably animated with a still body, and only moving mouth and facial features. The cels with his body need not be redrawn for every frame in this case. The illustrations show a crude example, but in fact this process is how even the most complex animation is created.

The major cost in producing an animated film is right here: in the

Fig. 12-4. A composite frame made of the six cells of Fig. 12-3. Note the ease of animating just the face or arms.

drawing of the many thousands of cels necessary for even a short film. Each cel must be carefully hand drawn and hand painted, at a great cost in time.

The general work of creating the frames can be highly simplified into two general categories.

The first is the drawing of *key frames*. These are frames selected by the head animators for their importance in the film, either because of the visual effect, a character's important expression, or the extremes of movement. Fig. 12-5 shows a storyboard for an animation we might want to produce. Fig. 12-6 shows a possible set of key frames.

Fig. 12-5. A rough storyboard.

Fig. 12-6. Key frames for Fig. 12-5.

Once the key frames are drawn, work begins on drawing *in-between* frames, as in Fig. 12-7. These frames are placed in between the key frames, as their name suggests. Generally, more skill is required for key frame design than for in-betweening, and the animators with the most experience do the key frame production, letting apprentices and less senior animators perform the in-betweening.

Fig. 12-7. In-betweening frames for the first two key frames of Fig. 12-6.

It should be noted that in-betweening is not a completely mechanical process. For example, consider the sequence in Fig. 12-8, of a man raising his hand very quickly. The key frames in Fig. 12-8 show the extremes of the movement, but they do not tell the whole story. Often animators distort or caricature in the in-betweens. Fig. 12-9 shows how this sequence might actually be in-betweened. It has been found from experience that the overshoot and distortion of the hand indicated in the figure make the motion look more fluid and natural when finally shown on the screen.

There are no hard and fast rules for this kind of distortion; animation is an art, and the best animation is usually done by the best artists.

ROTOSCOPING

Several techniques exist for cutting down on the time required in animation. One such technique is called *rotoscoping*, which involves the tracing of previously filmed action onto animation cels. The cels are then inked

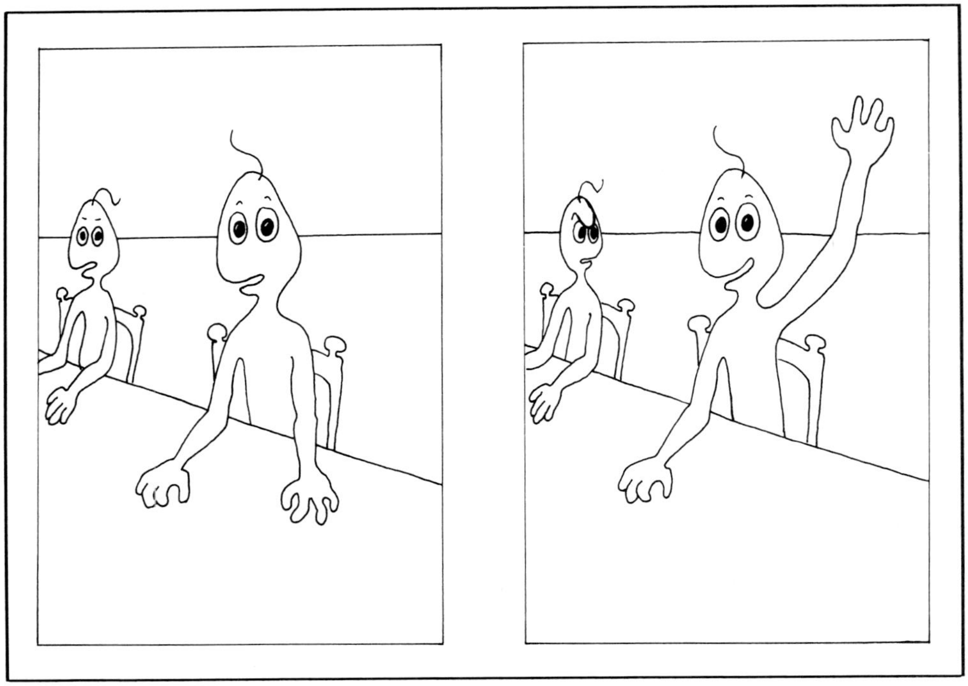

Fig. 12-8. The key frames for a man raising his hand.

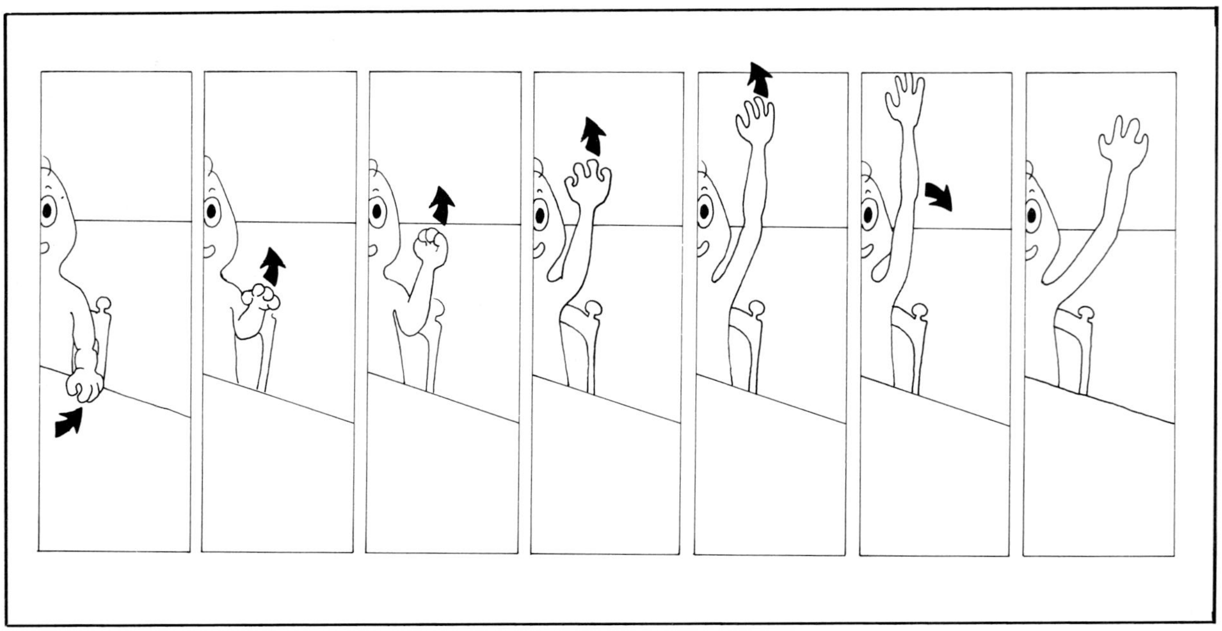

Fig. 12-9. The in-betweens for Fig. 12-8. Note the distortion of the hand.

and painted as usual and then filmed. The time required to design the key frames and in-betweens is eliminated. Rotoscoping is most often used from live footage; i.e., it would be difficult to animate a herd of running horses traditionally, but with live footage of running horses to trace from the animation can be produced much more quickly.

The results of rotoscoping have a fluidity and style not normally seen in conventional animation. It is usually not hard to tell the difference between rotoscoped and hand-designed animation; though, which looks "better" is often a matter of context and taste.

MIXED MEDIA

Another enhancement of animated film is to film live action, produce animation, and then refilm the combined live and drawn frames onto film. This technique, commonly called *mixed media*, can save time, and can produce quite stunning effects when done well.

AN OVERVIEW OF TWO-DIMENSIONAL COMPUTER-ASSISTED ANIMATION

It seems reasonable that given sufficient information about key frames and perhaps a few general distortion rules, a computer should be able to do most of the in-betweening in animation. This statement is true to a limited extent.

Consider Fig. 12-10. There is no way the computer can, without help, properly produce the in-between frames. There is too much information that we usually take for granted that is not explictly given in the frames, and is required for correct in-betweening.

Making elaborate three-dimensional models of the characters and entering them into the computer works in some cases, but the effort is tremendous, and as we noted before, there is a good deal of style in animation that such well-defined models cannot easily perform so that it's generally a waste of effort.

It is common to call this field computer-assisted animation, which is a good name, because it implies that the computer helps the animator and the animator also helps the computer! A popular method for computer-assisted animation is called *line interpolation*.

In line interpolation the animator describes the key frames to the com-

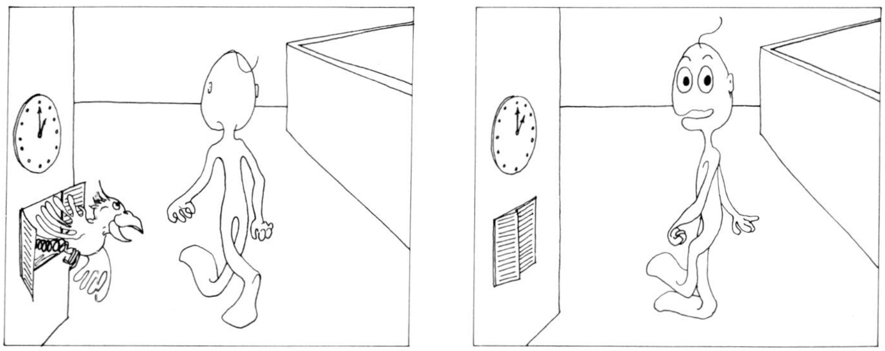

A. He walks away but hears his name . . .   B. And turns around.

Fig. 12-10. A man turns around to the sound of the bell.

puter with a tablet and pen, as described in Chapter 1. The frame is actually entered in *strokes*. A stroke is like the common motion of a pen stroke, but is formalized to begin when the stylus touches the tablet and continues until the pen leaves the tablet. Strokes need not be straight; a simple picture and one way of entering it is shown in Fig. 12-11.

The animator enters both key frames in this way. The idea is that every stroke in the first key frame will be turned into its corresponding stroke in the second key frame.

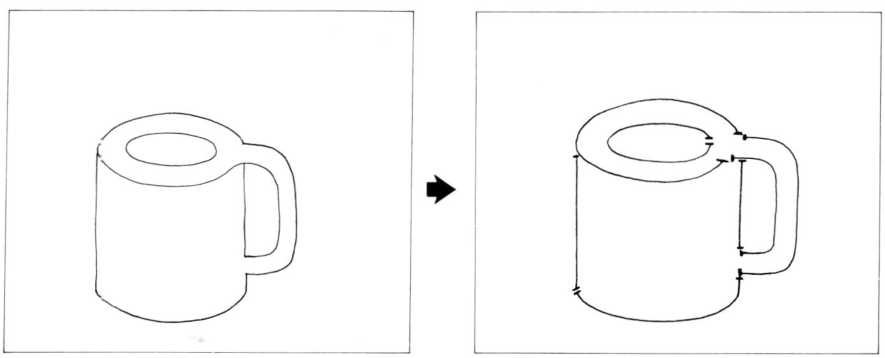

A. A cup.   B. The strokes used to draw the cup. (Strokes are marked for clarity.)

Fig. 12-11. Breakdown of a figure into strokes.

To make this happen, the animator specifies the number of frames to be in-betweened. The computer then takes the first stroke of the first key frame, and interpolates it into the first stroke of the second key frame, producing as many in-betweens along the way as needed. It then does the same thing for the second stroke, the third, and so on. Fig. 12-12 illustrates this process.

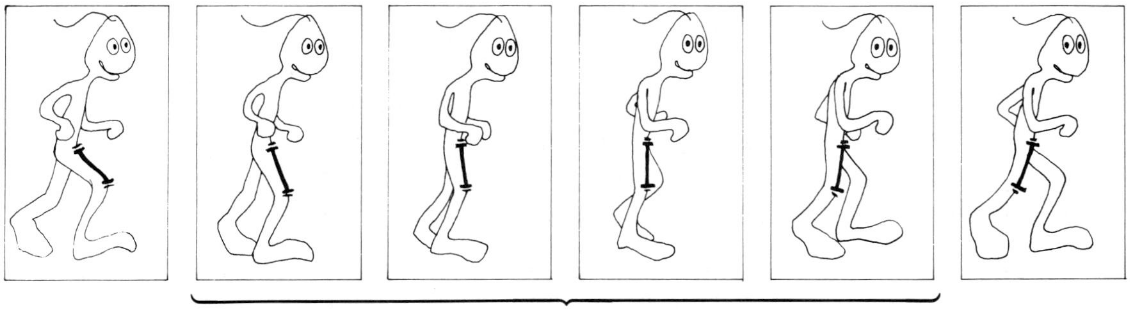

A. Start. B. In-betweens. C. End.

Fig. 12-12. An interpolated stroke.

The process is quick, and although the human element is missing in the in-between frames, the two key frames have been entered by an animator with careful choice of stroke placement. A series of key frames interpolated all at once can create a continuous sequence of animation. With practice, a skilled animator can create high-quality animation in this way in a fraction of the time otherwise needed for conventional animation, and with a fraction of the manpower!

Another advantage presented by the computer is that it can stack as many cels as you care to specify upon one another. In conventional animation only a certain number of cels can be stacked because even though the cels are drawn on clear plastic, that plastic starts to show up when too many cels are stacked. The colors on the bottom-most cels begin to appear darker, and sophisticated color corrections must be made either when painting the cels or when developing the film to make the colors come out right and alleviate the problem with the slight opaqueness of the plastic sheets. The computer has no such problem: the transparent parts of the image are perfectly transparent, and the colors do not degrade when additional cels are added.

AN OVERVIEW OF THREE-DIMENSIONAL COMPUTER-ASSISTED ANIMATION

The same idea of interpolation is at the heart of three-dimensional animation as well, but instead of interpolating lines, we interpolate transformations at nodes of articulated trees.

For example, given the tree of Fig. 12-13, recall that this completely describes an object. We can consider this a *pose*, the analogy to a key frame. Fig. 12-14 shows a second pose, again represented by its tree. If we specify a number of in-betweens to be generated, the computer can interpolate the values at each note to create in-between trees.

Experimentation with different interpolating schemes has shown that linear interpolation usually does not look good in three-dimensional animation, which is a shame because linear interpolation is fast and cheap. But if it doesn't look good, then it's useless for animation, and a new interpolation scheme must be found. Most animators now agree that a

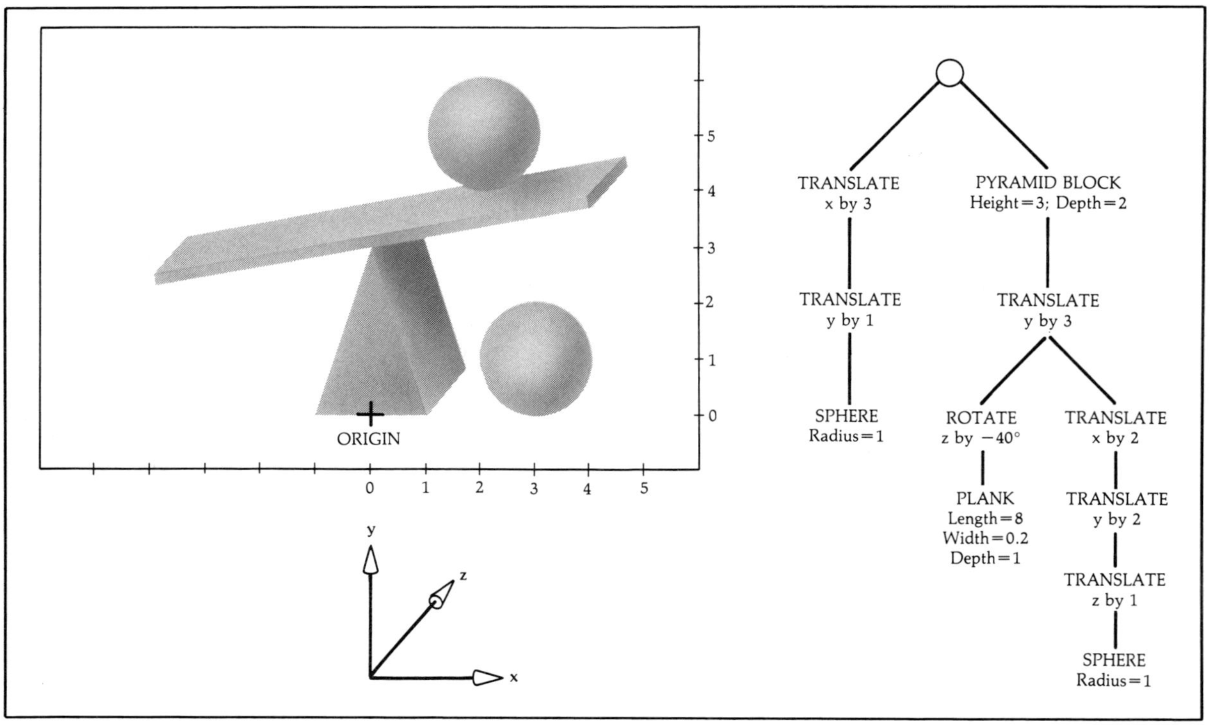

Fig. 12-13. A model and its tree.

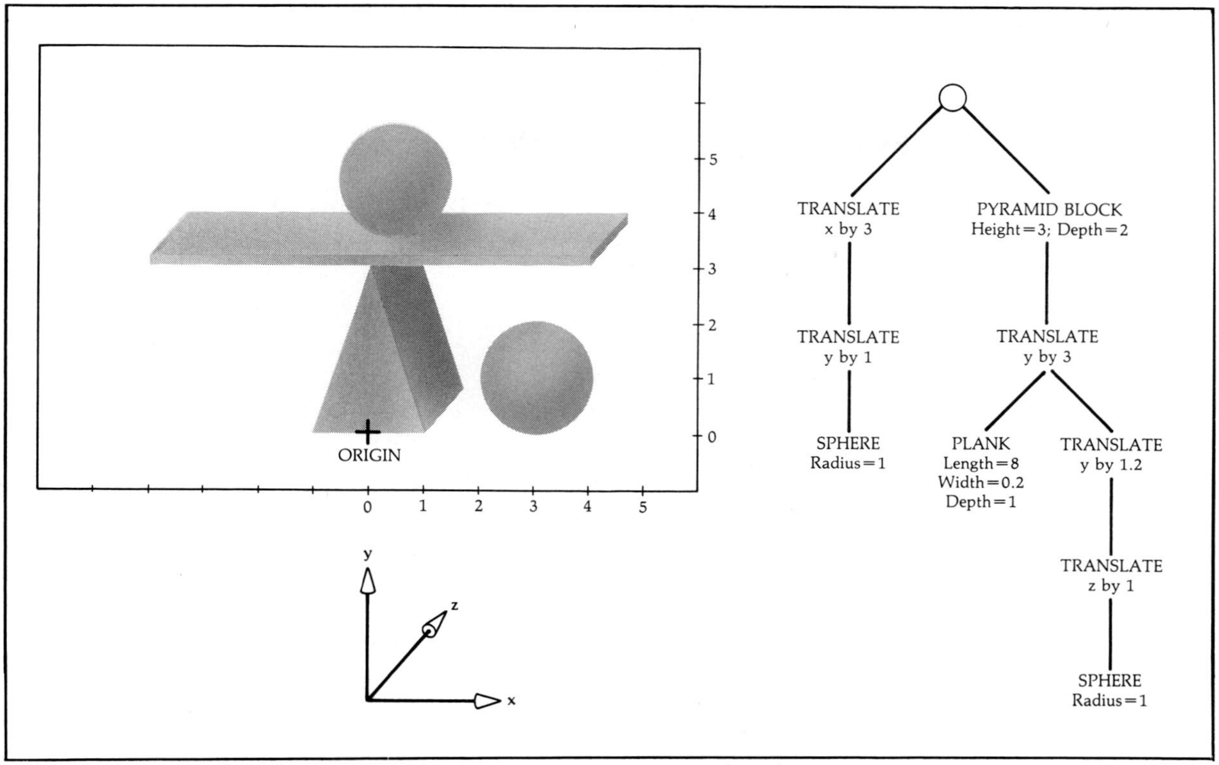

Fig. 12-14. The same model as Fig. 12-13, differently posed.

spline interpolation does very well for three-dimensional animation. So the usual practice is to fit a spline to the data as in Fig. 12-15. A spline is created for every value in every node, and this is used to create the interpolated in-between poses or frames. In other words, the articulation trees for different frames are connected with splines, and then the in-between frames are generated from the in-between trees.

The complete sequence is then played back to the animator in real time. The animator may insert or delete key frames, ask for more or fewer interpolated frames, or many other modifications of the animation. In particular, the animator may modify the splines used for interpolation by hand, which introduces the "human touch" simliar to the distortions introduced by conventional animators.

In addition to posing the model, the animator may also reposition the "camera" the computer is simulating when it draws the screen. The focus, perspective, hither and yon clipping plane locations, and more may be set at each pose. These too may be interpolated by the computer for very

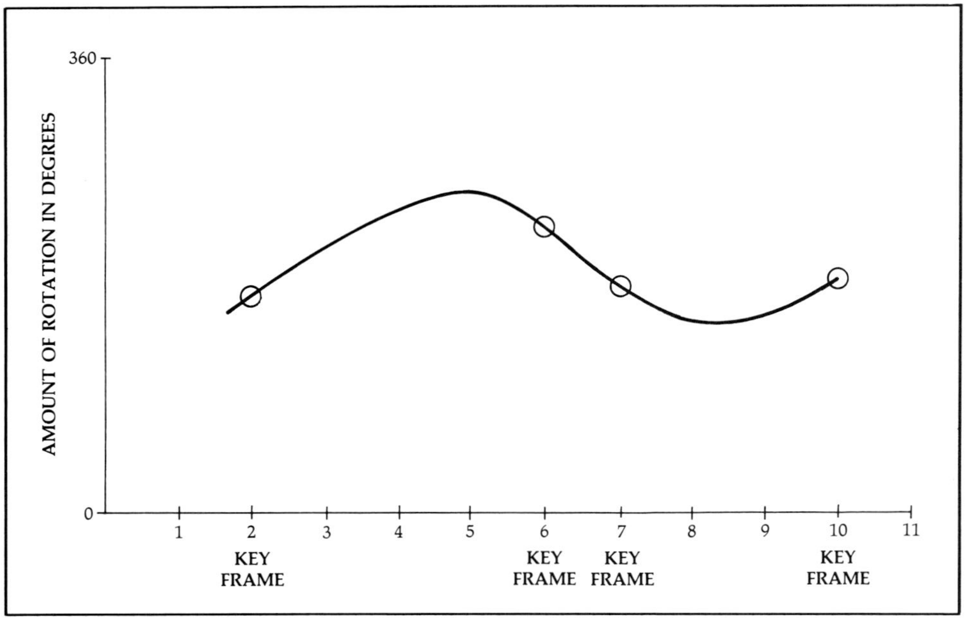

Fig. 12-15. Some data points and a spline joining them.

complex animation. The animator may also position several cameras at once. Then, the complete animation may be a composite from several different viewpoints. Of course, each camera may be moved and refocused and otherwise controlled as the animation progresses, just like manipulating a real camera during the filming of a movie.

The animator also has the opportunity to pose and animate just one character at a time. When the first character is completed, the second character is brought onto the screen, the first is deleted, and everything begins again from frame one except that the camera information is retained. This way the characters may be animated with complex choreography individually, and the combined animation will all share the same camera movements, which is a very difficult thing to do when animating many three-dimensional objects in a studio.

NEW FRONTIERS OFFERED BY COMPUTER ANIMATION

To give some idea of the power inherent in the computer-assisted three-dimensional animation field, let's quickly look at just a few interesting things that an animator can now do quickly and easily.

Objects may have more in their description than just their shape; they usually have some coloring, perhaps different surface textures, transparency in some places, and so on. These attributes may be tied into the animation system so that they are interpolated as well. For example, a window can go from totally transparent to totally opaque, in a smooth transition as the object moves. Or the surface texture may change to simulate the buildup of dirt on a vehicle traveling a road.

A very interesting effect is to have one object actually transform itself into something else. For example, a rock sitting in a field may suddenly change into a colorful hot-air balloon and smoothly rise into the sky! Or two objects, blatantly distinct, may roll towards each other and impact. The two objects then rebound, each now with characteristics of the other.

SUMMARY

In this chapter we looked at how conventional animation is produced, and why it works. We then saw how the computer could help us do conventional animation, and then looked to how the computer can help us do three-dimensional animation and beyond.

Animation (and all film) works in the first place because of *persistence of vision*, which is the natural ability of the human eye to retain a picture for just a fraction of a second before forgetting it. If we present the eye with a new picture very similar to the old one before the old one is gone, it will look as though the old picture turned into the new one. Animation consists of getting pictures in front of the human eye in rapid enough succession to sustain the illusion of movement.

We saw that in conventional animation a great deal of labor goes into making the 24 different pictures that must be displayed every second to keep that illusion going.

The process begins with a *storyboard*, which is sort of an illustrated script. When the storyboard is complete, the animation process begins. First, *key frames* are drawn by the senior animators. These are frames of animation that indicate the beginnings and ends of important motions, illustrate important character's expressions, and otherwise set the tone of the animation. Animators then produce *in-between frames* that fill in the gaps between key frames.

These frames are called *cels*. Each cel must be drawn, inked, and painted, then checked and tested before it is finally photographed. The final photography is done by laying many cels on top of one another to create a complete picture. Then, one frame of film is exposed to the complete picture. The picture is then disassembled, new cels are stacked, and a new frame of film is exposed. The process is long and tedious.

One way of cutting down on the time involved is called *rotoscoping*, which has a style and "feel" different from purely conventional animation. In rotoscoping live footage is traced onto cellulose, which is then inked, painted, and photographed. The advantage is that unless an error is made when tracing the film, you are sure how the animation will look. Other techniques for adding animation to film are lumped together under the heading *mixed media*.

Two-dimensional computer-assisted animation presents animators with freedom from the tedium of inking and painting cels by hand. An animator enters a frame with a stylus and tablet in *strokes*, or sweeps of the pen. The computer interpolates strokes between key frames automatically. Additionally, the computer can overlay as many cels as wanted without the distortion of color and opaqueness problems of the cellulose that always come with conventional animation.

The computer can also help us *pose* and animate three-dimensional models. What we effectively do is interactively modify the articulation tree that describes a computer model until we like the way the model looks. The computer then creates articulation trees that are interpolations of the key frames, just like interpolating strokes for two-dimensional animation. The resulting articulation trees draw a model in various stages of movement between the two key frames, and when rendered and shown in rapid succession the model appears to move.

The computer helps us do animation and transformations that would have been impossible or prohibitively expensive before. In the last section we list some possible uses of the computer in animation. The potential is limited only by your imagination!

Chapter THIRTEEN

Production Techniques

People have been making films for many years. Over the years some techniques have proven themselves so useful and common that they have been given names and a terminology to describe their various uses. In this chapter we will cover some of the most useful production techniques for animated film.

TRANSITIONS

When it's time for a piece of film or video to change from one scene to another, often a cinematic technique is used to effect the change in an interesting way. The most basic way is to simply switch immediately to the next scene, which is called a *cut* and is illustrated in Fig. 13-1.

The next scene can "push" the first scene out of the way—this is called a *wipe* (Fig. 13-2)—or the first scene can fade out, or get dimmer, and the second scene can fade up, or get brighter, making a *dissolve* (Fig. 13-3). Other effects fall under the general heading of *transitions*.

Transitions can be very simple, like the ones just discussed, or as complex as you like. The computer offers the versatility to design any kind of transition you care to have, so it would be impossible to list them all, or even all the different kinds. In this chapter we will look at some of the standard transitions, and then look at the various tools available to the designer of transitions.

Standard video effects are performed with a piece of hardware called a *switcher*. Switchers may now be bought with 30 or more transitions built into their hardware.

Computer-executed transitions can get as fancy as you like. For example, you may use the computer to retain information about some of the rendered shapes in the scene you are leaving and the scene you are going

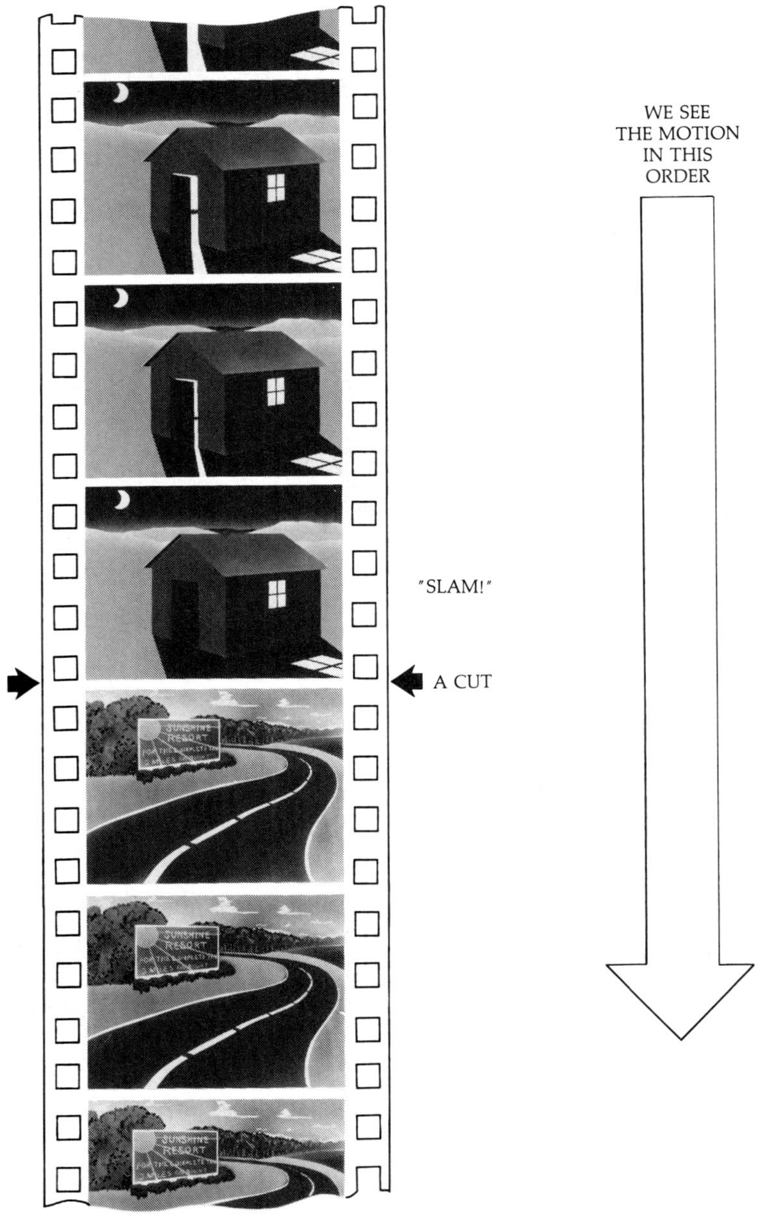

Fig. 13-1. A sequence of film showing a cut.

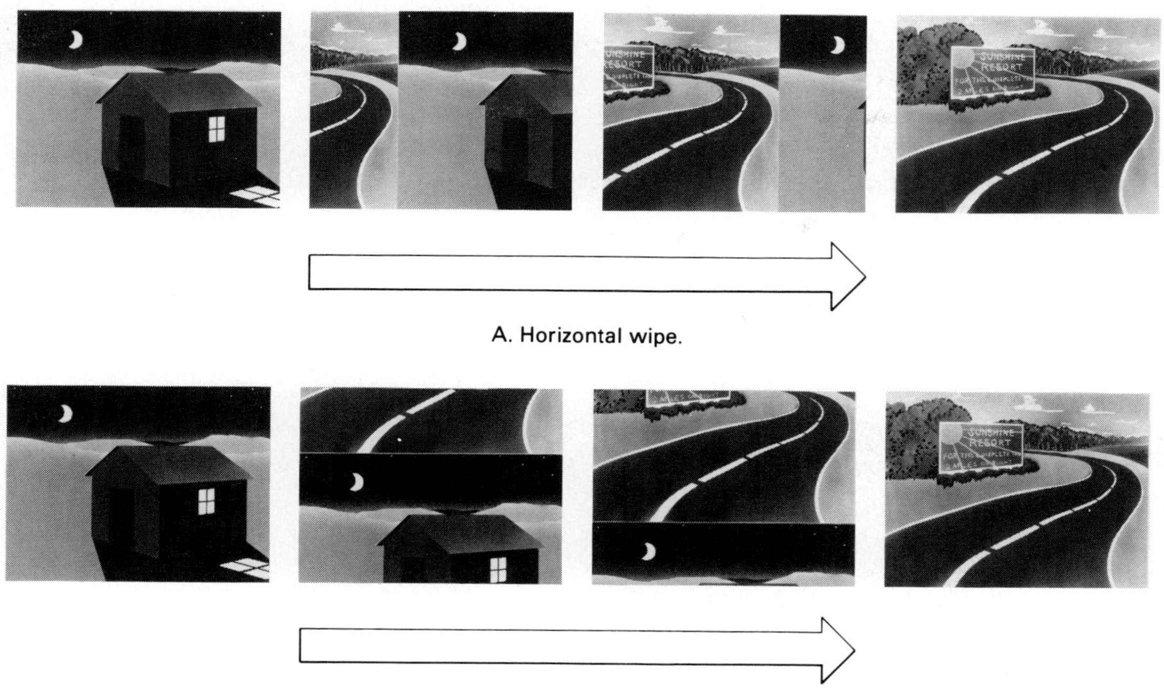

A. Horizontal wipe.

B. Vertical wipe.

Fig. 13-2. Examples of wipes.

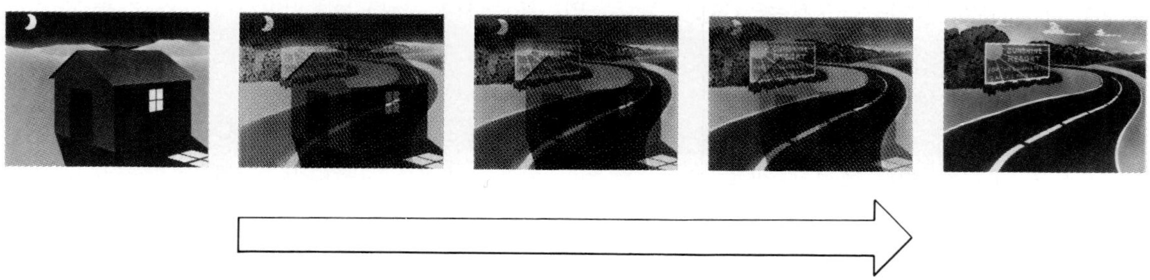

Fig. 13-3. A dissolve.

to. It can then use these shapes as surfaces upon which to map the two scenes, and then it can change one surface to the other.

Or, you may choose to cause each pixel to slowly run through a set of colors until it comes to the correct color in the scene you are going to. Or you could map the scene onto the surface of a sphere, spin the sphere to reveal the next scene on the other side, and then un-map the new scene back onto the full screen (Fig. 13-4).

You might want to make the old scene "drip" down the face of the screen like it was drawn with watercolors and splashed with water, and let the new scene drip down from the top of the screen in the same way.

Such transitions must normally be programmed by someone with computer programming experience. But a designer can create a transition and describe it in detail, and then ask a programmer to write the necessary programs. If the transition is well described, a programmer can usually make it happen.

PANS AND ZOOMS

Pans and zooms are standard cinematic techniques that can be emulated and embellished through the use of a computer. A *pan* is to slowly move the camera across the face of a picture (Fig. 13-5). A *zoom* is to focus in on a smaller part of the picture or to pull back to reveal more of it (Fig. 13-6).

With a computer doing the work, both of these techniques can be done at a constant rate, or at any speed and direction you choose. Some systems will even let you control the focus on a three-dimensional scene, as well as simulate different lenses on the "camera" taking the computer-simulated picture.

BLURRING, EDGING, AND SOME SPECIAL EFFECTS

With a picture in a frame buffer, and sometimes some information about the rendering of the picture in another frame buffer or in computer memory, the computer can do many interesting tricks to the picture.

The picture may be selectively blurred in any direction by any amount. Blurring the picture sometimes helps make a nice transition to another picture (or scene). Fig. 13-7 shows some selective blurring. Note that we have good control over blurring; in Fig. 13-7 we have blurred the figure horizontally so the vertical edges are still sharp.

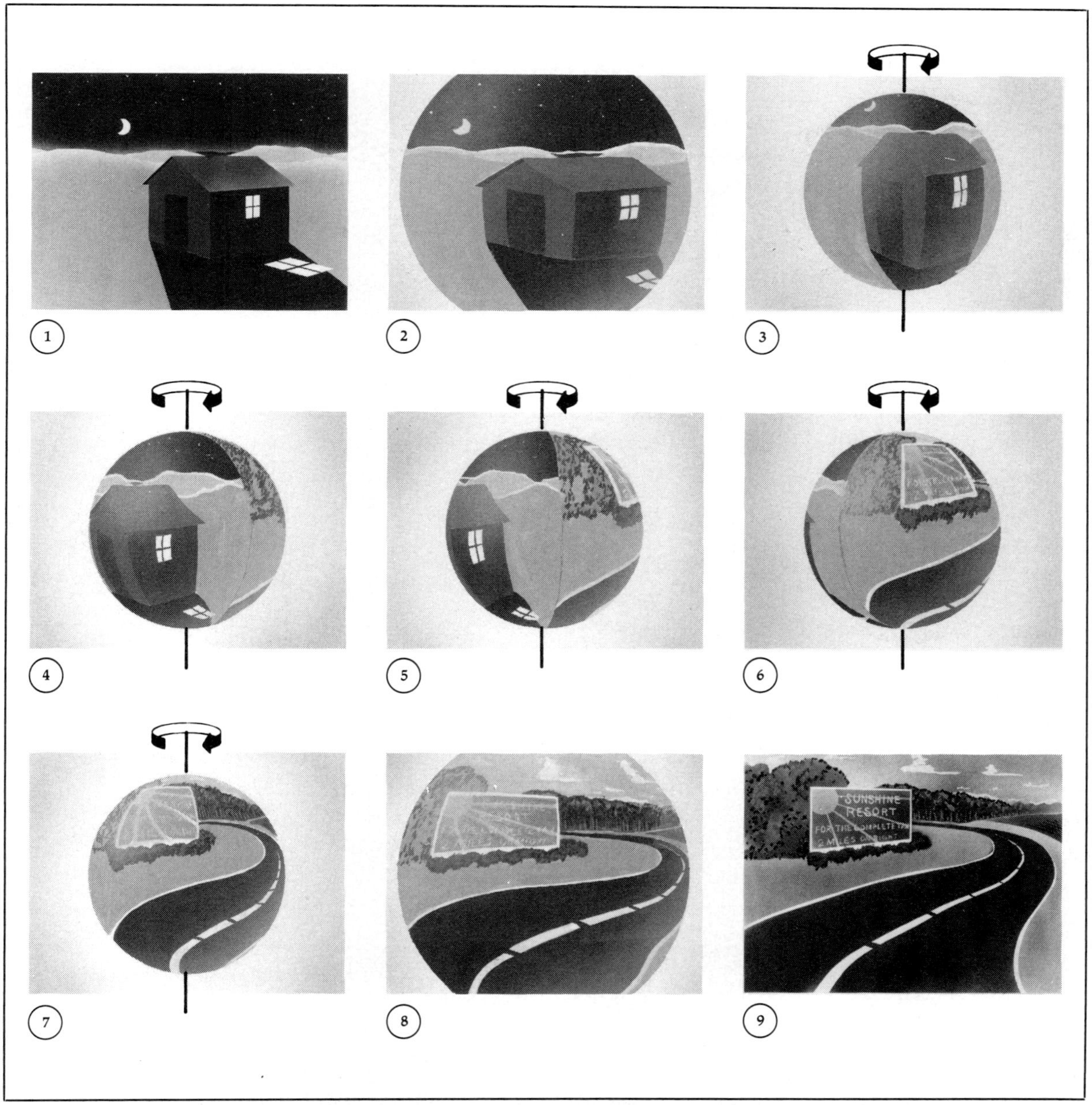

Fig. 13-4. A special transition: wrap the image around a sphere, and spin the sphere to show a new scene.

Fig. 13-5. Panning effects.

A. Original image. B. Zooming in. C. Zooming out.

Fig. 13-6. Effect of zooming in and out.

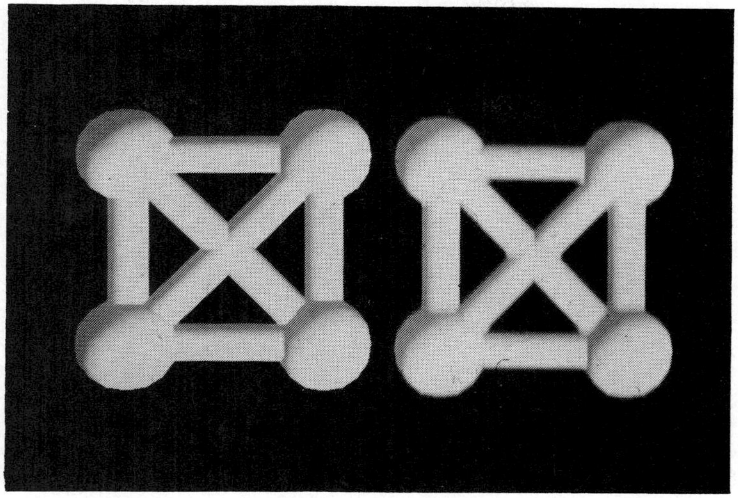

Fig. 13-7. Blurring of an object.

Another trick is *edging*, which means to sharpen up the edges in a picture. You may choose to only sharpen vertical edges (Fig. 13-8), horizontal edges (Fig. 13-9), or both (Fig. 13-10). The computer can automatically detect vertical or horizontal edges.

As with transition, there can be as many special effects performed on a single scene as you wish to imagine. Effects like star filters and long exposure time are only two examples.

MATTES AND MATTING

Let's say you want to make an outer-space scene where a spaceship slowly flies by in front of a background of stars. You might render the stars (Fig. 13-11), save the picture, then render the spaceship (Fig. 13-12), and save that. Now, you want to combine the two pictures (Fig. 13-13).

You need some way to add the two pictures together in just the right way. The process of adding pictures together is very common in computer production, because often full frames are drawn in several different stages. In this case the computer rendered the star field, and that image was saved as a complete picture. Then the computer rendered the spaceship, and that was also saved. There are many possibilities of combination offered by every computer production system.

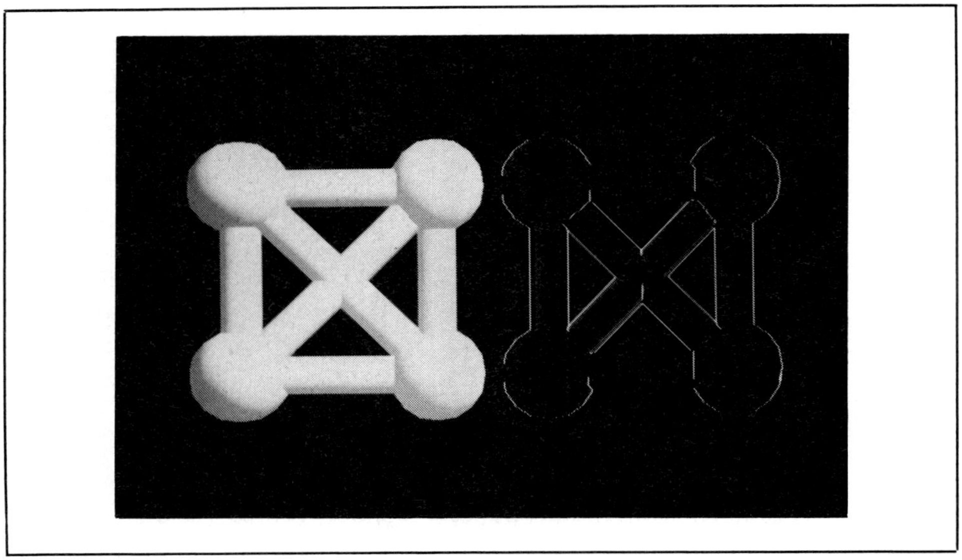

Fig. 13-8. The computer can automatically detect vertical edges.

Fig. 13-9. We can also look for horizontal edges.

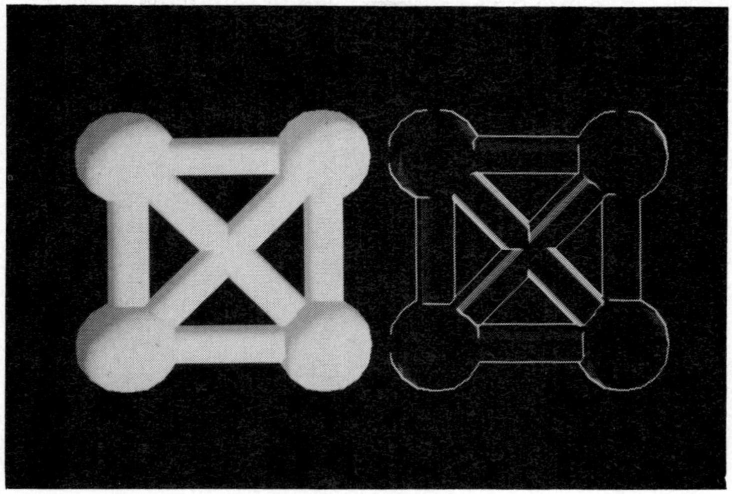

Fig. 13-10. Here we have told the computer to find all edges.

Fig. 13-11. A star background.

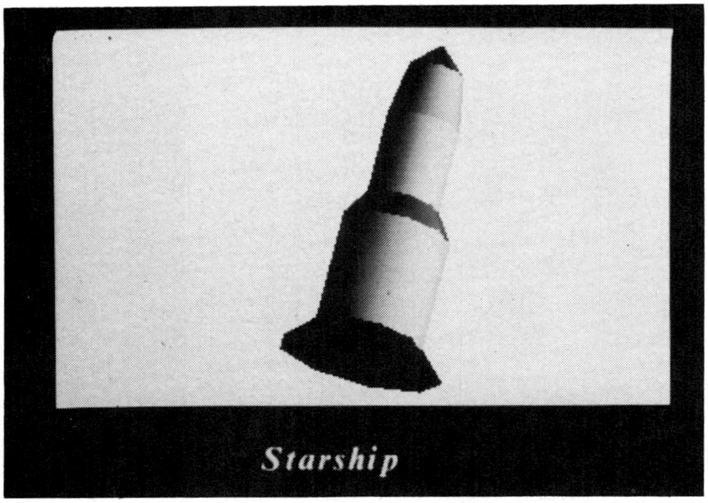

Fig. 13-12. A spaceship.

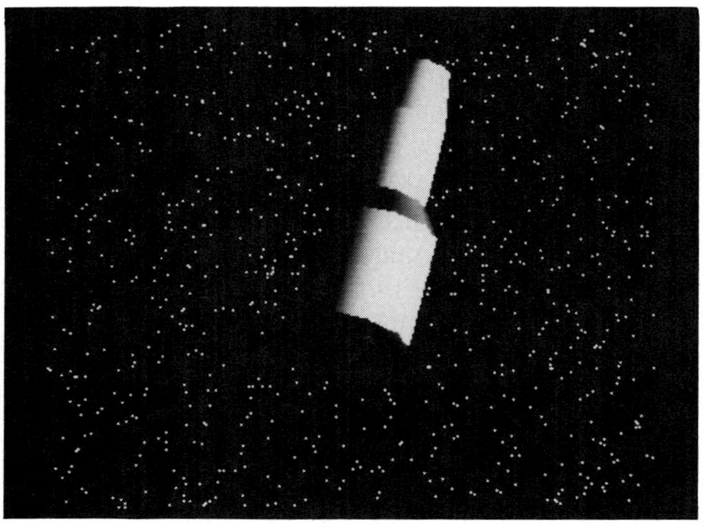

Fig. 13-13. A spaceship matted onto the stars.

One of the most useful methods is *transparency*. It might be used in our example in this way. To build up the complete picture, first draw the star field image into the frame buffer. Then tell the computer that the color black is to be transparent in the next picture, and draw the spaceship into the frame buffer. The computer will only change the contents of the frame buffer to the new picture where the new picture is a color other than black, which is another way of saying that everywhere the original picture was black, the contents of the frame buffer were left unchanged.

Note that the star field would come through around the ship, which is what we wanted. However, the star field would come through where the ship was black! We told it all black was transparent, and it just did its job. Transparency is great for many tasks, but it's just not the right technique here.

An alternative solution to our star-ship production is to copy a technique used in film production called *matting*. (The use of the word *matte* here is not like the matte when applied to a finish). The basic idea behind matting is that the producer cuts a "mask" that will be used for each frame that goes into the total picture. The mask instructs us to cut out only the pieces of the frame that are not covered. Then, we take the cut-out pieces and lay them into the total frame. Figs. 13-14, 13-15, and 13-16 each show some pictures, a matte for combining them and the result.

This process can also be considered optically by making a mask out of some opaque material (like heavy cardboard) for each frame. Then, each frame is put in a slide projector with its mask and all the frames are projected onto one screen (Fig. 13-17). Note that only those areas that are not covered by the mask appear on the screen. What we have called a *mask* is also called a *matte*.

We could then create mattes for the two frames in our picture, the spaceship and the stars. To create a matte in the computer we draw the matte into a frame buffer called the *matte buffer*. This frame buffer is consulted for every pixel as the image is copied. When a pixel is copied, its corresponding pixel in the matte buffer is checked. If the matte buffer is white, then no pixel is copied; if the matte buffer is black, then the pixel is copied. We then make mattes for both the spaceship and the star field and draw them into the frame buffer one after the other, as in Fig. 13-18. Note that the background really didn't need to be masked in this case.

Mattes need not be black and white. An optical matte might be made out of materials with different transparencies so that two images might blend into each other. In our matte buffers we can use shades of gray to indicate transparency. We might say that 0 is black, 255 is white, and intervening

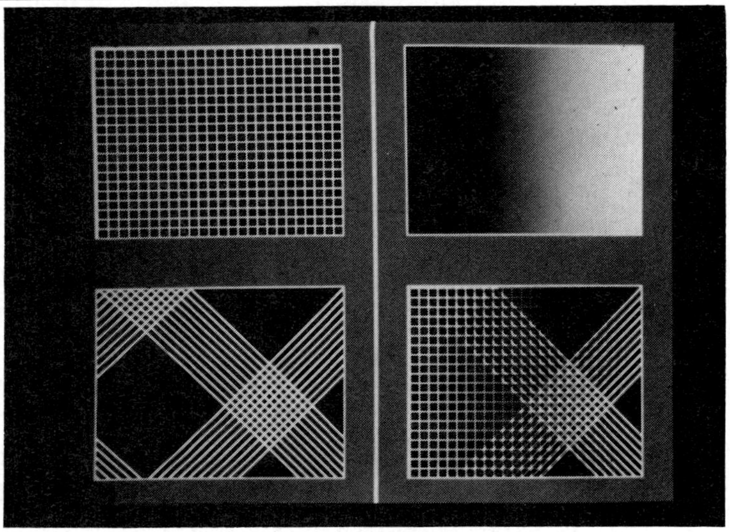

Fig. 13-14. Matting—The pictures on the left are combined with the matte in the upper right-hand corner, creating a final image in the lower right. White in the matte means use the lower source picture, more black means more of the upper picture.

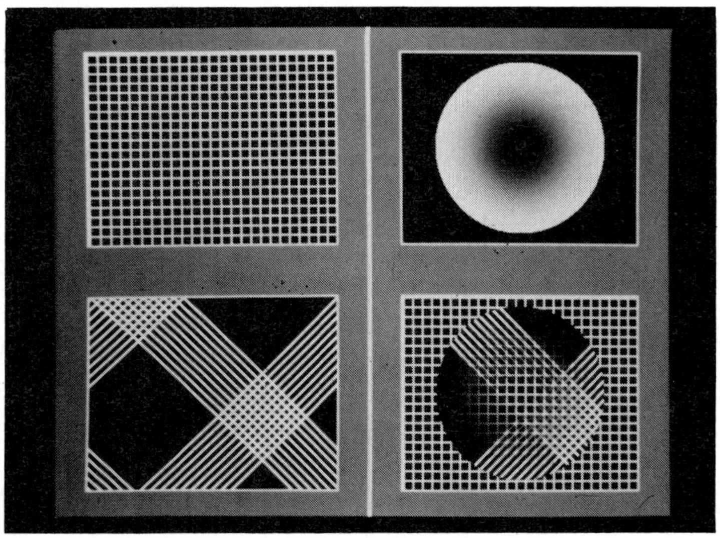

Fig. 13-15. Another example of matting.

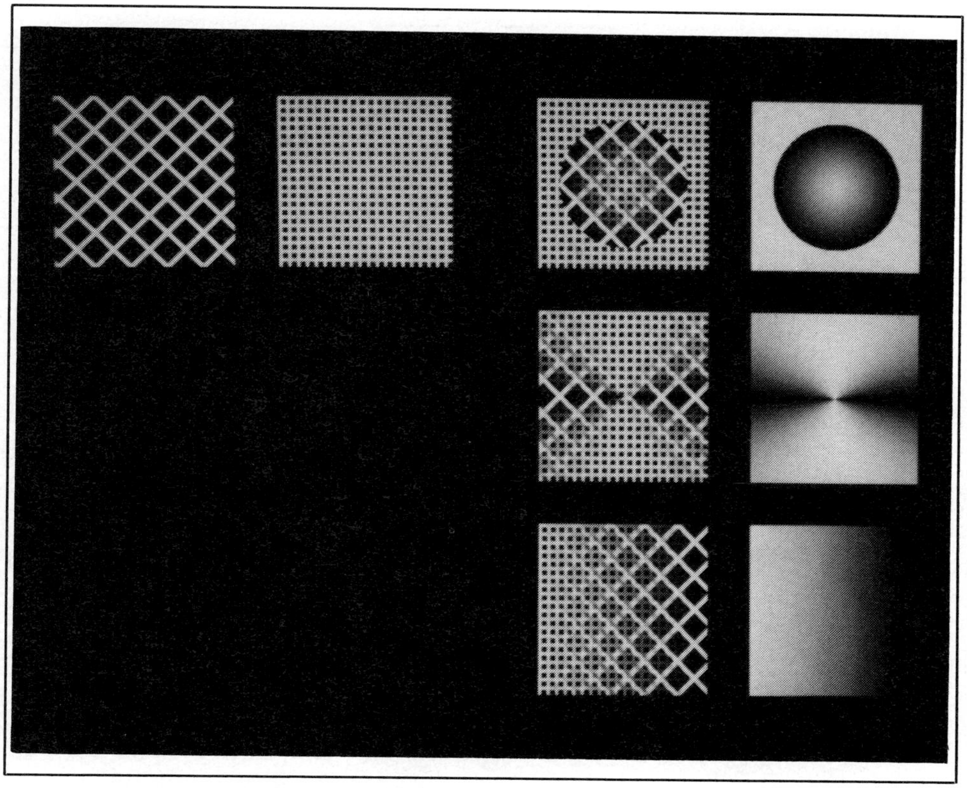

Fig. 13-16. Another example of matting. The source pictures are on the far left.

levels are gray. If a pixel is a shade of gray, then it is blended into the existing image in the frame buffer. The closer the matte pixel is to black, the more transparent is the new value. The new value is a linear interpolation of the pixel in the image buffer and the pixel that is being drawn on top of it.

Matte production is sometimes challenging. They can always be drawn by hand at a paint station, and may often be generated by the computer. Matte buffers that are generated according to a computer program can produce very beautiful transitions.

THE FUTURE

So where are we headed? What can we expect from computer graphics in the next few years?

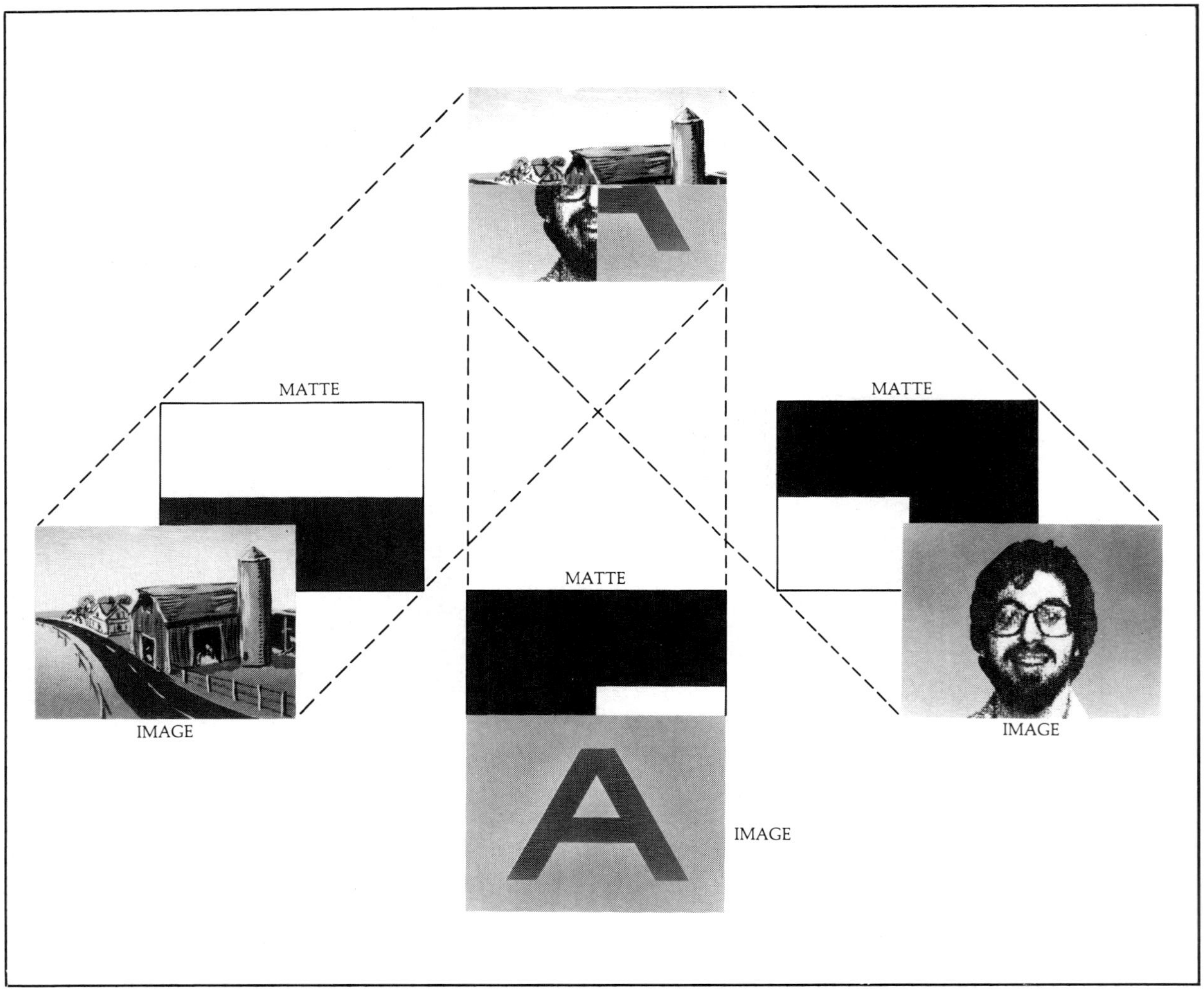

Fig. 13-17. Matting of several images.

I would expect to see a lot of stunningly creative animation when we find artists and programmers suddenly finding their complementary roles in computer animation and teaming up. We'll see model animation that will look both so realistic that you'll have to be told that is's computer generated, and (at least one) whole new style of art based on the unique capabilities of the computer.

What we're seeing now in computer graphics in film and on tv is the birth of a new art form. The future belongs to those who together have the

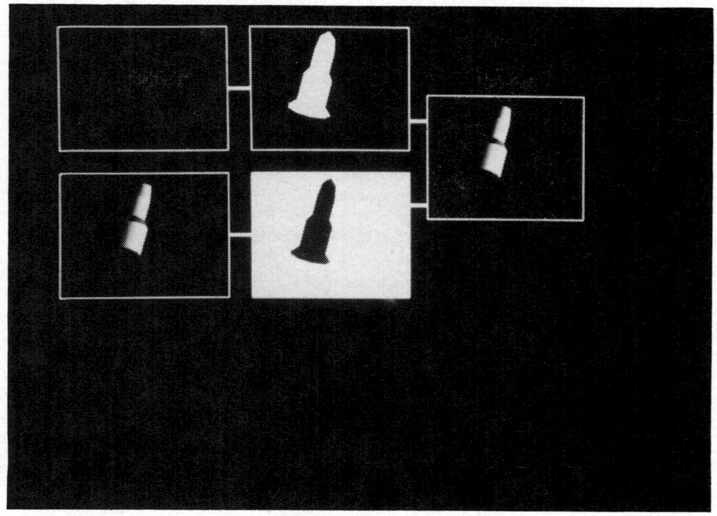

Fig. 13-18. The matting process for Fig. 13-13. White in the matte means "don't use;" black means "use."

imagination and technical skill to bring out the maximum versatility from the computer.

SUMMARY

In this chapter we covered some basic production techniques for animated films. The first class of techniques we discussed is called *transitions*. Transitions are basically a way of getting from one scene to another, and there can be as many kinds of transitions as you care to invent. We described some of the transitions that are now possible with the help of the computer. These are only initial ideas; the future of computer graphics belongs to the imaginative artists who can communicate their ideas to able programmers.

A standard technique for moving across an image is called a *pan*. Coming in closer to an image is called *zooming in*; getting farther away is called *zooming out*. You may also do all kinds of special effects on an image, from enhancing the edges to blurring the edges, to the various effects we mention as suggestions.

The technique for combining two different images to make them look like they were photographed together is called *matting.*

Matting uses the idea of *transparency.* Let's say we're adding buffer A into buffer B. If a pixel in buffer A is defined as transparent, then the corresponding pixel in buffer B is unchanged. The more opaque the pixel in A is, the more it is added to buffer B, until when A is totally opaque, the pixel in B is completely replaced with the value of the pixel in A.

A *matte* is a frame buffer that holds the transparency values for each pixel in buffer A. When two pictures are added, the matte buffer is referenced for each pixel, and the final result at each pixel is completely determined by the transparency value encoded in the matte buffer.

Index

T

V

W

Y

Z

75
15507